Hidden Lives

War, internment, and Australia's Italians

Mia Spizzica, editor

Brisbane

Glass House Books
an imprint of IP (Interactive Publications Pty Ltd)
Treetop Studio • 9 Kuhler Court
Carindale, Queensland, Australia 4152
sales@ipoz.biz
ipoz.biz/ipstore

First published by IP in 2018
© Mia Spizzica and the other authors contained herein, 2018

All rights reserved. Without limiting the rights under copyright reserved above, no part of this publication may be reproduced, stored in or introduced into a retrieval system, or transmitted, in any form or by any means (electronic, mechanical, photocopying, recording or otherwise), without the prior written permission of the copyright owner and the publisher of this book.

Printed in 12 pt Book Antiqua on 14 pt Avenir Book.

National Library of Australia Cataloguing-in-Publication entry

Title:	Hidden lives: war, internment and Australia's Italians, edited by Mia Spizzica
ISBN:	9781925231496 (PB)
	9781925231649 (eBk)
Subjects:	World War Two
	History: Australia
	Italian Internment
	Social Anthropology
	Political Science: Australia
	Human Rights

Contents

Introduction	1
Tearing Apart the Cardillo Family	13
The Truth Will Set You Free	37
A Teenage Girl's Memories of Wartime in Queensland	53
Orazio's Story	61
Surveillance, Internment and Dislocation	69
"The Hard Life at Tatura One Day Will End"	89
Claudia's Story	115
There Are So Many Questions I Wish I Had Asked…	129
A Kafkaesque Experience	147
The Life and Death of Raffaele Musitano	163
Memories of Port Pirie and the War	179
With a Suitcase and a Mandolin	191
Beyond the Barbed Wire	203
Within Our Limitations	215
Like a Dream So Long Ago	235
"Hey Dago!"	251
"We were just ordinary blokes!"	259
Tears and Sadness	295
Childhood Recollections of Tatura Camp 3A	305
Shattered Dreams	313
Selected Further Readings	323
Appendix 1: Australia Location Maps	334
Appendix 2: Map of Italy	336
Appendix 3: Loveday Camp	337
Appendix 4: Cowra Camp	339
Appendix 5: Hay Camp	340
Appendix 6: Tatura Camp	341
About the Contributors	342

Acknowledgements

I wish to thank the National Archives of Australia (NAA), National Archives Australia Research Grant, 2015, Australian War Memorial (AWM), State Library of New South Wales (SLNSW), State Library Victoria (SLV), State Library South Australia (SLSA), Monash Arts Research Grant, Italian Historical Society (IHS), the Lloyd Robson Travel Grant, the Australian Historical Association and Museum Victoria 1858 Student Scholarship.

I am very grateful to the extensive advisory group, who have offered their comments on the narratives or peer reviews of essays during the evolution of this anthology. Each has played a significant part in the development of this project: Laureate Professor Robert Pascoe, Assoc. Professor Hariz Halilovich, Professor Gaetano Rando, Professor Ivo Vellar MD, Dr Raffaele Lampugnani, Dr Gerardo Papalia, Dr David Faber, Dr Don Longo, Dr Catherine Dewhirst, Dr Joseph Toscano MD, Dr Anita Bressan, Dr Lara Palombo, Dr Susanna Iuliano, Dr David Reiter, Dr Paolo Baracchi, Research Associates Francesca Musicò-Rullo, Simone Alcorso, Antony Calabrò, Rick Datodi, Isaac Lam, Josie Verbis, Ennio Verbis and Meredith Sherlock.

With the deepest of appreciation, I thank the authors who contributed their personal testimonies to this book: Simone Alcorso, Claudia Barker, Marino Belligoi, Ross Calì, Roy Cardillo, Sam Cavallaro, Rick Datodi, Mafalda Fortuna, Nora Lo Giudice, Nicole Musitano, John Musitano, Joe Musitano, Nora Musitano, Dannielle Musitano, Mario Previtera, Susan Previtera, Francie Puccini, Rosa Rodighiero, Rina Scalgiotti, and Josie Verbis.

I am most thankful to my parents Domenico and Antonina Spizzica for their patience and support during the book's development. This collaborative project is dedicated to the memory of my grandfather Antonino (Nino) Spizzica, whose wartime internment in Australia prompted this publication.

Introduction

Family secrets and hidden lives:
War, internment, and Australia's Italians

During the first four decades of the 20th century, increasing numbers of Italians migrated to Australia. It was viewed as a distant British Dominion that offered bountiful opportunities for energetic, forward-looking migrants who sought to build an economically secure future for themselves and their families. Yet, the aspirations of many migrants were shattered by the economic consequences of the Great Depression in the 1930s, followed by World War II (WWII) from 1939 to 1945. When Italy declared war on 10 June 1940 on Britain and France, its alliance with the British Empire during the Great War dissolved into a distant memory. This all-out conflict between Britain, its allies, and the key Axis nations, Germany, Italy, and Japan, changed the economic and political trajectory of nations worldwide. Not only did the ravages of this world war change the physical environment, but also the fate of millions of civilians of many nations caught in the crossfire when populated areas became battlefield front lines, or as non-combatant residents in enemy nations. This conflict was to become a critical turning point for Italians migrants living in Australia, other British dominions, and in allied nations. In an instant, Italians living in allied nations had become enemy aliens. Their experiences have rarely been mentioned in mainstream Australian histories.

This collection of five research essays, and memories of fifteen Italian Australians, offers new insights into the deeply personal experiences of people whose families witnessed WWII in Australia. It is the first such compilation by authors originating from northern, central and Southern Italian provinces, and from five Australian States – Queensland, New South Wales, Victoria, South Australia and Western Australia. Although each story is a unique eyewitness account, authors share many Italian cultural values, language, history, and a profound sense of Italianness – *italianità*.

While official histories of Italian internment in Australia present one version of the home front war story, the narratives in this anthology offers an Italian Australian perspective. The testimonies rely primarily on recollections of events that occurred more than seventy years ago, which have been corroborated by primary sources that establish the authenticity of each story. Theirs are memories of anguish and hard times, similar to millions of other human beings who have experienced wars throughout the millennia. These unique wartime narratives shed new light on the lived experiences of Italians who were interned in Australia. To understand why wartime internment is such an important issue for the authors in this collection, it is framed with an overview of the historical backdrop of war between the Axis alliance and the British Empire, and the social and political environment on the Australian home front.

Historical Context

Unified in the 1860s, the fledgling Italian nation was to become Britain's ally in the Great War against the Austro-Hungarians. Like other European monarchies, Italy had claimed its first colonial territory in Africa in the 1880s, continuing to expand its territories under Fascism. By the early 1920s, Benito Mussolini and his Fascist government, gained control of Italy's social, political and economic development. He promised Italians a prosperous economic future under his leadership, and his supporters believed that Fascism would transform Italy into a modern industrial nation. Under his dictatorship, Italy was acting on its desire to become a new Roman Empire, spanning the entire Mediterranean and beyond. He was initially well regarded by many Western leaders including the prime ministers of Britain and Australia. However, as international economic conditions descended into the Great Depression, life in Italy became increasingly difficult.

By the mid-1930s, this new Italian Empire had expanded its territorial control in North Africa, challenging other colonial powers in the region, including Britain and France. Nonetheless, during these two Fascist decades, hundreds of thousands of Italians migrated abroad to escape what Italy could not offer their families - a better economic future. Interwar Italian migrants settled in other European nations, the Americas, the Levant, Asia, Africa, and the Antipodes. Rather than hapless migrants, these were ambitious men and women, who could pay for costly journeys, travel visas, food and lodgings in a foreign land to find good work in a master plan to improve their families' economic futures. Many had no confidence in the future promised by Fascism, or a desire to participate in Mussolini's utopian vision that may never materialise. Animosities between the former allies, Britain and Italy, grew after Mussolini's conquests in North Africa in the mid-1930s, deteriorating further after he signed the Pact of Steel with Adolph Hitler on 22 May 1939. By 10 June 1940, Italy had joined Germany in war against Britain.

World War II

Within an hour of war being declared, nationals from Axis countries including Germany, Austria, Spain, Finland, Hungary, Rumania, Albania, and Italy who were living or travelling in allied nations were classified as enemy aliens by government authorities. In Canada, more than 600 men in a population of about 100,000 Italians were detained in prison camps, while in the United States residence, movement, and workplace restrictions were imposed on an estimated 600,000 Italian Americans. Although few Italian Americans were interned, there were approximately 10,000 forced relocations away from high-risk security zones. After Japan attacked Pearl Harbor in December 1941, tens of thousands of Japanese Americans were displaced from their homes and detained in remote locations in the United States. These examples reveal how preventative internment of enemy aliens on suspicion of the *potential* for disloyalty to the host nation was generally accepted as a natural consequence of war.

Amongst those fleeing Nazism and Fascism were many Jews who were nationals of different nations, including Germany, Austria, and Italy. The internment of refugees escaping war was not reassessed until many had spent years confined in camps in Allied nations, including Australia. Britain imprisoned thousands of Italians living in territories that it controlled including in Egypt, India, Palestine, Malaya, Singapore and New Guinea. Enemy aliens incarcerated in Britain were initially deported to Canada for internment, but were torpedoed on the *SS Arandora Star*, resulting in the death of more than 1000 internees and guards. These 800 survivors were soon after sent on the *HMT Dunera* to Australia for internment. Italians who were detained in Palestine, Malaya, and Singapore were deported as entire families to Australia for internment, as were the gold miners from New Guinea. At the same time, the political volatility of Australia's government did not placate the nation's increasing trepidation against Italian migrants as potential enemy fighters, even if there was no demonstrable evidence to support this proposition. Between 1939 and 1942, Australia's confidence in its own ability to survive as a British democracy was rocked by a number of important domestic events.

Some of the most notable issues for the nation to manage were the numerous changes in federal government leadership. After the sudden death of Prime Minister Joseph Lyons in April 1939, Earl Page was in charge of the government for eleven days, until the United Australia Party (UAP) voted in Robert Menzies as the nation's leader. At war with Germany since May 1939, public unease increased after Italy's entry in the war in June 1940. This was closely followed by the Canberra air disaster in August, which claimed the lives of three senior War Cabinet Ministers just before a federal election. Newspapers of that fateful day reported Nazi bombings over Britain.

By August 1941, the UAP replaced Menzies with Arthur Fadden, who remained Prime Minister for only three months. In October 1941, the Federal Parliament's House of Representatives voted to replace the UAP with the Labor Party, led by John Curtin, to administer the nation's war effort. This was an extraordinary act. Government censorship and war propaganda were imposed on all forms of media, which silenced differing opinions on the war. The influential Returned Soldiers' League (RSSAILA) demanded that all enemy aliens be immediately interned. Left wing newspapers were banned and groups such as Australia First and the Jehovah Witnesses were outlawed. The sinking of the *HMAS Sydney* off the coast of Western Australia on 19 November 1941 with the loss of 645 men brought the war closer to the nation's shores. With the Japanese conquest of Singapore in December 1941, the attack on Darwin and northern Australia in early 1942 and the sinking of the *HMAS Kattabul* in Sydney Harbour, the front line drew ever nearer to a virtually undefended, under-populated British dominion of seven million residents in a remote corner of the Commonwealth in the Antipodes. Multiple war fronts, significant loss of life, changes in leadership and governments, war rations, and 'brown outs' exacerbated the nation's anxieties about its enemy alien immigrant residents. Not only did the war damage those on the front line on both sides but also those who endured the negative effects of war on the home front.

Enemy Aliens

A crescendo of palpable antagonism grew towards enemy aliens, especially in Queensland, where the Ferry Royal Commission (1925) had branded Southern Italians as inferior 'Mediterranean scum', and unions had won British Preference working rights over non-British workers in the mid-1930s. A groundswell of fear and loathing against enemy aliens nationwide culminated with the largest mass internment of that ethnic group in the Southern Hemisphere. Italian migrants, particularly those targeted by the Returned Soldiers' League and trade unions, became a metaphoric embodiment of Fascism and all it stood for, and by association with German Nazism and Japanese Imperialism. Thus, an unspoken war within a war on the home front escalated to a climax by mid-1942.

Almost 5,000 Italians living in Australia, along with hundreds arrested in other British-controlled territories, were interned in prison camps in isolated locations for an indefinite period. A few were released within months, others remained imprisoned for many years, while some internees never returned home. Australia's need for self-preservation in the face of a perceived imminent invasion by the Axis nations, triggered reactions that were fuelled by fears of an enemy within. It was a time of terror both for Australians and Italians alike. In communities where there was a higher proportion of Italians in the midst of a British-Australian population, many began to experience open resentment against them. Italians not interned were under surveillance, or sent to remote areas as forced labour. Families survived on savings, loans or on the charity of kind-hearted neighbours. There were differing consequences for every family in the Antipodean, Levantine, and Asiatic Italian Diasporas, as was the case in Europe, the Americas, and Africa. Countless forgotten documents divulge evidence on the internment experience describing covert investigations, anonymous accusations of disloyalty, confiscations, censored letters, and mass arrests without trial.

Archival records disclose numerous facts about the Italian Australian experiences as enemy aliens. Officials decided which documents should be retained or destroyed, which may explain the absence of many internee records. Indeed, some Italian dossiers are rich in content, while others are sparsely populated, void of content, or are recorded as missing. Nonetheless, official records offer only one type of primary source from the captors' perspective. Personal experiences from the 'enemy other' perspective are seldom included in archival records, perhaps because they articulate different interpretations of events.

Scattered throughout Italian detainee files are copious pages that detail events before, during, and after the war. Diaries, letters, and archival sources offer intimate details on tormented internee lives, and of deep mental anguish because of the severity of conditions behind barbed wire. Minute shards of evidence in internee dossiers suggest that a pervasive, slow-burning, psychological anguish was common amongst civilian prisoners during and well after their detentions. Some internees succumbed to the mental tensions of their harsh incarcerations and were sent to psychiatric asylums, which led to lifelong emotional scars, as described in some eyewitness accounts in this volume. While Catholic Archbishop Dr Daniel Mannix very actively protected Italians in Victoria from widespread internment, the same was not the case in other states.

War on the Home Front

Throughout the stories, our authors describe the unbearable war hysteria and distrust of Italians that constantly surrounded them. Some reveal instances of Italians who were protected by friends or good neighbours. For the rest, nothing could halt the unrelenting rounding up of Italian enemy aliens and more than 1,000 naturalised Italian British subjects across Australia. Families were caught by surprise as their men were rounded up for internment, often in the clothes they stood in. Men, women and children were herded off to local prisons to be fingerprinted, photographed, and numbered. The lucky ones were given time to wash, pack a small suitcase and dress in their best suits. Wives and children had few precious moments to wave heart-wrenching goodbyes as hundreds of men were herded at gunpoint, sometimes nudged by bayonets, onto trains with barred windows.

Survivors tell of the incredible terror they felt because no one knew if they would see their loved ones again. It was acutely obvious to Italians that the war emergency had completely overridden their assumed right of *habeas corpus* and the rule of Westminster law, even for naturalised British subjects and their Australian-born children.

Research and Testimonies

This book is divided into five sections comprising peer-reviewed academic essays offering thematic perspectives on internment, followed by personal narratives written by Italians whose families experienced wartime as enemy aliens. David Faber's discussion draws attention to the psychological impacts and legislative frameworks of preventative imprisonment during wartime, comparing this policy to the recent controversial detentions of asylum seekers. He argues that, without a Bill of Rights, as in the United States, individuals have no protection against internment during times of war. Through his case studies, Gaetano Rando illustrates the unintended adverse impacts of internment of breadwinners on Italian women and children across the continent. He argues that, despite the now commonly held view that internment was unjust, official recognition of this fact took more than 50 years to be acknowledged. Francesca Musicò-Rullo offers a detailed archival analysis on two families whose peaceful existence as hard working fishermen and farmers in New South Wales were destabilised by their enemy alien status. Her research suggests that the treatment of Italians during the war was incongruous, unreasonable, and counter-productive. My own chapter is based on interviews with the last known male internees who were held at Tatura Camp 3A, Hay Camp 6, and Camps 9, 10A, 14A, 14D at Loveday.

Some memoirs in this compilation begin well before the war between Italy and the Commonwealth transformed ordinary people into potential Fifth Columnists, or 'sleeper cells' – allegedly an enemy ready to assist an Axis invasion of Australia. Although there was no evidence of an Italian uprising or 'lone wolf' attacks, mass detention was the principal strategy employed to manage the nation's overwhelming war anxieties regarding Italians as potential supporter of a Japanese invasion. A number of stories in this anthology articulate unrequited emotional pain, even though more than seven decades have passed since their peaceful lives were shattered by conflict. While the archival records offer clear insights into the written history of wartime internment in this nation, they are not the final word on what tens of thousands of Italians experienced during wartime Australia. Theirs is a hidden story of fears, torment, and loss because of the mass incarceration of male breadwinners or even entire families. In this anthology, commonplace folk share their personal memories and feelings to acknowledge their families' wartime travails. Cast as a hated enemy, they too were human beings, silently suffering alongside their Australian neighbours. These fifteen narratives begin with Simone Alcorso's explorations on her father Orlando's wartime internment as an Italian Fascist. Uncovering the truth about her father's wartime experiences as an Italian Jew has profoundly changed her understanding of the family's history. Other stories offer different insights into wartime internment.

    The Tibaldi and Carbone families had arrived prior the Great War, Mariano Emmi, who first migrated in 1922, waited for his family to arrive in 1937. Sam Cavallaro, Mario Previtera, Nicole Musitano, and Roy Cardillo share their families' heartbreak and grief after the premature death of loved ones just before, during, or shortly after the war. The Datodi, and Fortuna families describe their detentions and deportation from Palestine as entire families, while the Marsella family was interned at Changi in Singapore by the British and later transported to Australia for indefinite detention at Tatura Internment Camp 3A. The Caminiti, Salvemini, and Cali` families share the many challenges that were eventually overcome with the support of extended family. Marino Belligoi explains how his grandfather's internment affected his family's life trajectory in Italy.

Transgenerational Memory

It could be argued that civilians who were on the front line of war suffered more than those interned in Australia. Yet, these recollections show how the suffering of innocent people could be aggravated by the unpredictable tides and foibles of war – and happenstance. These testimonies contest the view that Italians experienced a relatively benign war in Australia and give a voice to the unspoken sadness that remains hidden in many Italian families' reminiscences of wartime in Australia. They are not alone in this WWII civilian internment experience in Allied nations.

Although Britain has not offered a formal apology to civilians who were unjustly detained, the United States Government has been held to account for wrongful detentions of the Japanese in particular because of constitutional protections within that country's Bill of Rights. Canada, then a British dominion, and without a Bill of Rights, has begun the healing process through an acknowledgement of wrongful internments with funded research, websites, memorials and museum spaces focusing on Italian internment. In contrast, Australian politicians from both sides of politics have considered it adequate to express an acknowledgement and regret for wrongful detentions and civic injustices visited on tens of thousands of migrants primarily because of their Italian ethnicity. As a diaspora in an enemy nation, Italians not only lost the support of their country of origin, but also the right to live peacefully as residents in their adopted homeland. While military Prisoners of War attained a war pension on their return to Italy, Australia's civilian Italians lost more than they ever dared to reveal.

Furthermore, more than 1000 naturalised Italian Australians, Australian-born children of Italians, and Italian civilian deportees of the British, had their Naturalised British Subject (NBS) or Overseas British citizenships annulled from the day of internment. Thus, neither Italy the nation they had renounced to become NBS, nor Britain recognised their legal nationality. Remarkably, Italian-born children of naturalised Italians, lost their British Subject status on the day they turned 18 years old, but could not become naturalised until they turned 21 years old. Examples include Peter Dalseno who migrated as a 2-year-old infant with his family and the Italian-deportee children born at Tatura Internment Camp 3. Similarly, British citizen wives lost their birthrights when they married an Italian national or other foreigner.

At the time, these regulations effectively made Naturalised British Subject Italians and their families Stateless – without a nationality. This noteworthy legal, political, and civil rights issue, which became greatly magnified during wartime, has remained largely unacknowledged and under-researched in Italian-Australian internment history. Thus, Stateless Italians were forced to reapply for citizenship after the war, even though some had been British Subjects for many decades, and the overwhelming majority were found to be completely innocent of disloyalty to the British Commonwealth. In the case of Raffaele Musitano, his British Subject status was rescinded after his death, leaving his wife, three Australian-born toddlers, and a newborn infant without government support as Stateless enemy alien Italians. This family's tragic story is included in this collection. To date, there has been silence in respect of a formal apology to Italians adversely affected by wartime security measures; it is long overdue. By the time this book is published, it will be almost 80 years since war changed the life course of commonplace Italian migrants in Australia and other British territories. From the stories in this book, it becomes clearer that historical amnesia regarding the unjust treatment of Italians in Australia cannot continue in our national narrative.

While some Italians who share their stories here were lucky enough to overcome wartime adversities, others were irreparably scarred, or have simply disintegrated. Countless other Italian Australians have chosen to actively forget their wartime experiences. For many, this period was too painful to recount. Some have hidden this memory from their families, carrying to their graves the truth about the war. Their stories may never be told. The eyewitness testimonies in this book divulge long-forgotten memories of hidden grief and loss, sometimes-cruel happenings, and survival, as enemy aliens in Australia during WWII. After many challenging decades, Italian families have settled comfortably in this nation. Even so, these wartime recollections are published to ward off historical amnesia of a time when being Italian was a negative stigma. Their testimonies of our shared humanity honour the memory of all civilians who suffer during wars, regardless of background.

– Mia Spizzica

Tearing Apart the Cardillo Family

When Fascist Italy declared war on Britain and France on 10th June 1940, the lives of Italians living in Australia were propelled into a new political reality as 'enemy aliens' of the British Empire. Australia was at war not only with the Italian nation, but also with its substantial migrant diaspora living in its midst. In an Australian population of seven million people, the estimated 30,000 Italian migrants was a significant minority. As the largest non-British migrant population during the interwar decades, Italians were an easily identifiable ethnic group that looked different, had seemingly unusual customs, and spoke a foreign language.[1]

The most noticeable Italians were those who lived in large ethnic enclaves within the host community. Although there was a noticeable presence of Italians in large cities such as Melbourne and Sydney, many also lived in small mining towns, fishing villages and the sugar cane areas of far northern Queensland. This ethnic visibility quickly gave rise to fears of an Axis Fifth Column living in the midst of British-Australian society.[2] As a result, ordinary migrants and their families were propelled into a hostile political environment triggered by a conflict that began on the very continent they had left behind in order to make a better future for themselves in the Antipodes.

---

[1] Charles A. Price, *Southern Europeans in Australia* (Melbourne: Oxford University Press, 1963). First Nations were not included in the 1967 Census: see Bain Attwood, *The 1967 Referendum: Race, Power and the Australian Constitution* (Canberra: Aboriginal Studies Press, 2007).

[2] Kay Saunders and Roger Daniels, Eds, *Alien Justice: Wartime Internment in Australia and North America* (St Lucia: University of Queensland Press, 2000).

In some cases, children of Italians who were born or had been raised and educated in Australia were classified as enemy aliens, especially after the Japanese invasion of Singapore in late 1941 and the attacks on northern Australia in early 1942.[3] Disquiet gripped the sparsely populated antipodean nation-continent, often creating an undercurrent of frenzied panic about a possible uprising from within its migrant communities. This chapter focuses on the wartime experiences of the Cardillo family who lived in Atherton in Queensland. Documentation in the National Archives of Australia and oral testimony from Salvo's youngest son Orazio (Roy), now in his eightieth year, assist in the reconstruction of the Cardillo family's experiences before, during, and immediately after the Second World War. Their chronicle begins in northern Queensland where the family had settled in the early 1920s.[4]

A family's new life in the Antipodes

Salvatore (Salvo) Cardillo was born in Sicily in 1898. He migrated to Australia in 1922 and become a naturalised British subject in early 1925. Salvo settled in Ingham, working in the area as a cane cutter and farm worker until he purchased a corn farm in Atherton in 1937. In 1925, he married Filippa Privetera, and within a year the couple had begun a family, establishing their home in Burnside. The family grew to five children by 1936, and in the following year moved to the Atherton Tablelands in Queensland, principally because the climate was better of Filippa's chronic ill health. However, Filippa did not recover from a lung disease and died in January 1940. The youngest child, Orazio, who was four years old at the time, and four siblings were left to care for each other and their father. However, in March 1942, the

[3] National Archives Australia (NAA): BP242/1, Q31298 (Dalseno); MP1103/1, Q8715 (Signorini); MP1103/1, QF8783 (Gatti); MP1103/1, QF8770 (Di Blasi)

[4] NAA: MP1103/2, Q8503, Cardillo, Salvatore.

Tearing Apart the Cardillo Family

Figure 1.1: Italian internees leaving Loveday Internment Camp 9, 1943. (courtesy AWM).

family suffered another major ordeal when Salvo was unexpectedly interned during the mass arrests of Italians in north Queensland that followed the Japanese attacks on Darwin the previous month. Salvo's investigation dossier is a trove of military and police documents concerning his arrest, his objection to internment as a British subject, and his letters to authorities.[5] In contrast, official records on the fate of the Cardillo children are negligible, as they were for most children in state care in this period. Interviews with Orazio (Roy) Cardillo have helped therefore to piece together some of the story. In 2015, while sitting in his sunny lounge room in northern Queensland, Roy begins to recall long-buried memories of his wartime childhood.[6]

---

[5] NAA: BP242/1, Q3517, Cardillo, Queensland investigation case file (*hereafter:* Cardillo Investigation).

[6] Author's interviews with Roy Cardillo, Charters Towers,

Even as a small boy, Roy lost all hope of growing up in an intact family, and it is only very recently, six months before his eightieth birthday that he has finally felt able to talk about his experiences. Indeed, his four older siblings have never been able to discuss their wartime years because the memories are too painful.[7] As he explains:

> My father was angry much of the time after mum died. There were rumours that a man denounced him because he didn't help him to get his car out of a bog. Hearsay was that he wore a black shirt or jacket or vest and black tie into town, and that this proved that he was a Fascist. He wore black in mourning because my mother had died, not for Mussolini.[8]

Archival documents suggest that Salvo was arrested in the first instance, because he wore black clothing into town and because he had a brusque personality. His black shirt was interpreted as membership of Mussolini's Black Shirts.[9] During his interrogation Salvatore tried to explain that he had started wearing black after Filippa died, which was corroborated by police reports.[10] Given the family's Sicilian background, it is likely that the children also wore black clothing or armbands to school soon after their mother's death, as was the Italian custom at the time.

The military, however, would not accept Salvo's explanation, and gathered unsworn statements and negative gossip to support their case against him. Police documents suggest that authorities did not take into account the considerable emotional stress Salvo had been

---

Queensland, 2015 & 2016 (*hereafter:* Roy Cardillo).

[7] Author's interviews with Roy Cardillo, Charters Towers, Queensland, 2015 & 2016 (*hereafter:* Roy Cardillo).

[8] Ibid.

[9] Roslyn P. Cooper. "'We want a Mussolini': views of fascist Italy in Australia." *Australian Journal of Politics & History* 39, no. 3 (1993): 348-366. Black Shirts (Camicie Nere) were similar to the Nazi SS.

[10] Cardillo Investigation.

under during Filippa's long illness, his grief after her death, and the difficulty of raising five young children and running a farm single-handedly.

Even though police did not produce sworn material evidence to incontrovertibly prove subversive Fascist activities, Salvo was imprisoned as an Italian enemy alien from March 1942 to late 1943. Although a British citizen, Salvatore was arrested on a 'Master Warrant' without any criminal charge, because of his enemy alien Italian place of birth.[11] With the outbreak of war developed a deep-rooted suspicion of all Italians, whether British subjects or not, as potential saboteurs that endorsed these dramatic emergency security measures. These emergency laws obscured the lack of due process and completely disregarded naturalised British subject migrants their citizenship rights.[12] Consequently, Salvo's detention sealed the Cardillo family's future and led to the irreversible disintegration of the family unit. Roy Cardillo remembers the day his father was taken away:

> Police came and took Dad and left us (the five siblings) all on the farm. Five days later, the police came out to the farm and told us: *"If you want to see your father be at the Atherton Railway Station by 8 am tomorrow!"* We walked three and a half miles and got there just as the train was pulling out. Some time after that they took the four youngest of us to the Mount St Bernard Convent in Herberton.[13]

A blurred memory of arriving at the station too late to even wave goodbye to their father is still a very painful recollection for Roy. His father was being taken away for unknown reasons to an unknown internment camp

---

[11] NAA: MP1103/2, Q8503, Cardillo, Salvatore.

[12] Ilma M. O'Brien. "Citizenship, rights and emergency powers in Second World War Australia." *Australian Journal of Politics & History* 53, no. 2 (2007): 207-222.

[13] Roy Cardillo.

and the children did not know if they would ever see him again. Nellie, who was fourteen, and her thirteen-year-old sister Maria were left to take care of six-year-old Orazio and eight-year-old Antonio, while Carmelo, who was fifteen, stayed behind to manage the farm. However, the boy was unable to look after such a large property and eventually found work with neighbouring farmers until his father returned home in late 1944.

Still classified as children because they were under 16 years of age, Nellie and Maria Cardillo were forced to work as full- time cook assistants at the convent, earning just enough to pay for their keep and for the basic education, food and lodgings of their two younger brothers, Tony and Roy. According to Roy, his sisters and an unnamed Aboriginal girl in her teens were 'kitchen slaves', who were made to work seven days a week. He also remembers that while he was at the convent he was always hungry. Roy recalled that at times he would sneak into the convent kitchen to get a slice of bread with jam smuggled to him by Maria. Roy recounts a memory that has remained with him to the present:

> I can still see myself running as fast as I could towards the back of the chicken shed where I ate my bread in secret, so that the nuns wouldn't catch me. I was terrified that they would catch me! ....[14]

The harsh living conditions and discipline that Roy and his siblings experienced whilst at the convent have remained indelible memories in the family's wartime narrative. While the children were enduring a hard life in the convent, their father was languishing in Camp 9 Internment Camp at Loveday in outback South Australia, without being allowed access to a court hearing.

Identifying himself as 'Q8503' (his internee number), Salvo wrote a detailed letter from Loveday on 16 October 1942. He itemised all his detention transfers from the

---
[14] Ibid.

day of his arrest in Atherton on 22 March 1942. He had been sent through Cairns and Stewart Creek (Townsville) prisons to the Gaythorne Internment Centre in Brisbane, then to the Cowra Internment Camp in northern New South Wales for four months before being forwarded to Loveday. Salvatore's letter to authorities pointed out that he had never been given a chance to appeal his innocence, and could call on the references of a number of British-Australians to vouch for his good character and behaviour.

> ... I never cared for any Political group or Society, and my only aim was to bring up my family honestly with my own work. ... especially being deprived of their mother. ... and I fail to see the reason of my internment.[15]

The lack of **sworn** incriminating evidence in the archival recorded suggests that he was telling the truth As a British subject, he had the right to *habeas corpus* and a fair judicial hearing in a court of law before being convicted of disloyalty to the Crown. Yet, during a time of war, such a high valued Westminster right of citizenship was not afforded to Salvo and more than 1,000 other British subjects who were of Italian origins.[16] According to documents found in Salvo's investigation dossier, on numerous occasions he declared his loyalty to the nation, offered British-Australian references that could attest his innocence, and begged to be allowed to care for his five children and return to his farm. As the archives suggest, the letters triggered no action or response from authorities. The available documentary evidence suggests that Salvo was not made aware of the police reports or unsworn denunciations that sealed his and his children's respective confinements. The Cardillo investigation appears to be a montage of incongruous documents containing repeatedly altered descriptions of material proof and other unverifiable particulars.

---

[15] Cardillo Investigation.

[16] O'Brien, "Citizenship", passim.

Multiple documents to 'prove' Salvo's alleged treachery, produced without a single supporting affidavit, mounted to the point when miraculously transformed from a semi-literate Italian farmer who wore black clothing because of his wife's death, to Atherton's most significant and dangerous Black Shirt Fascist leader.[17]

'Fascism or Freedom'

To support the creation of such a treacherous Fascist, the Atherton police note a booklet entitled *Fascism or Freedom* was seized from the Cardillo home.[18] Herein lies the concrete evidence for the construction of the perfect case of treachery against Salvo. Further examination has unearthed the truth about this seemingly treacherous publication. The Fascist Party did not publish this booklet, as assumed by police. Rather, it was a religious booklet produced by the Jehovah's Witnesses in 1939 rebuking the Fascist, Nazi, and Communist governments of Europe, along with a robust critique of the Catholic Church. A digital copy of the original document is located in a Jehovah Witness archives in the United States.[19] Furthermore, government records reveal that the Jehovah Witness Bible and Tract Society (Society) had become a prohibited organisation by 1941, primarily because it preached against war service, judged as treason during wartime.[20] During the war, the Society's publications were banned and its radio stations were confiscated by the military.[21] Roy reports that the Jehovah Witness radio station in Atherton was taken by the military during the war, and

---

[17] Cardillo Investigation.

[18] Ibid.

[19] J. F. Rutherford, *Fascism or Freedom* (Brooklyn, NY: Watch Tower Bible and Tract Society, 1939), http://ia601406.us.archive.org/23/items/WatchtowerLibrary/booklets/1939_fof_E.pdf, accessed 2/3/16.

[20] NAA: A467, SF43/1, Investigations – Jehovah's Witnesses.

[21] NAA: A425, 1944/3859, Prohibited Publications. Seditions - Watch Tower Bible Tract Society ...

Figure 2.2: Fascism or Freedom, booklet cover, published by Watchtower and Bible Tract Society, Brooklyn, NY, 1939.

is presently still owned by the Australian government.[22] By the time the police report reached Cairns, the booklet was retitled 'Fascism' in the investigation dossier, thus creating a narrative of treason, supported by verification of Salvo's alleged Fascist sympathies. Thus, a Jehovah Witness evangelising booklet and a modification of its title in police reports, was enough to create a negative storyline of Salvo's alleged betrayal of the Commonwealth.

'Sober, industrious, loyal'

By the time the Cardillo dossier left the Cairns Police in early 1942, he had been recast as a perilous Fascist leader

---

[22] Email communication with Roy Cardillo, 29 March, 2016.

with Fascist literature in his home. Nevertheless, it is of note that no such evidence had been sought or produced by police in June 1940 when the vast majority of Fascist leaders were arrested. Later investigations established that Salvo had no adverse record of political or subversive activity before his internment. Furthermore, the positive references from three British-Australian neighbours attesting his innocence were completely disregarded, as was a petition by fifteen well-respected British-Australians in the Atherton community confirming that Salvo was 'sober, industrious and loyal' to the Crown. Even when Salvo openly criticised Mussolini, the authorities construed this as a clever ploy to hide his real Fifth Columnist role. Furthermore, anonymous corroborating denunciations by members of the RSSAILA and local men linked to the police were produced as reliable evidence to support a mounting case against him.[23] After 70 years of official concealment, the details of these secret denunciations have only recently been released.

Moreover, Salvatore's record contains a statement written by an unknown denunciator written during his imprisonment, that he was an unfit and incompetent father. The document claims that the children were better cared for in the convent, where they should remain. This raises the question of whether one of the aims of Salvo's detention was to keep the children away from the family's potential conversion to the Jehovah's Witness religion, although other reasons are also plausible.[24] At this stage, the reasons why these individuals created false evidence against Salvo Cardillo remains a moot point. Although he had been detained for unknown reasons, the wellbeing of his children was the most important issue in Salvo's

---

[23] Cardillo Investigation.

[24] In 1941, the Federal Government declared the Jehovah's Witnesses a prohibited organisation because it preached against war service, which was considered seditious. See NAA: A467, SF43/1, Investigations - Jehovah's Witnesses; and NAA: A425, 1944/3859, Prohibited Publications.

Tearing Apart the Cardillo Family

Figure 1.3: Salvatore Cardillo, Atherton, Queensland, c. 1960.

mind.

An independent Official Visitor to the internment camps, the Hon. Mr Justice Davidson, approached the Eastern Command of the Military Forces on 9 July 1942 to make enquiries about the welfare of the five Cardillo children. His report states:

> ... all the children are well cared for. The two elder girls are employed by the Convent and are paid 12/6 per week, which amount goes to supporting the other two children ...[25]

This glowing report was at the very least ambiguous. Not only did it fail to acknowledge the real conditions of the girls' employment, it was misinformed regarding their wages. According to Roy, his sisters 'earned 5 shillings each per week, which they never received for their own personal use'. While it was true that their earnings were used to support the younger brothers and pay for their lodgings, the report does not reveal that Roy

---

[25] Ibid.

was constantly famished because was not given enough food to eat.[26] It seems likely that the children were not personally asked how they felt about their confinement in a convent.

No follow-up investigations into the welfare of the siblings were recorded in Salvo's file. This suggests that the children were of little interest to the authorities. To date there is no evidence to imply that the Catholic Church felt any sense of responsibility for them beyond placing them in care at Mount St Bernard. The records are also silent on the question of whether the extended Cardillo family or the Atherton Italian community spoke up for the children's wellbeing during their father's absence. The Cardillo children were pseudo-orphans of war, and as minors had no right to autonomy, nor agency to direct their own lives. In addition, as an internee their father had also lost his right to liberty as a British subject and rights to support and protect his family as a parent.

On 16 October 1942, Salvo produced a letter appealing to the Commandant of the Loveday Internment Camp. He had finally managed to gain his right to appeal as a naturalised British subject. His words offer an insight into the anguish he was experiencing:

> I have 5 children and have been left a widower since 1940. I never cared for any Political Group or Society, and my only aim was to bring up my family honestly with my own work. ... Evidence of my good character could be given by Jack PINK and TOM PINK and Mr. Steer, who are neighbouring farmers ... I feel that my five children ... have the right to have the guide of their father, especially being deprived of their mother. ... I fail to see the reason of my internment. ... I beg to ask for your assistance ...[27]

However, no reply to this tormented letter has been

---

[26] Roy Cardillo.
[27] Cardillo Investigation.

found in his dossier. He stated that he had given three written referees' letters as supporting evidence to police, but these were not found in his case notes. Later documents suggest that these letters may have disappeared. There are no comments by military investigators regarding any positive references in support of Salvo's case. Given the absence of commentary, it is feasible that the supporting letters that Salvo had entrusted to the police were never submitted to the military authorities, nor was his case ever reviewed. The absence of sworn declarations is also a feature of Salvo's detention record.

In early 1943 Salvo wrote a statement to accompany a formal review in front of the Official Visitor for Internees, Mr Geoffrey Sandford Reed, K.C. and Captain J. Paterson at Loveday Internment Camp:

> I bought a farm ... I still owe £350. I bought it
> for £900. My wife is dead. I would rather see
> Australia win the war. I came out [to Australia] 21
> years ago ... I have never been in trouble with the
> police.[28]

Salvo remained interned at Loveday until May 1943 when he was transferred to a forced labour gang in the Civilian Alien Corps (CAC) in South Australia.[29] In an undated letter to the Federal Attorney General, he again begs clemency to be permitted to return to his children and farm. He was on the verge of financial collapse because of overdue rates and fines totalling £62/11/4 imposed on the farm by the Shire of Atherton.[30] Despite a lifetime of hard work, the Italian was on the threshold of losing both his farm and his children. After almost a year in the CAC, he was finally permitted to return home on restricted parole in December 1943. Salvo's restriction orders were not

---

[28] NAA: A367, C73857, Cardillo Salvatore.

[29] Italian internees were 'conscripted' to the Civilian Alien Corp after the Italian Armistice in September 1943. CAC forced labourers worked under harsh conditions, under threat of re-internment.

[30] Cardillo Investigation.

revoked until September 1944, even though no evidence had been produced to show that he was a security risk.[31]

With all the available documentary and oral testimony evidence considered, it is likely that Salvo was interned because he spoke Italian, socialised with other Italians, and wore black clothing. The booklet published by the Jehovah Witnesses sealed his imprisonment. These issues together with unidentified personal resentments by nameless persons, and a more general resentment and suspicion of Southern Italians living in Australia, were enough to detain an innocent man.

No explicit government policy has been located supporting the view that a migrant's ethnic origins may have significantly influenced who was singled out for internment. Nonetheless, there is mounting evidence to suggest an unexplained reason for the internment of Salvatore Cardillo and the forced removal of four of his five children from their home. Since Salvo was Sicilian, a brief appraisal is offered of the widespread negative profiling of Southern Italian regional groups in Australia during the twentieth century.[32]

Ethnic profiling

Newspapers such as *Smith's Weekly* had vilified Italians as unwelcome foreigners for decades before the war, eschewing political correctness in their interpretation of what constituted loyalty to the Crown and who was an ethnic outsider. Headlines that read, in large bold capitals, 'MAKE NO MISTAKE ABOUT THE DAGO MENACE', included caricature images of Australia's Italian immigrants that augmented the visual differences between Italians and British-Australians.[33] This representation of Italians as a military threat to Australian society fed into

---

[31] Cardillo Investigation.

[32] 'Southern Italy' refers to Italian regions south of Rome.

[33] Ilma M. O'Brien, "Ubi bene, ubi patria: the Second World War and citizenship in a country town", 33, in Beaumont, J., I. M. O'Brien,

a pre-existing racialised narrative. Prevalent attitudes regarding the superiority of Nordic and Alpine 'races' and the corresponding inferiority of non-British migrants, Asians, Aboriginal Australians, and Torres Strait Islanders were taken for granted. This racialised reality was not surprising given the White Australia Policy that was built into the Australian Constitution[34] and the Ferry Royal Commission of 1925 (Ferry Report) that singled out Southern Italians as undesirable migrants.[35] It was in this negatively charged, racialised social climate that the Cardillo family was torn apart.

An additional feature of social attitudes during the interwar and war years was the then-popular theory of eugenics, which was viewed as a way of classifying human beings from the highest (white Britishers) to the lowest in order to make appropriate laws to develop a better society. Given the prevailing racialised attitudes expounded by newspapers and policy-makers, it is likely that Australian authorities were not consciously aware that they were selecting Italians for detention based on skin, eye and hair colour, in conjunction with their regional origins. Salvatore Cardillo's file confirms that he had black hair, a dark complexion, and dark eyes. The pervasive and selective racialisation referred to in the Ferry Report was to be corroborated by Jens Lyng's *Non-Britishers in Australia*, a research project published by a well-respected university in 1927.[36]

---

and M. Trinca, Eds. *Under Suspicion: Citizenship and Internment in Australia during the Second World War*. Canberra, National Museum of Australia. (2008).

[34] James Jupp, *From White Australia to Woomera: The Story of Australian Immigration*, Cambridge: Cambridge University Press, (2002).

[35] NAA: A458, L156/3, Queensland Royal Commission; B741, V/3477, Aliens in North Queensland.

[36] NAA: A437, 1946/6/171; Report of the Royal Commission on Aliens in North Queensland - Alien Control; Jens Lyng, *Non-Britishers in Australia: Influence on Population and Progress* (Melbourne: Macmillan in association with Melbourne University

The undercurrent of this ethnic profiling practically authorised by the Ferry Royal Commission Report promoted Queensland's desire for greater social control of Southern Italians in particular. According to Roy, this issue may have been a point of contention in the case of the Italians in Atherton. He reflects: 'The Sicilians and Calabrians in Atherton looked different from the other more modern-looking Italian families. The Southern women didn't wear makeup, nail polish, or more modern dresses and the men looked old fashioned.' Societal attitudes concerning Southern Italians were possibly reinforced by Lyng's commentary:

> In Southern Italy and Sicily the small strain of Nordic blood infused by the Normans in the 11th century has been outbred, and in its place the once pure Mediterranean blood has been impoverished by an infusion of inferior African and Asiatic blood. [37]

Lyng's attitude towards Southern Italians is further exemplified in the lecture notes of a military intelligence training officer identified in the archival documents as J. H. Hehir.[38]

'WOPs'

The Australian War Memorial archives reveal how military and police investigators were trained in ethno-psychological profiling of Italians in Australia during the war.[39] In 1941, J. H. Hehir, a military intelligence expert, prepared seven pages of hand-written lecture notes to assist with the training of intelligence officers. Italian migrants characterised as 'WOP' (White Oriental Peasant) were the focus of Hehir's notes. Lieutenant Hehir

---

Press, 1927).

[37] Lyng, *Non-Britishers*, 93–108.

[38] AWM: 419/46/37, PR 88/178, talk by J. L. Hehir, (1941).

[39] Ibid.

offered his trainees insights into the historical, political, physical, and psychological characteristics of Italian migrants to assist their work in locating, identifying, and subsequently arresting them. Characteristics of the WOP refer to the unskilled working-class Italian migrant, but the notes refer only to those from the 'Heel' and 'Foot' of Italy and the island of Sicily. It becomes evident that these three Italian sub-ethnic groups were to be the focus of military intelligence investigations. Hehir explained to his readers:

> ... what is there about this short thickset figure ... [let us] try to discover ... what is inside ... that olive skin, what kind of brain is housed in that heavily thatched and gleamingly oily head ...[40]

Reflecting on our ethnic and racially ordered, pre-multicultural past, there is a sense of racialised mockery of the WOP on every page of Lieutenant Hehir's notes. Italians were classified as 'good' or 'bad' sub-ethnic types, which was accepted as a pre-ordained, irreversible, genetic predisposition. There were five psychological categories: the timid WOP, the aggressive WOP, the Camorra or Mafia WOP, the ignorant WOP, and the clever or cunning WOP. Hehir remarks:

> In this war no Wop should be pronounced harmless unless first pronounced extinct. Inactive, yes, lacking opportunity, yes, but harmless – no.[41]

His unequivocal description of all Italians as dangerous Fascists left no room for doubt about the innocence of any Italian living in Australia. This extraordinary document clearly illustrates that the internment of Italians in Australia particularly targeted those from the Southern regions of Italy. A microscopic clue in this regard can be found in Ilma Martinuzzi O'Brien's, *The Internment Diaries*

---
[40] Ibid.
[41] Ibid.

of Mario Sardi. She notes that of the 406 Italians who were interned in this sugar-cane town in north Queensland, 222 were from Sicily, 65 from Veneto and Udine, and 38 from Tuscany.[42] Of interest is the high proportion of Sicilian internees from one small community. Further research on internment records and local history archives may disclose whether Sicilians were the largest sub-ethnic group among the town's Italian population, and if this group was particularly targeted for internment.

Messages home

Another insight regarding the regional origins of internees comes from a file compiled at Camp 9 at Loveday. In October 1941, the Apostolic Delegate for the Vatican, Monsignor Rev. Panico, visited the remote semi-desert camp to collect messages from internees to send via Radio Vaticano to families still living in Italy. In a snapshot of the Papal Delegate's visit, the largest numbers of internees at Camp 9 were 1,471 Sicilians who were primarily fishermen, and fruiterers from the Aeolian Islands, located in the Province of Messina. Other regions represented in the Papal Delegate's file were: Lombardy with 989 men, 632 from the Veneto region, 525 from Piedmont, 42 from Calabria, and 275 from Molfetta in Puglia.[43] The Delegate's visit occurred six months before the mass round up of 1942. After Japan's attack on Darwin in February 1942, about 1,170 West Australians and 2,410 cane cutters from Queensland were sent to Camp 14A and 14D at Loveday. While it remains unclear if the largest proportion of all interned migrants were from Sicily, it is certain that they were an especially significant proportion of the internees at Loveday and Cowra Internment Camps. The unresolved question is whether Southern Italian regional groups were targeted more so than other

---

[42] Ilma M. O'Brien, ed. *The Internment Diaries of Mario Sardi* (Alphington: Lucerne Press, 2013), 185.

[43] NAA: MP508/1, 255/702/1791, Internees – Messages through Apostolic Delegate.

Italians because of the negative ethnic profiling of these cohorts as seen in the 'WOP' note by intelligence officer J. H. Hehir.[44] It is unknown if Salvatore was affected by this ethnic profiling, but it seems probable that his dark complexion, hair and eyes, and lack of education charactered him as a WOP.

Conditional parole

In June 1943, the Minister for Information, Arthur Calwell, wrote a strong letter to the Minister for the Army asking that naturalised British subjects be granted the right to appeal their internments. A softening of harsh detention practices was slowly beginning to take root in the hearts and minds of some members of the Curtin Government.[45] After the removal of Benito Mussolini from power and the Italian Armistice in mid-1943, the Internee Review Tribunal began the release on restricted parole under the auspices of the Allied Works Council.[46]

Salvatore Cardillo's conditional parole was revoked in September 1944; a full year after the Italian Armistice was declared. According to Roy, by the time he returned to the family farm in Atherton at the end of 1945, he could neither speak nor understand a word of Sicilian and did not recognise his father. The farm had been ruined by disuse. Each Cardillo family member was deeply affected by the death of Filippa, the removal of Salvo, and the fragmentation of the family unit. This deeply traumatised family was under enormous emotional, social, and financial stresses from the time of Filippa Cardillo's death for decades beyond the war's end.[47]

---

[44] AWM: 419/46/37, PR 88/178, talk by J. L. Hehir.

[45] Arthur Calwell, Letter to the Minister of the Army, 25/6/1943, Internment Archives, Italian Historical Society, Carlton: Army, 115/52, letter.

[46] NAA: B6586, P19 PART 2, Allied Works Council – Alien Regulations.

[47] Roy Cardillo.

War's end

From 1939 to 1945, war anxiety took hold of the Australian collective consciousness. British-Australians were justifiably fearful of an invasion by Axis nations, but innocent Italian immigrants became caught up in the murky currents of dread, suspicion, and ethnic prejudices. Archival records attests that the vast majority of the accusations against the Italians were later found to be distorted, or even fabricated by military authorities and the police. Many of the denouncers were unnamed in case files, while those who were named often gave unsworn evidence. Contradictory evidence abounds in the process that removed Salvatore Cardillo from his family and detained him without trial.

During a public meeting in Townsville in August 1945, Arthur Calwell, who became the Australian Labor Government's Minister of Immigration in the 1950s, reportedly declared:

> Unfortunately, campaigns were fostered in Australia from time to time on racial or religious grounds. Such could not be too strongly condemned as it was harmful to Australia at home and abroad.[48]

Calwell's comments approximate a remorseful reflection on his former role as Information Minster during the war. Nonetheless, by means of government news reports on radio, in cinemas and newspapers, Calwell was instrumental in creating the negative stereotype of the migrant 'enemy within', justified at the time as a necessary part of the war effort. However, his softened stance towards Italians was not sufficient, to stop a barrage of references to Italians as 'eyeties', 'dagos', and 'wogs' well into the 1960s. Destined to inform the fledgling Immigration Department, a report on 'alien control' was

---

[48] 'Calwell's views on aliens', *Townsville Daily Bulletin*, 4 August 1945, 5f.

prepared by public servant Noel Wray Lamidey in 1947.[49] The report noted that the issues of the 'outsider's' inclusion and acceptance by the host society was as important after war's end as it had been before and during the war. Lamidey later published a book based on his earlier report entitled *Partial Success: My Years as a Public Servant* (Canberra: 1971), in which he re-affirmed that newcomers needed to be made more welcome and accepted by the post-war nation. However, as Mark Finnane writes: 'From 1945 to the mid-1960s Australian policing and security interest in aliens was sustained through the continuing reactivation of historical memories of two world wars.'[50] If this is accurate, clandestine surveillance and ethnic profiling of non-British residents was likely to have continued unabated for decades after the war officially ended.

Conclusion

According to Roy, the Cardillos were never able to become a united family again, especially after Salvo remarried and had another child. Soon after the war, the five children left on their different paths because of the complex family circumstances that surrounded them, regardless of whether they were emotionally ready or not.

Roy still lives with many emotional scares from his childhood. He has life-long dyslexia, which he suggests is due to being denied pencil and paper for the entire time he was confined to the convent. In spite of this, he has a brilliant mathematical mind, which he has used to his advantage later in life. Roy never married, becoming an outback drover and then a tradesman until his retirement.

---

[49] Noel W. Lamidey, *A Report to the Honourable Arthur A. Calwell, M. P., Minister for Immigration upon some aspects of alien control in Australia during time of war* (Canberra: Aliens Classification and Advisory Committee, 1947).

[50] Mark Finnane, 'Controlling the alien in mid-twentieth century Australia: The origins and fate of a policing role', *Policing and Society*, 19, no. 4 (2009): 442–467.

He now lives a quiet life near Townsville, surrounded by many loyal friends, pets, and an extended family. In recent years, he has changed his name by deed poll from Orazio to Roy. Now 80 years old, he reports that he is comfortable recounting his family's wartime experiences and has written a short memoir that is included in an anthology of Italian wartime narratives.[51] Many thousands of Italian migrants who arrived in Australia during the interwar decades, like the Cardillos, were adversely affected by war hysteria that seized this nation. Salvatore Cardillo's internment had emotional and financial ramifications for the entire family. The children lived with profound emotional scars that lasted a lifetime. Even after more than 70 years, Roy Cardillo still has vivid memories of those terrible war years and sad memories that sometimes come flooding back.

An unresolved question that this chapter raises is whether Sicilians, like Salvatore, were particularly targeted for detention because of their ethnicity, or skin colour regardless of the lack of evidence against them.[52] The fact that most of Australia's 30,000 Italians were not incarcerated leaves room for conjecture about the real reasons for imprisoning a naturalised British subject with no known ties to Fascism. Another issue that remains unanswered is whether Salvo's alleged interest in the Jehovah's Witness literature was manufactured, as he did not read in English, nor was known to participate in religious groups. It also remains a moot point whether the unsworn and unverified denunciations against him were malicious and contrived. It also remains unclear why the children were not taken to their nearest relatives to be care for, instead of being confined to an institution. Perhaps there are valuable lessons to be learned from a family torn apart by war's consequences. Regrettably, past injustices

---

[51] See: Roy Cardillo, 'Orazio's Story', in this book; many thanks to Roy Cardillo.
[52] Beaumont. *Under Suspicion*, 1–8.

towards innocent Italian migrants have remained largely unaddressed in mainstream histories of Word War II in Australia, perhaps because as Kay Saunders suggests: 'questions about the persecution ... of ethnic minorities (are) still unpalatable.'[53]

– Mia Spizzica (peer reviewed)

---

[53] Saunders. *Alien Justice*, xvii.

Hidden Lives

Figure 2.1: Italian internees, Loveday Internment Camp, 1943.
(courtesy AWM)

The Truth Will Set You Free

The journey of an internee descendant

My journey of discovery has been one of anger, pain, and at times joy. There is no doubt that it has been one of self-discovery as well. We are our ancestors and unless we know them we cannot truly know ourselves.

There are always reasons why parents or grandparents keep information from their children: often it is to protect them but it is also to protect themselves. It is very painful to revisit places of trauma and in times past when there was no recognition of emotional trauma, no counselling or assistance to deal with depression or feelings of negativity, one simply had to get on with life which is what my parents and grandparents did.

I was born in Tasmania into a family that was well off. As a child I lacked for nothing and so in this cloistered environment, I simply took for granted the world around me. To me it was extremely normal to live in a big house with a great garden to play in and to have my godparents living with me. I never saw them as servants even though that is what they were, which I discovered at the age of nine when they decided they'd had enough of living in Australia and wished to return to Italy and their families. For me, it was heart breaking and I simply could not understand that they could leave me. Angela had been like my mother and I spent more time with her and Mario than I did with my own parents. I learnt to cook from Angela by her side in the kitchen; I would watch her ironing all the washing and doing the cleaning, but I never thought anything of it. It was just the way it was. I learnt to speak Italian from them, my first memories are of Angela and Mario; and so I believe I imprinted their way of life and their proletariat values that were quite different to those of my parents. Things changed hugely when we moved to

Hidden Lives

Figure 2.2: Orlando, Claudio, Niny, and Amilcare Piperno Alcorso, George Street, Sydney, 1939.

Sydney and they were no longer with us.

My teen years were tumultuous; I was not a happy person. I hated school and I became quite rebellious. All I ever wanted was to go to Italy to see Angela and Mario again. I managed to do this first with my parents and then several times again by myself where I discovered the reality of their lives and how hard they had worked for my family. I loved Italy and being with them and all my relatives in Rome. I never felt a close connection to Australia as I constantly felt displaced; I saw my life differently to my contemporaries and never became part of a close-knit group of friends. I tended to be a loner and in many ways, I still am.

It was from my Aunt Luisella in Rome whom I adored that I found out that we were of Jewish descent. I must have been around twenty-two years old when it simply came out as part of the conversation. She was horrified that I had not been told and still I can see the expression of sadness on her face at my shock. We had been baptised as Catholics and even though there was no religion of any sort practiced in my home, we were always told we were Catholic. My parents were both anti-religion of any kind and now that I know the truth about them, it is very easy to understand why. Both of them were Jewish. My father, Orlando Piperno Alcorso from Italy, and my mother, Corina Marcu from Romania. They both came from well-established, upper class families and would never have dreamt of migrating to Australia for economic reasons or to give their children a better start in life. They left because they had no choice. My mother entered Australia in 1939 as a refugee alien with Jewish stamped on her entry visa. My father arrived in 1938 as a textile merchant to set up a new industry before the Second World War broke out. His immediate family negated their Jewish connection. This decision would have severe repercussions when the war broke out and they were arrested as enemy aliens. This decision still does not make sense to the rest of the family as other family members who came to Australia fleeing the racial laws of 1938 in Italy, declared they were Jewish and rather than being interned became part of the Australian Defence Forces in non-combative roles.

As children, we knew that my father and uncle had been interned but they rarely spoke of their experiences, or if they did, they made light of them or never finished the stories, always changing the subject and going onto other things. We knew that my father had been kept by the authorities for far longer than my uncle and was not released until the end of the war despite the Allied Armistice with Italy in 1943, when my uncle Claudio was released. We were simply told that he, unlike my father, was ill and had to return to civilian life. We never questioned their reasoning. We grew up in an age when parental authority was absolute and we learnt never to question our elders, simply to respect them and do as we were told.

Despite my new knowledge of my Jewish ancestry, I did not take a great interest in it. I was at an age when the development of my own life was paramount, I was looking forward to all the experiences one can have as an adult. I was never particularly close to my parents and so my own adventures seemed far more important. Besides I had learnt early on to repress my emotions and to withdraw from my parents. It is only now in hindsight and with all the research I have done into my family's origins and history that particular events I can remember begin to make sense.

Occasionally, while in Australia, an Italian would immediately say to me "but of course you are Jewish" and I would often wonder how they knew. One of the greatest ironies of my journey is that Italian Australians knew that the family origins were Jewish, yet as we were growing up we never did. I later discovered that Piperno is as much a Jewish name in Italy as Goldberg is here. The other curiosity is that my research has revealed that everyone in the internment camps knew that my father and uncle were Jewish. They were known as the Jewish brothers, yet they continued to maintain the pretence. One can understand of course that if a non-religious family is persecuted for their racial origins they would do as much as possible to protect their children from further persecution. But why maintain this pretence while imprisoned in a camp, which stole your youth? And why maintain this pretence when your uncle, your mother's brother, readily admitted Jewish ancestry, and was never interned and served in the Australian Defence Forces?

This riddle can never be answered one can only make suppositions because unfortunately those family members who should have been asked, never were, and are now no longer with us. It also begs the question that the authorities must have known about the Alcorso brothers' Jewish connections but never laboured the point, not even in the Internment Appeals tribunal. Both brothers were questioned about their Jewish ancestry but they made little

Figure 2.3: Orlando Alcorso, circa 1935.

of it, stating that a maternal grandfather was Jewish and leaving it at that. The brothers were determined to prove that they were not Fascists far more than seeking liberty from the confines of internment through an association with Judaism.

The decision of the Appeals Tribunal was that the brothers were in fact bona fide refugees from the tyranny of Mussolini's Fascist regime in Italy with no malicious intent in Australia nor were they a security threat and thus could be released from internment. Despite this, the Australian military authorities blatantly overturned this decision and kept the brothers interned. In fact, it was to the authorities' advantage that they did not openly admit their Jewish connections. Research in the archives proves that my father in particular, Orlando Alcorso, was used for propaganda purposes.

My journey of discovery has had many emotional moments but perhaps none quite as harsh as discovering the footage in the National Film and Sound Archives on the perils of the Fifth Column in Australia. The Fifth Column was considered as a Fascist implant with the intention of spying. My father had mentioned his notoriety in the press and made a joke out of the display of his personal effects in an exhibition on the Fifth Column in Sydney but never elaborated on the subject. My mother even mentioned with a smile on her face that she first heard of Orlando Alcorso long before she met him, through the personal items of his she had seen in this exhibition as well as reading newspaper articles on his subversive Fascist activity. It is only now that I can understand how devastating this must have been for both my parents. They did not escape the terrors of Fascism and the persecution of the Jews by the Nazis to come to this new, supposedly democratic country to be made an example of and used as propaganda. My father was extremely anti-Fascist and he had every reason to be. He grew up in a prosperous family, his life was blessed, and he was young and enjoyed everything that his father provided for him. But, life was about to take a dramatic fork in the road for the Alcorso family.

Just before the anti-Jewish laws were to take effect in 1938, my father very unwillingly left the country of his birth and the life he enjoyed. He had no choice, like many other Jewish families they had to make very hard decisions very early on when they began to understand what the future may hold for them and how they may survive yet another period of oppression. Other members in the family did not make these hard decisions at the right time and suffered the consequences of the very harsh racial laws imposed by Mussolini. Once the Nazis took over Italy after the fall of the Fascist Regime in 1943, the persecution of the Jews took up the similar pattern of other European countries. My grandmother's sister and her husband, a cousin of my grandfather, Amilcare, were taken to Auschwitz where they were murdered. Other family members fled into hiding in the Italian countryside where they were protected by sympathetic Italians and the Church, until the Allies liberated Italy in 1945.

It is very hard for a daughter to see the father she loved portrayed in such a negative light. Especially knowing how staunchly democratic he was all his life and how much he hated any form of oppression or removal of civil liberties. I left the viewing room of the National Film and Sound Archives (NFSA) shaking and barely containing the tears. I felt shattered and was so disturbed I could not function for the rest of the day, having to quiet my distress in the comfort of my home with my beloved dogs. That moment will always remain with me as I was born in Australia; my parents fled to have a better life and to give themselves and their children freedom. These feelings create a paradox: how could the land of my birth, a democratic nation, treat my father so harshly; an innocent man, a victim of circumstance, fleeing to freedom? Perhaps one can rationalise that it was a time of war when severe measures were necessary unbeknown to the greater civilian population.

There is no doubt that the effects of internment, and how the authorities viewed my father stayed with him for the rest of his life. Now that trauma is well studied and psychologists are well acquainted with the reactions of post-traumatic stress disorder (PTSD), my father's behaviour patterns very easily fall into those of a patient with this disorder. He was an extremely volatile man with outbursts of temper that could be terrifying. He had very fastidious personal habits and was very particular about his food. Unless lamb was cooked the Roman way he would not tolerate any form of mutton in the house. We rarely ate potatoes. He adored mandarins and ate them profusely. He suffered from digestive problems and chronic dental issues. It is only now that we know that the diet of the internees was a constant preparation of boiled mutton and potatoes. They were deprived of citrus and as their diet was very low in Vitamin C, they probably suffered the consequences of gum disease.

His perception by the authorities of being a Fascist undermined his self-esteem. Apart from his abrupt and often inexplicable outbursts of anger, he would often withdraw into himself and pacify his demons by drinking Scotch alone. At these times, my mother knew well to leave him be and she would sense his moods and warn us to be quiet around him. Despite these outbursts, he did have a great sense of humour and his antics and jokes are well known. He would often make us laugh and it was this softer side to him, which is better remembered by his contemporaries rather than his bouts of annoyance. My father was a kind, generous, fair man who was well loved by all his employees. He truly understood what it meant to be hard done by and would not tolerate anything that he considered to be an injustice.

In many ways he was a private man, never seeking the limelight but preferring to get on with things in his own way. It is only now that I can begin to understand the complex person my father was and the profound effect he had on us all. I look back now and see that I grew up with strangers. I never understood the rationale my parents had for their behaviour towards us and they never explained anything that we had done to upset them but simply became angry. They would never engage in conversations of the past but simply say: "Why do you want to know? It is history!" Even at the discovery of my Jewish ancestry, my father would not discuss the matter, preferring to ignore the subject completely. It is only from my Italian relatives and my own research that I have discovered how much they really were involved with the Jewish community, both professionally and personally. They never practiced the religion and kept well away from it. We were never taken to a synagogue and I knew very little about the Jewish faith until I started to do my own reading. What I discovered was that there is a difference between being ethnically Jewish and believing in the Jewish faith. Being Jewish is something that is instilled in families for millennia, regardless of whether they have practiced the religion or not. It is something, which is carried through the genes, and part of one's identity. It is a shared history of oppression and movement from one nation to another. It is the ability to adapt and to excel wherever one finds oneself. It is a history of traditions and a strong belief in education. It is a binding philosophy, which keeps communities strong against all odds. Certainly my family maintained all of this whether they denied their ethnicity or not.

As mentioned previously, I ignored the matter of my family history for many years. I always knew that when I retired I wanted to delve more into my father's life and now that I have the time, the research I have uncovered is staggering. The time to start digging was triggered by a colleague getting in touch with my cousin who referred her onto me wanting to know more about the Alcorso family. This connection sparked a great friendship and a lot of this research has been done together. She alerted me to the fact that over 50 files on the Alcorso family were in the National Archives. I was simply staggered as she informed me that my family alone was worth a book of revealing stories!

The road into the archives was not an easy one, there were many files yet to be opened, and the time required to go through all of them was substantial. In fact, it took around two years of painstaking reading and photographing. My journey took me to Sydney, Melbourne, Canberra, Hobart, Adelaide, and Darwin. One can imagine sitting down in a public reading room to uncover one's family secrets. Some of the files are so old they almost crumble under your fingers, as you smell the dust of decades that have settled upon them. It does not seem right that an indifferent government body can know more about your family than you do, and what I read just added to the shock of discovering that my parents were strangers to me. My father's movements from the moment he arrived in the country pre-war to several years after the war were documented. He was watched by the Intelligence services vigilantly and consistently. When the Intelligence services became ASIO they continued their watch on all members of my family as they are mentioned in the files. It is unsettling to know that as a small child you are known to the powers that be, and they are aware of where you go, where you live and what you do. I have no idea if my father knew of his surveillance after the war but I certainly hope not. He was not the only one who was scrutinised; my uncle Claudio was given the same treatment. In the eyes of the Australian military, they thought he had evolved from being Fascist to Communist, a somewhat interesting and dynamic shift indeed!

Apart from trawling through the files in the National Archives there were also the State Archives and the State Libraries. Here, I concentrated my efforts in NSW and the Northern Territory. My father had mentioned that he had spent time in the Northern Territory working on an airfield close to Alice Springs. I also discovered that he had been assigned labouring work on the Mt Isa to Tennant Creek Road, which had to be built for the Australian and American forces to have easy access for their supplies and equipment. He was a cultured, educated man who had never done labouring work in his life. I also discovered that he had been assigned to clean the latrines. Apart from the physical impact of such hard work, the psychological effect was profound. His health deteriorated rapidly, he continuously asked for reassignment of duties and the doctors who examined him reported that he was suffering from a nervous disorder and stress as well as a decline in his physical condition. The authorities simply maintained that he was difficult and wanted to shirk his duties; they threatened to send him to the insane asylum in Darwin. Many internees who were sent there never came out again. Orlando managed to get some leave and then he went 'Absent without Leave' – AWOL. When his case came to court, very close to the conclusion of the war, the judge declared that a man of his background and education should not be assigned to such debilitating and humiliating tasks. My father won the case, the war ended and he was liberated. He returned to Sydney a frail and shattered man who had spent the best years of his life behind barbed wire.

Some who read these paragraphs, may well ask why not let sleeping dogs lie? Why dig up the past and create an emotional journey for a child who may be better off not knowing the truth about her parents' lives? For some, this may well be the case, but for me it was not enough. I had a very difficult relationship with my parents and when they died I had a desperate need to understand why we were always at loggerheads and what was it about my actions that had disturbed them so much. I could not rest easy until I knew the truth. This journey has been extremely cathartic. It has helped me to understand them and thus forgive them and love them so much more than before. I can see why they could never discuss their innermost secrets, but I also firmly believe that my uncovering the truth has set them free. For years they carried the burdens of their secrets locked in a silence, which became their reality. Their trauma was often triggered by my actions, which they could not understand. Yet they could not explain to me why they were so upsetting. At least now I know and I sincerely believe that they too, have forgiven me.

Grief undergoes various patterns as have been documented by professional psychologists. First we experience denial, then anger and then a slow acceptance of the reality of what has passed. I believe that my journey of grief in dealing with my parents' past has experienced all these phases. I am now in acceptance mode and therefore coming to terms with their lives and what they have passed onto me. However there was also a period of great anger.

The anger that I felt about how my parents were treated, especially my father, was turned onto the government authorities. One of my colleagues organised a group of Italian internees' descendants to attend the 70th anniversary of the opening of the Loveday Internment Camps at Barmera in South Australia. We were a small group of ten. After we arrived, we realised that this event was predominantly organised to celebrate the efforts of the military families who had been in charge of some

Hidden Lives

Figure 2.4: Italian internees at Loveday Internment Camp, Loveday, South Australia, 1943 (courtesy AWM).

4000 internees. The Italians and the New Caledonian-Japanese families were the only guests representing what it really meant to be on the other side of the barbed wire. Most of the speeches that were given were to commend the Commander, the Officers, and the enlisted men of the Australian Military Forces who had done such an excellent job on profiting from the labour of the internees. Loveday was a compound of several camps, established by the Murray River in order to have a constant water supply but also to irrigate the fields of vegetables that were grown by the internees, very few of whom managed to reap the vitamins that this fresh produce would give them. Instead, this produce was sold at a profit in order to compensate for the cost of running such an intensive system of camps. Apart from vegetables there was also a piggery, chicken farming and egg production. Certainly the soldiers benefited from all this wonderful fresh food, with most of the excess produce sold for profit.

My anger at this gathering reached a point where I

could no longer contain myself and after all the speeches were given. I grabbed the microphone from the Master of Ceremony announcing that I had something to say. I introduced myself as the daughter of a civilian internee. I asked the 250 guests to reflect a moment on what it must have been like to be an internee in the prime of one's life, to be kept behind barbed wire never knowing when you were going to be released and the anguish that would cause your family who had very little information on your health and sanity. I finished by saying that the scars of such an internment remain forever and are passed onto the next generation. I sat down boiling with fury. The room was deathly silent. The Italians clapped! I felt my father applaud and that night I dreamt of him and for the first time I truly felt his pain. We had at last crossed the barrier that had separated us for so long. He was free and so was I.

When I crossed the anger zone I realised that I felt lighter, a lot of the pain and trauma that I had been carrying myself for so long began to lessen. I began to feel the strong connection I had felt with my Italian side begin to take shape again. My Italian antecedents started to form again in my mind. I saw my Nonno Amilcare with Silky his dog. I could see him so clearly in his study in the Round House in Tasmania. I could smell the leather of his chair which was passed onto my father. I could feel the softness of his clothes when he'd lift me up onto his lap and call me Simonetta and I would touch the silk of his *farfalla*, the bow tie he always wore. I could smell the perfume that my Nonna Niny wore, and how I would sit with her and thread beads. I remembered my Aunt Silvana, my father's older sister and how much I enjoyed spending time with her in Rome. She was eccentric and interesting and I loved listening to her stories. Her apartment in Rome was a mix of Italy and Brazil, the country she, her husband Vittorio and her two boys, my cousins Robert and Richard, ended up residing in when they had to escape from Italy. I could see so clearly my aunt Luisella's apartment in Rome, her wonderful collection of Etruscan antiquities, her beautiful Italian furniture, her collection of books and boxes. I could smell the delicious food emanating from her kitchen where Angela used to create Italian specialties, especially artichokes, which I adored and still do.

The need for me to return to Italy after a prolonged absence became intense. I organised my trip and reconnected with my cousins whom I hadn't seen in over 28 years. The joy I felt being back in Italy was sublime. The fragrances of the food and the markets, the colours of the buildings, the antiquities, the cobblestones, the freshness of the fountains, the subtle light, so different to the harsh contrast of Australia. I stayed with my cousin and the next morning I climbed up the mountain of the village where he lived. It was early morning, the diffusion of light as it spilled over the hillsides was a subtle melding of purples and yellows. In the distance I could see the ancient church and before I even realised it, the church bells started to peal echoing over the countryside. I was staggered by a sound that until then I had not realised how much I had missed. The pealing of the church bells in Rome is one of the greatest memories I have of my times in Italy with my aunt when I would climb to her roof top, gaze out over the beautiful and ancient vista and be lulled into a state of serenity by the many different sounds of church bells.

I knew in that moment on that hillside, that it was crucial for me to document the Alcorso story, and that I owed it to my family and that it should be a legacy for our descendants. I decided to spend some time in Italy to do the research necessary for the Italian side of the story. This story revealed relatives who were never spoken about and who were unknown to all the family in Australia. Through a close cousin who lives in Tuscany, we traced where they lived and I met many of them. The family is large and there are many descendants on the Piperno side. My grandfather, Amilcare Piperno Alcorso, had three brothers all of whom married and from them there are many children. It was extraordinary to meet them and immediately appreciate that we were kin, simply by family resemblance.

This true Alcorso family history is in the process of being written. This one will be the real version, rather than the stories created by members of the family traumatised by incarceration and war. They needed their own stories to maintain sanity and to keep going in a time when that was what one was supposed to do; keep quiet and move on.

– Simone Alcorso

Hidden Lives

Figure 3.1: Carbone family: (left to right) Michael (Michele), Josephine (Giuseppina), Phillipa (Filippa), Francesca, Santo; Seated: Concetto holding Leonora (Nora), Innisfail, Queensland, 1935.

A Teenage Girl's Memories of Wartime in Queensland

The Carbone family's story in Australia began before the First World War. Our memories are of the good and bad times and the challenges that Italian migrants faced before and during the war. My father, Concetto Carbone was born in 1884 in a small town named Giardini in Sicily. He arrived in Sydney in 1913, just before the First World War. My mother Francesca and sisters Filippa and Giuseppina joined him on a farm near Innisfail in Northern Queensland in 1919, where they began a new life as vegetable farmers and sugar cane growers. My father and the rest of the family became naturalised British Subjects during the 1920s. The family grew larger with three more children. My brothers Michele and Santo were born in the late 1920s and I was born in 1931. I was 13 years old when my father was interned, so I remember everything that happened to this very day.

My father was a very quiet, private man who adored his family. He spent most of his time working on the farm and with his family. He had no connections to anyone involved in politics. Even at the now mature age of 90, I still have no idea why the police took him away in April in 1942. By then, my dad was 57 years old, with a blind left eye and many decades of very hard manual work under his belt. He was not as physically strong as younger men any more, but the police took him away because someone had denounced him as the enemy.

All the families were terrified for the entire war, as they could not trust anyone outside their kinfolk. The British-Australians were against us; unknown accusers, maybe to save their own necks, were denouncing fellow Italians to the police with false claims. The police believed the lies and the Italians suffered the consequences. For the Queensland women, the Japanese were invaders rather than allies of the Italians. How could they be safe without their menfolk to protect them? War was unpredictable and very dangerous for everyone, especially the Italians who were under constant surveillance. We all knew we were being watched and we were petrified.

A word or act taken the wrong way could be seen as being disloyal or even helping the enemy to invade. Later, we heard that someone had dobbed Dad to the police. They said he had a hurricane lamp and was signalling the enemy. But that wasn't at all true! As Dad had done for so many years, he went out with the lamp in the dark to shut down the electric pump. As he walked, the lamp waved from side to side, as lamps usually do. He went to the shed and back to the house. We were off the main road in the countryside where *no one* came past. There was no one to signal to. Who was he supposed to be signalling, out in the middle of the farmlands and bush? No one! We were minding our own business when Dad was denounced with a lie. The police told us that there was evidence of my father's disloyal behaviour. They didn't show us any evidence. There was no warrant for a crime of any type and he wasn't given access to a lawyer or a court of law. Our British citizenship rights had completely vanished on 19 April 1942.

I recall the day the police came to take my father away. The family was in shock when the police said to my mother: "We've got some of his friends in town. Get him ready, we're going to intern him with the others." I remember like yesterday when the arrested Italians were taken from the Innisfail gaol to the train station and locked in carriages with barred windows. There were, how can I put this *mildly* – a few *mongrels* of the Innisfail people – shopkeepers shouted out: *"Shoot them all! Get rid of them all!"* We were in shock and couldn't believe our ears and eyes. There were people we knew very well! The loudest were the owners of the local drapery shop who came to the station to scream at the Italian men as they were taken away on the trains. It's sad to think, we had been buying

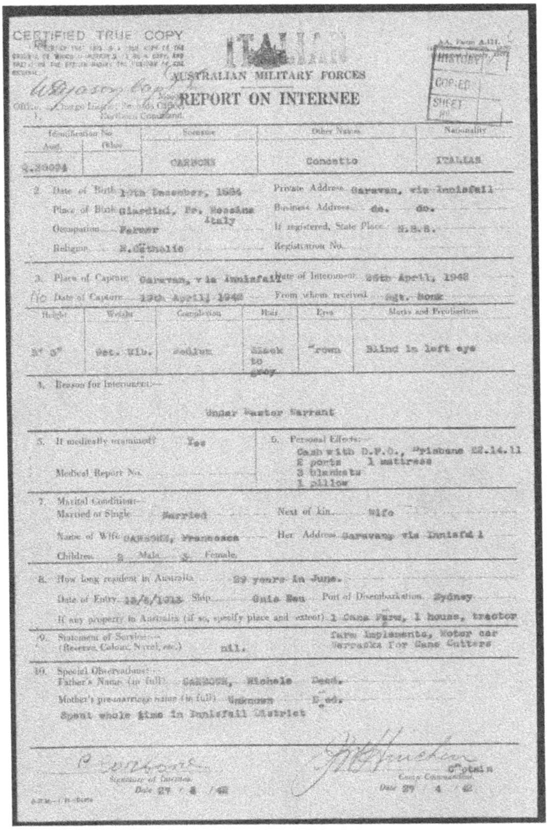

A Teenage Girl's Memories of Wartime in Queensland

Figure 3.2: Concetto Carbone internment card, Queensland, 1942. (courtesy NAA)

goods from them all those years and now we were the enemy! They were friendly before the war but suddenly everything changed. Before then, the local Italian migrants were keeping their businesses going. For the rest of the war, none of the local Italians went into these peoples' shops again if they could avoid it. They wanted our men dead, why would we go into their shops?

As the men were pushed into the train carriages, we wanted to touch our father to say how much we loved him and to say goodbye. It was a very intense desperate need to touch my dad because it could be for the last time. We couldn't kiss him or touch him! We couldn't touch him! It was a nightmare! They were locked into the carriages, with barred windows! We couldn't see anyone in the dark train with those barred windows. We couldn't see my dad, and we didn't know where he was! My world was falling down around me.

My sister tried to stop me from crying, but I couldn't, especially as the train started to move away. We didn't know if we would ever see Dad again. All the women were hysterical and the children were all crying and screaming for their daddies. The men were crying too. We could hear them as the train moved away into the distance. It was so very terrible! It felt like the sky was falling down on us.

For me, the memories of that day are as vivid today as if it is April 1942. All the Italian families believed that maybe their men might never come home alive. It was *war* and no one knew what would happen in the war. What would happen if the Japanese attacked? What would happen to us women and children? What would happen to the men in the place where they were interned? We just didn't know what would happen and sometimes we imagined the worse. All I could think about was if Dad would return home alive. This painful image will remain with me forever. Thinking about now, I can remember how awful it was for my aging parents. Poor old Mum! Poor old Dad!

In Northern Queensland, many families lost their farms or businesses if they had a mortgage and not enough savings to keep going them through the war years. We heard that some local folks were hoping that Italian farms would be sold for pennies once the men were taken away. We tried our very hardest so that this wouldn't happen. My two older brothers worked hard to grow the sugar cane, together with my sisters, my mum and me. We managed to keep our farm going from 1942 to 1945. While we had plenty of food from the farm, money was scarce and we needed to borrow £20 a month from

Figure 3.3: Wedding of Carmelo and Nora. Left to right: Carmelo Lo Giudice and Nora Lo Giudice nee Carbone. (far right): Rose Cristado; (front) Carl Cerolo, Innisfail, Queensland, 1947.

a lawyer. When Dad returned we had to pay back all the money for the years he was interned *and* the enormous interest as well.

When my dad was taken, my two older sisters were already married and one brother in law was interned with Dad. The two men looked after each other in the camp, as Dad was old by then. I recall how the family sent Dad homemade biscuits and warm clothing to tell him that he was constantly in their hearts and minds every hour of every day. We sent monthly packs of biscuits to Dad. The postage cost a lot in those days. Maybe it was a about a week's wages, around £5. We needed to send him the biscuits because we didn't know if he had enough good food. Dad wrote us letters regularly and we would write back. That's how I learnt to write in Italian – writing to my dad. One time Dad sent a letter saying that it was very cold at the Cowra Internment Camp. So we sent him a good woollen coat. It cost a lot of money! I think it was about £25 to buy and even as much to send. That was more than a year's savings! No matter how much it cost, we had to send these things to him to show him how much we loved him. Dad was later sent to South Australia to the Loveday Internment Camp.

After release from Loveday, Dad was sent to work in the Civilian Alien Corps in an unknown location in either South Australia or the Northern Territory. Like the other Italian men, he earned only enough to pay for his food and lodgings in the outback. It was very hard work and he was not allowed to return home until the end of the war. Back on the farm, life was hard and I was doing my part in helping the family to survive until my father's return. I never returned to school after the war, like many children who had left school when they were 14 years old in those days.

From a young teenage girl's perspective, my dad returned home the same as he was before his arrest. Everyone in the family was ecstatic for my dad to be home again, even though he was much older and worn out. The worse part was the family's torment in not knowing if, and when, he would return home. My dad's anguish was that he could not be with his family as their breadwinner and protector.

After the war, life soon returned to the farming routine once all the family was reunited again. But there were a few more family struggles with repayments of the large loan that the family needed to take to keep afloat during dad's internment. We had worked very hard during the war to survive and afterwards to pay back that enormous loan. Life was not easy as an enemy alien family, even though our family was naturalised, with three children born in Queensland. By 1945, Dad was more than 60 years old, with age-related health problems after more than three years of imprisonment away from his family. In our usual way, we left the past behind, rolled up our sleeves, and got on with life as we had always done.

I became a cane cutter gang's cook. That's where I met a dashing, young cane cutter from Innisfail named Carmelo (Charlie) Lo Giudice. Charlie, his dad and uncle had been interned at Loveday with my father. We were married in 1947, and have had three wonderful children – Sebastian, Maria and Lydia. After seven decades, we are still happily married with grandchildren and live in our original Queenslander house on stilts in Innisfail.

Even after more than seventy years, the painful memories of our terrible wartime experience are still clear in my memory. By telling our family's story, I want the facts to be written down, so that people can try to understand what some Italians suffered during the Second World War in Queensland.

– Nora Lo Giudice (nee Carbone)

Hidden Lives

Figure 4.1: The Cardillo family: left to right: Tony, Nellie (Lucia), seated Filippa holding Orazio, standing: Paddy, (Carmelo), seated Salvatore, and Maria, Atherton, Queensland, 1938.

Orazio's Story

A Family's Wartime Experiences on the Home Front

I was 79 years old when I was finally able talk about what I experienced as a young boy in Queensland, during and after WWII. This is my story.

I was born Orazio Cardillo, on 6 March 1936, Ingham in far north Queensland, in sugarcane country. I've changed my name by deed poll to Roy, because that's the name that I've always been called for as long as I can remember. My father Salvatore Cardillo was born in Fiumefreddo in Sicily on 6 January 1898. He came to Australia in 1922 for a better life for himself and his three brothers Orazio, Mario, and Antonino. He didn't have much education and I don't know anything about his family. My mother Filippa came to Australia from the same town in 1925 to get married to my father in Bimberside near Ingham. They were both naturalised in 1927 when my oldest brother Carmelo was seven months old. My parents had five children by the time I was born in 1936. Antonino, who we called Tony, Lucia who I always knew as Nellie, Carmelo we called Paddy, Maria, and me: Orazio. We moved to the Atherton Tablelands in 1937, when I was one year old.

I can only remember my mum one time when we were on a hilltop called Hastie's Hill. I was about three years old. Mum was collecting wild herbs to put into Sicilian patties. I recall that I was lying on the ground and she lay down beside me. I can't remember what mum looked like or what she wore or the sound of her voice. She was sick for a very long time with a lung infection. Then one day, she wasn't there any more. Mum died in January 1940 when I was almost four years old. I have no memory of the funeral or her grave. After mum passed away, Nellie, who was 12 years old and Maria 11 years old, were running the household and looked after all of us. I began primary school in 1941, when Paddy left school to work on the farm with my father. My brothers told me that we still owed about £300 of mortgage on the farm so everyone needed to help the family carry on and to pay the bills.

Figure 4.2: Salvatore Cardillo, Nelly holding Orazio and Filippa Cardillo, on the farm at Atherton, Queensland, 1939.

My father used to dress in his good clothes when he went to town to meet his friends. He wore a black vest or black shirt and a black tie because my mother had died which was a Sicilian tradition in those days. Maybe we kids went to school with a black armbands or black clothes as well. From what I remember, father sometimes met up in town with Southern Italian men who looked a bit poor. The Northern Italians were more affluent looking and did not talk to the Southern Italians.

One day in early 1942, the police came to the house and took my father away, leaving us five kids alone on the farm. He was criticised and called disloyal because he only talked with the Italians when he went into town. Who else was he going to talk to if he didn't know may

Orazio's Story

people and was constantly stressed because of his debts, had lost his wife and had five children to feed? Later, I was told that he was arrested because he wore black and was part of the Black Shirts and the Italian Fascists group in Atherton. This wasn't true. He wasn't interested in anything political, especially since he could barely read or write. My father only wore black because he was mourning my mother's death, not because of the Fascists who he knew nothing about. Even though dad was a Naturalised British Subject and there was only hearsay regarding his links to the Fascists, the police still kept him in prison. From what I saw, the Southern Italians were mostly the ones who were arrested in Atherton.

A few days after my father was arrested, the police came and told us five children "If you want to see your father, come to the railway station in the morning before 8am!" We walked more than three miles to the train station and I had to be carried part of the way. We arrived just as the train was leaving so we never got to say good bye to our father. By then we were all too upset to talk, so we walked home without saying a word. Five days later, the priest came with the police. They took Nellie, Maria, Tony, and me, about 20 kilometres away from our farm, to the Mount Saint Bernard Convent in Herberton, which is still a boarding college today.

After my father was taken away, Paddy who was then 16 years old, tried to run our corn farm but couldn't manage it alone. He had to plough the soil for the crop using the horses, which was too hard for him to do single-handed. He ended up going to a nearby farm to work for them. The first family named Tognola were good to Paddy then he went to work on the Yardley farm. When there was no work at the Tongola farm, I'm not sure if they paid him, but he was fed and received clothing and lodgings. He slept there and milked cows in exchange for food and lodgings. That is how Paddy survived during the time my father was interned.

GRADE 4 BOYS - 1948

Figure 4.3: Orazio (Horatio) Cardillo (front row far left) on a happy day at Tolga Primary School, Queensland, 1948.

It was much colder at the convent than our farm in Atherton because it was situated on high tablelands. We used to eat in the convent and slept in the house across the road from the school. An old woman ran it as a boarding house for boys with 15 beds in the lounge room. There were about 150 girls and 15 boys attending the convent when I was there. We went to church three or four times a week and I always felt unpleasantly chilly and I had a cold all the time.

I was thinking of food a lot of the time because there was not very much of it. I couldn't eat porridge in the morning because I'm lactose intolerant, so I used to have a piece of toast without butter and a glass of water. After breakfast, sometimes we would hear the air raid siren and all the students would run to the air-raid trenches down at the trees. The teachers would give us a hanky to put on our mouths and we had to stay in the trenches until they told us to come out. That was fun!

I can remember eating nuts from the Bunya pines, native pines that grew in the convent gardens. Because of the cooler temperatures in Herberton they used to grow really well. The nuts would fall with a big bang to the ground and we rushed to eat them up. They were so good to eat.

Maria and Nellie were at the convent working in the kitchen for seven days a week. They were slaving in the kitchen from sunrise to sunset every day that I can remember. They got paid five shillings a week that was to pay for board and schooling for my brother and me. So they never got that money. They never got paid for all the time they put into their work, which was very unfair. Nellie and Tony were in the convent from 1942 to when our father returned home from the internment camp at Christmas 1943. Maria and I were in the convent from 1942 to the end of 1945.

Working in the convent kitchen with my sisters was an Indigenous girl, named Darna, who came from the Cooktown convent, and two other girls who were about 17 years old, from a place called Chilligoe. Sometimes, I went around to the kitchen to get extra food from my sister Maria. I used to sneak out slices of bread that she spread with jam or peanut butter. I was so scared that I would be punished by the nuns that I ran as fast as my legs would take me to the back of the chicken shed to eat my bread.

I can remember one fun time while I was at the boarding school. Army trucks came and got all the girls and boys and took us all to the racecourse to watch a military parade. There were thousands of troops in the middle of the racecourse where a military General watched them parade before they were sent to fight in the Middle East or New Guinea. We were there for hours and hours. Some troops would faint but no one would go and help them. It was a day of fun away from boarding school. We travelled in open trucks, back to the convent. That was the biggest outing that we had at the convent. Another time, after the war, they took us on a picnic to a nearby creek. The teachers gave us condensed milk, which made me sick.

In 1946, I went to the convent school in Atherton. This was a bad year for me. On Monday mornings we said prayers, and the nuns would call out: "All you pagans that never went to church yesterday come out in front of the class." It was always a little girl whose surnames sounds like Milampi, and me who came to the front. All the kids would look at us while they said their prayers. The other cruel thing was that the other kids would not talk to us.

During Christmas 1946, Nellie and I went for a few weeks to stay with our Uncle Antonio and Aunt at Macknade. As quick as a flash, my aunt got Nellie engaged to an Italian guy, even though she was more Australian than Italian. Tony left his job on the farm and became a shift worker at the local cinema. Tuesday was always cinema night. We had discounts on Tuesdays because my brother worked there. I enjoyed going to the cinema because it was a time when we could escape to another world on the screen.

Figure 4.4: Roy Cardillo, Charters Towers, Queensland, 2016.

In 1947 my father sold the farm. It was sad to leave the old farmhouse and the memories of our family life there. Dad paid £3,000 for a farm in Tolga, which was about seven kilometres north of Atherton. In the same year Nellie got married and soon started her own family. I went to a local state school in Tolga where I was given pencil and paper and began to learn to write. That's where I met my good friend Bill Frazer who is still my friend. I was 11 years old and was put into Grade 3 because of my dyslexia. I left school when I was half way through Grade 5 when I was 15 years old. In the same year, my father gave me a horse and a spring cart and told me to pick 25 acres of corn.

Maria stayed on the farm to look after my father until he married a woman who lived in Italy (by proxy) in 1949. They had one child named Joe. After my stepmother came into the household, Maria had to leave and returned to the convent from 1952 to 1953. She got married to an Italian bloke in Home Hill and had four children. Paddy returned home and worked with my father on the new farm, but after 18 months of heavy manual work he left to go into the Australian Air Force for six years.

Our family broke up completely after my father remarried and had another son. Soon after he settled with his new family, we five children left on different paths, although I wasn't ready to make a new life by myself. First, Paddy the oldest left, followed by Nellie, then Tony, and Maria. The worst years were when I was 15 to 17 years old because I wasn't allowed to have my friends come to visit me at home. I was young and very sociable while my father and his wife were very private people. In 1953, I left home to become a stockman in western Queensland and did a bit of droving. Later, I worked for a windmill mechanic Owen Castles until he died suddenly. His wife Eileen looked after me like a son rather than as an employee. After Mr Castles died, I started working for myself building windmills, tanks and plastering old tanks for the next 25 years.

Afterwards, I started the best years of my life for the next 15 years. Even though I was dyslexic, I was very good at mathematics. I was lucky enough to use this knowledge in the stock market, which allowed me to retire at 60 years of age. For two or three months a year, I played roulette using my numbers skills in every casino from Hobart to Cairns. It is marvellous what I was able to achieve with a very good knowledge of numbers and how they work.

What about my family? Well, we were never able to become a united family again. Things had changed, and it was difficult to be in the family home without my real mum. The war years were very difficult for everyone in my family. First we lost our adored mother in 1940. Then in 1942, the army took our father away and we never knew if he would return home. What was even worse was that four of us were sent to a convent against our will, which was a very unhappy, hard time for all of us. Then after the war, my father remarried and our original family could never be united again without our mother.

Life has its complications. The good thing is that I still have good friend like Bill Frazer and his wife Anne who both came to my 80th birthday party. I'm still close to my surviving brother, Tony and my sisters Nellie and Maria. They and their kids came to my 80th birthday in March 2016 and we felt like a family again, even if only for one cheerful night together. I have retired happily to Charters Towers near Townsville and enjoy time with good friends and family when they visit.

– Roy Cardillo

Surveillance, Internment and Dislocation

The experiences of two Calabrian families in New South Wales during WWII

When Italy declared war in June 1940, a collective anti-Italian 'paranoia', as historian Gianfranco Cresciani terms it emerged, as Italians in Australia automatically became 'enemies'.[54] In the eyes of the Federal Government, Italians were a security risk that needed to be controlled, therefore, police surveillance and investigation was carried out on Italians, dossiers compiled, homes searched, and belongings ransacked.[55] Under the National Security (Aliens Control) Regulations of 1939, significant reductions in civil liberties occurred and Italians (and this could be also applied to naturalised Italians) were no longer permitted to have wirelesses, cameras, and other goods, especially guns, which could aid them in threatening Australia's security. This was followed up with the *Alien Registration Act* whereby aliens, even the elderly, were required to register at their local police station, be fingerprinted, inform police of their whereabouts and report with their identity cards on a regular basis. In mainstream society, the media exacerbated the panic. Groups such as the Returned Sailors', Soldiers' and Airmens' Imperial League of Australia, caused Italians to become dislocated, subjected to racial taunts, and their businesses vandalised, with many losing their livelihoods.

---

[54] Many thanks go to Julia Musicò (nee Lucchese), for editing this paper and Paul Rullo for his ongoing support. In this paper 'Italians' refers to Italian nationals known as 'aliens', those Italians who became naturalised British subjects and the Australian-born children of these Italians. Quote from Gianfranco Cresciani, "The Internment of Italians in New South Wales," in *Australia, The Australians and the Italian Migration*, ed. Gianfranco Cresciani (Milano: Franco Angeli Editore,1983), 74.

[55] Ibid., 71.

Italian organisations, social clubs and Italian language newspapers were declared illegal and closed down once Italy joined the war.

The State Government of NSW was particularly proactive in ensuring Italians were controlled and was far more hostile towards them than the Federal Government. NSW wartime premiers, Alexander Mair (1939–41) and William J. McKell (1941-47) were exponents of the anti-Italian frenzy, urging the Federal Government on several occasions to have all Italians interned, which was deemed not necessary or feasible by the Federal Government.[56] The NSW Commissioner of Police, W.J. MacKay, formed an Intelligence Section at Police Headquarters in Sydney in 1939 to conduct investigations regarding Italians and liaised with the Military (this became the Military Police Intelligence Section – MPI). By the time Italy joined the war, the MPI had already drawn up lists of Italians to be investigated and arrested (172 Italians were arrested on the first day after war was declared).[57] By November 1940, 420 Italian nationals were interned in NSW, plus an additional 95 naturalised British subjects.[58]

When arrested for internment, Italians from NSW bore the humiliation of being taken to Long Bay Jail (often the venereal diseases section), where conditions were deplorable. This came to the attention of the Premier's Department as contravening the Geneva Convention.[59] They would then be transferred from there to either Hay or Orange internment camps, then later to camps such as Cowra, or Loveday in South Australia, until they were released into the Civil Alien Corps. By 1944, Italians from NSW accounted for 806 of the total 3651 internments of

[56] Cresciani, 72-73.
[57] Ibid. 77.
[58] Ibid.
[59] Ibid., 78. Alcorso, an internee kept at Long Bay confirms this, Claudio Alcorso and Caroline Alcorso, "Italians in Australia During World War II," in *Australia's Italians – Culture and Community in a Changing Society*, ed. Stephen Castles (North Sydney: Allen and Unwin, 1992), 20.

Italians throughout Australia.⁶⁰ In addition to internment, Cresciani argues that the NSW Government from June 1940 took 'prompt action' to 'every other aspect in the life of the Italian community'.⁶¹ For example, in the first half of June 1940, Police closed 139 Italian businesses on the advice of the NSW Premier (although the Federal Government was to allow them to re-open).⁶² Similarly, the NSW Premier was concerned about the large number of Italian land acquisitions (especially in the Riverina) and thought they formed part of a conspiratorial 'system'.⁶³ In the eyes of one internee, Claudio Alcorso, NSW was the most 'chauvinist' state, with Mair and MacKay obsessed with 'sabotage' and they even viewed naturalised Italians as 'foreigners'.⁶⁴

It is difficult to talk of one common collective war experience to which all Italian families were subjected. Rather, there was a myriad of 'experiences' based on variables, such as individual Italians' circumstances, location, and association. Essentially, these variables were driven by different state governments' reactions to the 'Italian threat'. For example, almost half of all the internments in Australia came from Queensland, while Victoria had a small number of internments.⁶⁵ The panic in which the NSW Government reacted to Italians meant it did not exercise consistent measures in their treatment and assessment of Italians. Much of the investigation taking place was based on hearsay, clumsily collected, circumstantial evidence was used as direct evidence, and heavy reliance was based on the opinion of individuals

---

⁶⁰ Cresciani, "The Internment of Italians," 85.
⁶¹ Ibid. 81.
⁶² Ibid.
⁶³ Ibid. 83.
⁶⁴ Alcorso, "Italians in Australia," 22.
⁶⁵ Ilma Martinuzzi O'Brien, "Internments in Australia During World War II: Life Histories of Citizenship and Exclusion," in *Enemy Aliens – The Internment of Italian Migrants in Australia during the Second World War*, ed. Cate Elkner (Bacchus Marsh: Connor Court, 2005), 20.

held by the local police.⁶⁶ When government ministers prompted further investigations, they were often carried out by members of the Australian military, often very senior officers, not engaged in active service. Their opinions were clearly influenced by sensationalised military fears and, most likely, the frenzy of anti-Italian racism.

To illustrate the varying nature of the wartime experience in Australia, experiences of both my paternal and maternal grandfathers and their families will be examined. Both were from Calabrian backgrounds and lived in New South Wales: the first in Cabramatta (at that time then on the semi-rural outskirts of Sydney), the second in Leeton, a rural town in the Riverina (Murrumbidgee Irrigation Area). Much of the research conducted on Italians during the war in Australia, thus far, has focused primarily on internment (mostly in other states). While this is certainly the most important part of the wartime experience and discussed here, this paper aims to shed light on the experience of those Italians who were not interned and were still trying to engage in Australian society.⁶⁷

---

⁶⁶ See also, Gianfranco Cresciani, 'The Bogey of the Italian Fifth Column', in *Italians in Australia – Historical and Social Perspectives*, ed. Gaetano Rando and Michael Arrighi (Wollongong: University of Wollongong, 1993), 76-77.

⁶⁷ The main research on NSW internment on NSW is Cresciani's 1983 work already cited. See also Francesca A. Musicò, "The Italian Experience in NSW During World War II," in Prigioniero di Guerra: POW – Italian Migrant Exhibition (Liverpool: Liverpool Regional Museum, 2005), 6-8. Examples of studies on internments include: Ilma Martinuzzi O'Brien, *The Internment Diaries of Mario Sardi* (Alphington: Lucerne Press, 2013); Margaret Bevege, *Behind Barbed Wire: Internment in Australia during World War II* (St. Lucia: University of Queensland Press, 1993); Diane Menghetti, "The Internment of Italians in North Queensland," in Cresciani, *Australia, The Australians and the Italian Migration*, 88-101; Mia Spizzica, "Italian Civilian Internment in South Australia Revisited," *Journal of the Historical Society of South Australia*, 41,(2013): 65-79 and Richard

The Internment of Giuseppe Musicò

Giuseppe Musicò married in 1938 and a few months after marriage migrated from Oppido Mamertina to Australia, leaving his pregnant wife behind. Their first child, Giuseppe (my father), was born in 1939 in Calabria. Three of Giuseppe's siblings Natale, Alfonso, and Isabella had earlier migrated to Australia and Giuseppe hoped to increase his opportunities by migrating to Australia and joining them. Giuseppe arrived aboard the *SS Esquilino* on 29 June 1938, disembarking in Melbourne. Shortly after, he travelled to Stanthorpe (Cannon Creek) in Queensland to join his brothers, Natale and Alfonso, on their apple orchard. After a year, he decided he would return to Italy but before doing so, visited his sister, Isabella Molluso, who lived in Bonnyrigg, NSW. By this time, World War II had broken out and he was consequently unable to return to Italy. He then rented a farm at Mimosa Road, Bossley Park to run a market garden.

After Italy's entry into the war, all aliens were required to register at their local police station. Giuseppe admitted he was not aware of his obligation to register when visited by three police constables on 3 September 1940, at his farm in Bonnyrigg. The police report describing his capture reads:

> Alien was found in a shack in scrubland at Bonnyrigg and stated he could speak no English, he was taken to his married sister's home, which was his address. His brother-in-law stated he did not advise alien to register as he minds his own business. A near neighbour states that she definitely advised alien to register but he shook his head and laughed. He was taken to Liverpool Police Station and detained. We are all of the opinion that his movements should be restricted.[68]

Bosworth and Romano Ugolini, *War, Internment and Mass Migration: The Italo-Australian Experience 1940-1990* (Roma: Gruppo Editoriale Internazionale, 1992). op. cit.
[68] National Archives of Australia, (NAA): ST1233/1, Item N27845

Police searched Giuseppe's room at his sister's home. A single-barrelled shotgun was located, but it was the property of his nephew, who used it to kill vermin. Nonetheless, it was seized, along with a quantity of written material.[69] The written material consisting mainly of letters, which were sent for translation, but no adverse finding was found.[70] The fact that Giuseppe had a bicycle concerned the police. They detained him at Liverpool Police Station to prevent him riding off and disappearing after the questioning. He did not possess any of the other contraband goods forbidden for aliens, such as cameras, explosives, motor cars, wireless sets etc. The Police concluded that he be interned as he spoke little English, was unregistered, and had in their view, "little if any regard for this Country".[71] Liverpool Police returned to Giuseppe's farm at 4:30pm on 10 September 1940 to arrest him, and took him to Long Bay Gaol.[72]

At the time of capture, in addition to some shillings and personal bedding, the authorities recorded his crops at the Mimosa Rd farm as being: 1¼ acres of potatoes, 1¼ acres of peas and 1½ acres of mixed vegetables.[73] Giuseppe's brother-in-law wanted to continue paying the monthly instalments on the land but required the written lease to do so.[74] When the police contacted Musicò at Orange (the first camp where Giuseppe had been interned) regarding the lease, he stated it had been confiscated when he was first detained at Liverpool Police Station.

Summary of Personal Particulars, 5 September 1940.
[69] Ibid.
[70] NAA: ST1233/1, Item N27845, Translator's Report, 4 September 1940.
[71] NAA: ST1233/1, Item N27845, Summary of Personal Particulars, 5 September 1940.
[72] NAA: ST1233/1, Item N27845, Commonwealth of Australia – Warrant for Internment of Enemy Aliens.
[73] NAA: ST1233/1, Item N27845, Property Statement –Internee, Musicò, Giuseppe.
[74] NAA: ST1233/1, Item N27845, Application by Gaetano Molluso, 10 October 1940

Surveillance, Internment and Dislocation

Figure 5.1: Giuseppe Musicò, Italy, 1930s.

He made a complaint through the Military Authorities and an investigation of the officers at Long Bay was conducted about the lost personal property. None of the officers could recall the lease and on Giuseppe's property statement, only 'papers' were listed, with no particulars.[75] Interestingly, the stealing or 'misplacing' of internees' property was commonplace, as Cresciani records in the case of prominent internee, Prince Alfonso Del Drago, whose gold watch was stolen when interned.[76]

From 2 October 1940 until 13 January 1941, Giuseppe was interned at the Orange temporary internment camp and was later transferred to the Hay internment camp (13 January 1941 – 11 June 1941).[77] His certificates containing

---
[75] NAA: ST1233/1, Item N27845, Internee's Property Sheet, 10 September 1940.
[76] Cresciani, "The Internment of Italians," 79.
[77] NAA: MP1103/2, Item N9434, Internee – Service and Casualty Form – Giuseppe Musicò.

photographs and handprints survive, as do the 'change of abode' certificates issued each time an internee went to a new camp.[78]

All internees had one opportunity to appeal their internment. In late January 1941, while interned at Hay, Giuseppe was brought to Sydney to appear before the Alien's Tribunal. Through an interpreter, Giuseppe was firstly questioned about his connection to Italy, particularly whether any family members were in the Italian armed forces or were members of the Fascist Party, and about his own Italian military service in 1930. Giuseppe stressed that he had little news from Italy; the last time he received communication was in April 1940. The second set of questions focused on Giuseppe's arrival in Australia and his failure to register as an alien. He was queried as to why he had not seen the Consul on his arrival: his answer was he was not aware of this obligation. Giuseppe was further questioned as to whether he had been approached by Italian organisations in Sydney and/or attended their functions. Again, Giuseppe stated he had no knowledge of such organisations and only came to Sydney to sell his produce at the markets. He was asked whether he possessed a wireless, which he did not, and was questioned about the gun in his possession, which belonged to his nephew. The intense questioning focused on his failure to register as an alien. Giuseppe again stated he was unaware of this obligation, as he had no understanding of English. The Tribunal insisted that he must have spoken to other Italians and a neighbour, the local nurse, who would have told him to register. Giuseppe stated he knew nothing and spent all his time working. The Tribunal further questioned him about another neighbour, a Mrs Harris, and asked whether she had informed Giuseppe to register. He replied, "I could not speak English and she could not speak Italian, how could she tell me I had to register?" The Tribunal argued that Giuseppe must have known that war had broken out with Italy, requiring him to register. Giuseppe replied that he only learnt that Italy

---

[78] NAA: E40/8, Item CA 8258, Form of Application for Registration, 22 February 1941; See also applications in NAA: E40, Item Musicò, G.

was in the war a month after it happened.

The following day of the Tribunal, Mrs Harris, Giuseppe's neighbour, was brought in as a witness. She stated quite emphatically that she had not communicated with him due to language barriers and only greeted him whenever he rode past her property on his bicycle.[79] Mrs Harris did state that she told Giuseppe's family that he should register but did not know whether the family had done so. While the Tribunal focused on the fact that Mrs Harris had informed the family about registration, Giuseppe's main concern was that she provided a good character reference to help his appeal. Her reply, "As far as I can say, he is a very hard-working man and very industrious. Beyond that I cannot say anything about him".[80]

In the Memorandum to the Attorney General's Department, the Deputy Crown Solicitor recommended that Giuseppe's internment continue because of his close ties to Italy (essentially, his recent arrival and the fact that his wife and son resided in Italy).[81] The Alien's Tribunal recommended that he continue to be detained, as in their eyes, his loyalty to Australia was questionable as he was an enemy alien of military age, a fairly recent arrival and had completed military service in Italy. The military authorities accepted the Alien's Tribunal's recommendations and Giuseppe returned to Hay where he remained until June 1941, after which he was moved to Loveday, South Australia.

In addition to sending money and goods, Giuseppe's sister and brother-in-law, Isabella and Gaetano Molluso, wrote many times to the Australian authorities promising to provide work and lodgings in return for Giuseppe's

---

[79] NAA: C329/643, Item 643, National Security (Aliens Control) Regulations Regulation 20, Objection 34 of 1941 in the Matter of An Objection by Giuseppe Musicò, 29 January 1941, 4.

[80] NAA: C329/643, Item 643, National Security (Aliens Control) Regulations Regulation 20, Objection 34 of 1941 in the Matter of An Objection by Giuseppe Musicò, 29 January 1941, 5.

[81] NAA: 1941, MP508/1, Item 255/741/362, Memorandum to The Secretary, Attorney General's Department, 30 January 1941.

release. In June 1941, Gaetano sought a reason why his earlier attempts failed to have him released.[82] His reply from the authorities was that they were under no obligation to justify their reasons for refusing release. In December 1941, Molluso wrote to the Hon. H. P. Lazzarini, the Minister for Home Security (ironically, of Italian extraction), asking advice on how to secure his brother-in-law's release.[83] Molluso claimed he urged Giuseppe to have his fingerprints registered at the local police station, but he refused for fear of being incarcerated. Further, he highlighted that he and his family were all naturalised British subjects and were "prepared to take any responsibility the government desires with reference to our loyalty to the British flag", and that the local MLA and councillor could vouch for their loyalties. Lazzarini forwarded this letter to the Hon. F. M. Forde, Minister for the Army, requesting enquiries be made into the case.[84] Forde requested that the Lieut. General of the Eastern Command, further investigate Giuseppe's case, who then recommended non-release due to his disregard of the National Security Regulations, and because he still remained a potential threat being of military age with ties to Italy.[85] In addition, a new charge during this investigation was levelled at Giuseppe. Prior to internment, he had been farming at Bossley Park, an area adjacent to the main water channel leading to Prospect Dam, a reservoir providing water for the metropolitan area of Sydney.[86] Tensions had escalated between the local Italians and the Water Board's inspector, Patrick Shaw, over water availability. An allegation was made that Italians tried to destroy his home and stab his wife.

[82] NAA: ST1233/1, Item N27845, Edgley, Son & Williams to Attorney General's Department, 27 June 1941.
[83] NAA: MP508/1, Item 255/741/362, Gaetano Molluso to Hon. H. P. Lazzarini, 8 December 1941.
[84] NAA: MP508/1, Item 255/741/362, Hon. H. P. Lazzarini to Hon. F. M. Forde, 11 December 1941.
[85] NAA: MP508/1, Item 255/741/362, Giuseppe Musicò (N.9434), 15 January 1942.
[86] NAA: MP508/1, Item 255/741/362, Giuseppe Musicò (N.9434), 15 January 1942.

What this had to do with Giuseppe, who had been locked away for nearly two years, is unclear, but it demonstrates the heightened suspicion against Italians, and type of evidence collected against him. Based on this information, Forde refused Lazzarini's request and recommended Giuseppe remain in internment.[87] Interestingly, during all these investigations, no communication was made to camp officials requesting information about Giuseppe's conduct in the camp, suggesting they did not intend to use such information to aid his release.

Thanks to the Censorship Office, one letter from Giuseppe's niece, Antonia Molluso, survives in the National Archives of Australia. Written in January 1942, she stated that the family had spoken to the local 'engineer' of Cabramatta who suggested the family write to the Prime Minister to plead for his release.[88] The Censor was particularly interested in the line "we have told the truth that it was through fear that you did not register, now if anybody calls you, you may say the same thing" suggesting some kind of cover- up.[89]

In most Italian families, internment was rarely discussed, so this chapter of Giuseppe's life tends to be informed by official documents. Little is known of his emotions, trials, tribulations, or his daily life in the camp, or of his fears for his family in Italy who he could not support. A precious artefact that survives from Giuseppe's internment is a wooden plaque he hand-carved in Hay Internment Camp 6. Internees kept themselves busy creating wooden handcrafts, using very basic tools. This plaque is beautifully crafted with an eagle as its centrepiece and two blank oval spots intended for photographs. Only a handful of stories have filtered down through the family about the activities of internees. One tale is that internees

---

[87] NAA: MP508/1, Item 255/741/362, Hon. F.M. Forde to Hon, H. P. Lazzarini, 2 February 1942.

[88] NAA: ST1233/1, Item N27845, Antonia Molluso to Giuseppe Musicò, 12 January 1942.

[89] NAA: ST1233/1, Item N27845, Censorship Office – G. Musicò Int. No. 9434, Camp No. 9.

Hidden Lives

Figure 5.2: Wooden plaque: MUSICÒ GIUSEPPE - HAY - PRIGIONIERO DI GUERRA, (Prisoner of War) handmade by Giuseppe Musicò, whilst interned at Hay Internment Camp 6, 1940.

made *grappa* unbeknown to the camp authorities. Another story concerns the sewing of an Italian flag in the camps. The internees ordered coloured fabrics a little at a time and eventually created a flag, strictly prohibited during the war. What we do know is that Giuseppe formed many friendships in the camps with men who would later marry into his family or become *compare*.

It should be noted that one of the interesting people interned with Giuseppe was the Prince Del Drago, a cousin of Italian King Victor Emmanuel. Twice-decorated in World War I, Del Drago arrived in Sydney in 1926 and became president of the Italian Ex-Servicemen's Association and the local *Fascio*. Due to his high profile in the Italian community and his Fascist sympathies, Del Drago was interned at Orange, Hay, and Loveday. Del Drago's status made him an ideal camp leader and he acted as an intermediary between the Italian-speaking internees and English-speaking Australian army. One of his main concerns was to get the internees' messages to their families in Italy. While at Loveday, Del Drago wrote to Archbishop Panico, the Apostolic Delegate, to transmit messages via the Vatican to families in Italy. One message is found in Del Drago's file from Giuseppe on 10 October 1941 to his mother in Oppido Mamertina, relaying he was interned in Camp 9 (Loveday), was in good health, and wished to receive news.[90]

From May 1943, the War Cabinet decided that internees, who were no longer subversive or security threats could be released to work on the Civil Aliens Corps. Under the National Security (Aliens Service) Regulations, the CAC was established in May 1943 to provide much needed labour for national projects such as railways. Whilst internees were 'released' from internment camp, their lives were still restricted and they had to remain in the state of their release, notify the Controller of Aliens of any change in their living and working situations. From May 1943, it appears internees were interviewed in the camps to examine their suitability to work on the CAC. While at Loveday, the following unsworn evidence was taken on 28 May 1943 from Giuseppe. He was not keen on working for the CAC and wanted to be sent to his brothers' farm instead:

> I am not a Fascist. I have never been a Fascist. It is not correct that I say my sympathies are not with Italy. I am an Italian and my sympathies are with Italy. I certainly like work. I am prepared to go to work if I am sent where I was before, that was Liverpool. I do not want to go anywhere else. I have two brothers in Queensland and I will be very pleased to be sent there. I am not prepared to go anywhere. I did not register because I did not know the language and I was not aware that I should report to the police.[91]

This was consistent with what other fellow internees who were interned with Giuseppe at the time have

---

[90] NAA: SP1714/1, Item N29007, Prince Del Drago to Apostolic Delegate Panico, 11 October 1941 & NAA: A6126, Item 76, Del Drago, Alforzo [sic] 1943-1951.

[91] NAA: ST1233/1, Item N27845, Unsworn Evidence Taken Before Lt. Col. Chambers & Capts. Davis & Sexton at Loveday', 28 May 1943.

recalled, that he always distanced himself from the Fascist elements in the camps.[92] The Camp Commandant found no adverse reports, concluding Giuseppe did not pose a security risk if he were released on parole. Giuseppe's terms of release were quite stringent: that he accept employment provided by the Deputy Director of Security; not leave the state of South Australia and not "associate or communicate with persons of enemy origin" (with the exception of family); and "not engage in any activity prejudicial 'to the safety of the Commonwealth".[93] He was formally released from Wayville Detention Barracks on 29 September 1943 to commence employment with the CAC (under the direction of the Allied Works Council). Giuseppe was employed on several national projects such as in Wangianna, Commonwealth Railways, Quorn, and 742 Mile Camp, Transline (W.A.).[94]

Again, while in the CAC, Giuseppe's family wrote to various authorities pleading for his release. In late 1943, Giuseppe's brother, Natale, from Stanthorpe (through his local MP) beseeched the Director General of Security that he would provide employment on his farm should Giuseppe be released.[95] There was a major agricultural labour shortage. In November 1943, Giuseppe's nephew asked the Cabramatta Municipal Council's Electrical Engineer and the local Member of the Legislative Assembly to again contact Lazzarini, promising work on his farm for Giuseppe growing vegetables under contract to the Government. In 1944, Giuseppe's sister, Isabella, wrote to Forde, urging him to consider his release.[96] She heard that Giuseppe had been ill and assured him that she could provide care for him, and when recovered, provide

---

[92] Information supplied by Giuseppe Mittiga, 2016.
[93] NAA: ST1233/1, Item N27845, National Security (Aliens Control) Regulations, 29 September 1943.
[94] NAA: ST1233/1, Item N27845, Notice of Discharge, 12 March 1945.
[95] NAA: A367/1, Item C78226, Member for Carnarvon to Director General of Security, 20 December 1943.
[96] NAA: A367/1, Item C78226, Isabella Musicò to F.M. Forde, 16 April 1944.

work on her two farms holding government contracts for vegetable growing. These pleas for release were all unsuccessful. Giuseppe was officially discharged from the CAC on the 12th March 1945, to rebuild his life.[97]

The Lucchese Family

Antonino (Antonio) Lucchese arrived in 1929 and his eldest son Alfonso, landed in Sydney on the *Remo* on 27 April 1934, from the town of San Ferdinando in Calabria. They settled in Leeton, a rural town in the Murrumbidgee Irrigation Area (MIA), like many of their *paesani* from San Ferdinando, to farm citrus, stone fruit and grapes. His wife, Teresa, and their two younger sons, Francesco and Ferdinando arrived on the *Viminale* in Melbourne, on the 23 December 1936. They had two older daughters who remained in Italy with their families who later migrated to Australia. The Lucchese family was highly respected by both Australians and Italians in Leeton, suggested by the fact that when the patriarch, Antonio, died in September 1939, both the local and Italian newspapers featured articles.[98]

Alfonso and his wife, Elisabetta, met the residency requirements and applied for naturalisation in mid 1939. In his application, Alfonso stated his desire to become a British subject and had no intention to return or even visit Italy. Perhaps this is one reason why his Italian passport survives in his naturalisation file.[99] Two weeks after Australia entered the war in September 1939, Alfonso wrote to the Minister for the Interior, enquiring about his application, stating if it was not yet finalised, he would have to report to the local police station.[100] While

[97] NAA: ST1233/1, Item N27845, Notice of Discharge, 12 March 1945.
[98] 'Death in Italian Community – Mr. Anthony Lucchese', *The Murrumbidgee Irrigator*, 15 September 1939, 2, 'Cronaca di Leeton – Doloroso Lutto in Casa Lucchesi [sic]', *Il Giornale Italiano*, 11 October 1939, 3.
[99] NAA: A659/1, Item 1939/1/11592, A. Lucchese.
[100] NAA: A659/1, Item 1939/1/11592, Alfonso Lucchese to Minister

Alfonso was granted citizenship, Teresa, Francesco, and Ferdinando registered as aliens on the outbreak of war in 1939.[101] In July 1940, Teresa signed her form of parole, a requirement for aliens, stating she would not undertake any action "prejudicial to the safety of the British Empire" during the War.[102]

Even though the Lucchese family were compliant, meeting their legal obligations as aliens and they escaped internment, their lives were still greatly affected by being 'Italians' during the war. The dossier on Teresa from August 1940 reveals that the Lucchese property (Farm 285), was searched by Leeton Police but no security breaches were evident. While a quantity of literature was investigated, no subversive evidence was collected. The main concern of the Police was the fact her two daughters remained in Italy and that she associated 'with Italian Fraternity' in Leeton.[103] What seemed to have been in her favour was that her son, Alfonso and his wife, with whom she resided, were both naturalised, and the family had been given a good character report by two respected Leeton families, the Grants and Millers. In their concluding remarks, Leeton Police stated, "We are of the opinion that no action is necessary to restrict the movements of this alien. She is an old lady and in ill health, and not able to get about very well. She is living with her son, Alphonso (sic) Lucchese, who is a naturalised British subject".[104] Her son, Francesco, was also not considered a candidate for internment as Alfonso, a naturalised British subject, employed him, and that they had not "heard of any subversive act or conduct

---

for the Interior, 18 September 1939.
[101] NAA: SP11/5, Item Lucchese, Francesco, Form of Application for Registration – Francesco Lucchese, 23 September 1939 & NAA: SP11/2, Item Italian/Lucchese T, Form of Application for Registration- Teresa Lucchese, 3 October 1939.
[102] NAA: SP11/2, Item Italian/Lucchese T, Form of Parole, 3 July 1940.
[103] NAA: C123, Item 9392, Dossier 9392, 7 August 1940, in Lucchese, Teresa (Italian) [Box 282].
[104] Ibid.

on his part".[105]

An investigation file survives from June 1941 detailing that the Lucchese's mail had been monitored by the authorities and read by the censors.[106] During the War, it was impossible to send mail to Italy from Australia. In an attempt to contact her two daughters in Italy, Teresa sent letters via relatives in San Francisco and Buffalo, New York (as the USA did not enter the War until December that year).

Francesco applied in July 1941 for a driver's licence. The local Leeton Police did their best to put forward a case to the MPI via the Commissioner of Police in Sydney, as to why this alien should be allowed to operate a motor vehicle during wartime. They stated that Francesco was 18 years of age, "reliable and of good character" and needed to drive his brother's lorry specifically for taking produce from the farm to the local Leeton cannery.[107] The MPI refused Francesco's application as his need to drive was not an 'absolute necessity' as his brother was naturalised and had a licence.[108] In July 1944, Francesco, now 22 and had just put in his application for naturalisation, tried again for a driver's licence for the same purpose.[109] This attempt was successful on condition that he only drove around the Leeton district between 6am to 6pm Monday to Saturdays, with no driving permitted on Sundays.[110]

---

[105] NAA: C123, Item 9393, MPI Inquiry Form, 7 August 1941, in Lucchese, Francesco (naturalised British subject) (formerly Italian) [Box 282].
[106] NAA: C123, Item 9392, Lucchese, Teresa (Italian) [Box 282].
[107] NAA: C123, Item 9393, Police Correspondence 25 July 1941(names withheld), in Lucchese, Francesco (naturalised British subject) [formerly Italian) [Box 282].
[108] NAA: C123, Item 9393, E. J. Baldwin to F. Lucchese, 12 August 1941 and Police correspondence 23 July 1941 in Lucchese, Francesco (naturalised British subject) (formerly Italian) [Box 282].
[109] NAA: C123, Item 9393, F. Lucchese to Commissioner for Road Transport, 28 June 1944 in Lucchese, Francesco (naturalised British subject) (formerly Italian) [Box 282].
[110] NAA: C123, Item 9393, Permit 14 August 1944 in Lucchese,

During the War, the Lucchese family continued farming stone fruit and grapes. Towards the end of the war in February 1945, Francesco gained his naturalisation.[111] During the war Ferdinando became a committee member in the Leeton branch of the 'Australian Relief for Italy', an organisation permitted by the Australian Government (as Mussolini had fallen by late 1943) and its focus was collecting donations to send to war-torn Italy.[112] Apart from the above restrictions, their lives went on as normal.

After release from internment, Giuseppe Musicò returned to Humphries Road, Bonnyrigg, as a market gardener and continued farming at Mimosa Rd. He worked as a painter for NSW Railways for over 18 years, continuing market gardening part-time. By 1949, Giuseppe saved enough money to bring his wife and ten-year-old son, whom he had never met to Australia. The couple later had four more children and raised them on their property at Cabramatta. Giuseppe died in 1980 and his wife in 2002.

Teresa Lucchese died in 1952 and the Lucchese brothers continued farming in Leeton. Alfonso stayed on the family farm; Francesco branched out into his own citrus orchard at Corbie Hill; and Ferdinando went into fish haulage in Ulladulla. Before his citrus orchard, Francesco briefly ran a fish-and-chip shop in Leeton, finally they moved to Sydney in 1961. He worked for Waverley Council for over 20 years and died in 1987.

What these two family experiences reflect is that all Italian families were adversely affected by wartime restrictions to different extents. As Mia Spizzica argues "regardless of political allegiances, national loyalty, citizenship, or their willingness to support Australia's war effort, almost every Italian family in Australia

---

Francesco (naturalised British subject) (formerly Italian) [Box 282].
[111] NAA: A714, Item 23/10498, Certificate of Naturalisation – Francesco Lucchese.
[112] Spizzica, "Italian Civilian Internment," 65; Rando and Arrighi *Italians in Australia – Historical and Social Perspectives*, 45, Cresciani, *Australia, The Australians and the Italian Migration*, 75.

Figure 5.3: Brothers Ferdinando, Alfonso, and Francesco Lucchese on their farm in Leeton NSW, late 1930s.

needed to contend with considerable financial, social and personal difficulties during WWII because of their enemy alien status. The degree to which their lives would change depended on how authorities would judge their 'loyalty' to Australia and whether they were disposed to harming the Commonwealth.

Thus, the experiences presented here seem to show the contradictions between decisions made by the authorities. In the case of Giuseppe Musicò, he was deemed 'too new' to Australia to have any regard for it. His failure to register as an alien and his family connections in Italy meant his internment was the only way to ensure the safety of the nation. Musicò would fail in his appeal against internment, as few internees (less than 150) were given early release. The Lucchese family seemed to have been the kinds of Italians the authorities preferred, compliant, quick to fulfil their legal obligations and well-respected by patriotic Australians. In their case, having close family in Italy did not seem to be a 'security problem'. While mostly left alone by the authorities during the war, even the Luccheses had some of their civil liberties infringed.

Essentially, the treatment of Italians in Australia during World War II was contradictory and counter-productive. As Cresciani argues, "to people interested essentially in work and the family, with no links at all, in most cases, with Italian officials in Australian and with Italy, the whole question of their being a security risk was absurd and incomprehensible".[113] He maintains that from all the searches conducted on Italians, not one cache of arms or explosives or any plan by Italians for subversive activities was uncovered.[114] What was even more illogical was that men who had sons fighting in the Australian forces were interned, as were Italian Jewish refugees. This chapter reflects the hardship and wartime experiences of only two families. The National Archives of Australia has thousands of files yet to be examined.

– Francesca Musicò Rullo (peer reviewed)

---

[113] Cresciani, "The Internment of Australians," 75.
[114] Ibid., 87.

"The Hard life at Tatura One Day Will End"

The Internment of the Datodi family

La vita dura di Tatura
un giorno finera`
pure seperandoci la nostra amicizia
per sempre durira`

The hard life at Tatura
one day will end
even if we will be separated
our friendship will last forever [translation]

– Costanza Datodi Tatura, 23/11/1942

Preface

A few dramatic turns of events uprooted my family from the relative comfort and security of a well-ordered family life in Haifa, Palestine (now Israel) in 1940. Through no fault of their own the entire Datodi family were jailed as civilian internees and treated like common criminals. They were transported to the other side of the world to Australia. All our family's men, women and children were classified as Italian 'enemy aliens' and spent nearly five years as prisoners. Three years and eight months were spent in country Victoria, at the Tatura Internment Camp 3A. My grandparents, uncles, aunties, parents, cousin and brother lived behind barbed wire under primitive conditions until 1945–1946. After their release, they made the difficult decision to stay in Australia, rather than going to a war-ravaged Italy. At first, they faced many difficulties re-establishing themselves in a foreign country. They were Italian, Australia's enemy during World War Two; however they were surprised and grateful for the kindness and acceptance shown by many Australians. Having lost everything they possessed due to their internment, the family pulled together, gradually found housing, employment, and eventually re-established themselves. They assimilated into Australia and the way of life without forgetting their Italian heritage. This family narrative was written in a personal way, originally just for my own understanding. As it developed, it became obvious that it may be of interest to others, as the story of internment of Italians living in Palestine is an interesting one. Our family's difficult wartime experiences may contribute in some small way towards preventing a repetition of the senseless grief, loss and hardship caused to innocent civilians during wars.

Our family's origins

The origin of the Datodi family name is probably 'Todi'. This name can be traced back to 1236 AD a small town in the province of Perugia in Umbria, Italy. To date, we have only been able to trace back our family to my great-grandfather Giorgio Datodi who was born in Genoa, Italy, in 1843. He moved to Haifa, Palestine, probably when he was in his 20s, most likely to further the family's business interests in the 1870s. The Datodi family were merchants who exported marble, grains, and other merchandise from Genoa, while at the same time being involved in the import business in Haifa.

Giorgio Datodi married my great grandmother, Maria Bez in Haifa in about 1875. Maria was a Templer, (Deutscher Tempel), a Lutheran sect founded in 1861 in Germany. Her family moved to Palestine from Germany with the Templers who attempted to established settlements in the 'Holy Land' in about 1865. She converted to strict Catholicism to marry Giorgio, and they began to raise a family in their first house, at the foot of Mt Carmel in the distinctive Levantine German colony in Haifa. They had five children.

My grandfather, Francesco 'Franz' Datodi, was born in Haifa in 1883. Francesco was a trained silversmith and goldsmith, and an excellent tradesman who was extremely good at working with his hands. As a young man, Franz worked from a small shop front in the city of Haifa. For some years before he married, he worked on digs at archaeological sites at Baalbek in Lebanon, and many other sites in the area. He used to organise the Arab labour force and managed the work sites for European archaeologists. One of the highlights of Grandpa's archaeological exploits was dining with the famous 'Lawrence of Arabia'. While working on the digs in the desert, Grandpa Franz would often share meals with the Arab Bedouins, under the stars or in their nomadic tents.

Figure 6.1: Francesco and Nicola Datodi (from left) with archaeologists and their assistants, Palestine, early 1900s.

He married my grandmother Anna Bencich in 1910. Her family was of Italian and Croatian background and had migrated to Haifa from Izmir, in Turkey. They had five children but two died as infants. Their second child was my father, Ottavio, who was born in Haifa in 1913. While life was comfortable for the Italian community in Haifa, it was to change dramatically for the worse. In 1915,

Italy joined with Britain and France during the Great War and so they became the enemy of the Austro-Hungarian-German Empire. The Datodi family had to leave Haifa because they had become the enemy of the Germans. As a result, both the family home and family business were lost. They returned to Haifa from Naples after the war and re-established themselves. After 1918, Palestine was no longer a territory of the Ottoman Empire but had become a British protectorate. I think the confusion arose because my family referred to the part of Haifa they lived in as 'the German Colony' simply because many Germans lived there. Grandpa later worked as a building contractor or project manager for building sites in and around Haifa until he was interned.

My mother's father Vincenzo Platone was born in 1874 in the port town of Bari in Puglia, Italy. My grandmother, Francesca Maria Morelli, was born in the port town of Taranto in the 'heel' of Italy. Their marriage certificate shows that Francesca was seventeen, the same age as Vincenzo, but in fact she was only 15 years old. So it seems that they falsified her birth date. The young lovers may have eloped, as it seems both families were against the marriage. In addition to Francesca's age, Vincenzo's occupation as a fisherman and wandering musician may have been unacceptable to her family. The couple married in Brindisi in September 1893, after which they spent the first few years in Taranto and then moved to Patras in Greece. By 1906, they had moved to Port Said in Egypt where they stayed for several years before moving to Alexandria and then Cairo. We think that my Platone grandparents had 13 children, but four children died as infants. The family moved once more, to Ismailia, which is on the Suez Canal about 80 kilometres from Port Said. Presumably, there were better business opportunities there. The Platone family lived relatively well in Ismailia, in a large rented three-story house with several Arab servants. They were not wealthy but comfortable, owning a small holiday cabin at Port Said, and regularly travelling there by train. They dressed smartly and were conspicuous going to church every weekend dressed in their Sunday best.

Figure 6.2: Datodi family – (left to right) Alfredo, Nicola, Ersilia, Francesco; seated: Maria (nee Bez), Haifa, 1910.

The Platone family were very close and considered the 'beautiful people' of Ismailia's colonial European Levantine colony. The family would often have huge family celebrations at picnics in the park, especially for the day after Easter, known as *'la scampagnata di pasquetta'*. My mother, Costanza Platone, was born on the 9th March 1916 in Alexandria Egypt. Her parents, being typically 'old school' Italians, and naturally strict, ensured she was chaperoned everywhere she went. Her father's strict, disciplinary attitude did not suppress Mum's gregarious and demonstrative nature, as she was full of life, had a happy, out-going personality and disposition. Mum had learnt Italian and English at school and could speak, read

Hidden Lives

Figure 6.3: The extended Platone family having a picnic, Costanza Platone (later Datodi), front far right sitting on rug, Ismailia, Egypt, 1930s.

and write both these languages extremely well. She could also speak Egyptian-Arabic. My mother was only 20 years old when both her parents died in the same year in 1936. When my Platone grandparents died Mum moved from Izmalia to Haifa to live with her older sister Maria and her family. This is when my parents met.

Ottavio was keen on Costanza from the moment he first saw her. The family told me he would stand under Mum's balcony and whistle love tunes to serenade her, much like in Romeo and Juliet. All the Datodi family liked Mum very much. Grandma Datodi and Mum's sister Maria were very much in favour of the relationship, and keen to see them wed. My parents were married in Haifa, Palestine in 1938 in the church attached to the Stella Maris Carmelite Monastery, on the slopes of Mt Carmel; Dad was 26 and Mum was 23 years old. This was just two years after the death of Mum's parents. They went to Italy for their honeymoon on the Lloyd Triestino ship, the Esperia.

On returning from their honeymoon, my parents rented an apartment in Carmel Avenue close to Grandpa

Datodi's family home. Mum spent a great deal of her free time at my grandparents' home and after they were married. Mum and Dad had dinner at my grandparents' home most nights. But war was in the air again. There was a curfew in Haifa the night my brother, Renato (Ray), was born. Renato was born on the 27 March 1939 in the Italian hospital that Grandpa had helped to build. The British imposed curfews due to the trouble between the Arabs and Jews. This came to be known as the Arab Revolt of 1936 to 1939. Dad had to physically carry Mum to the hospital, running in the shadows for fear of being spotted.

Haifa

England and France declared war on Germany on the 3 September in 1939. The British immediately interned all Germans living in Palestine. German men of military age were sent to Acre Internment Camp and the German women, children and elderly were moved to camps established on several Templer farming settlements. Perimeter fences were erected around the settlements and several families were forced to share each house under extremely crowded conditions. Nine months later, on the 10 June 1940, Italy declared war on Great Britain and France. The Italian civilians living in Palestine were considered a security risk by the British and so they were arrested and interned. At about 10pm on the 10 June 1940 the English police called at the homes of Italian families living in Haifa and asked the men to accompany them to the police station on the pretext of signing documents. They were assured that it would not take long and they would be home in no time. Instead, they were locked in the Haifa gaol, and as events turned out for my family, they were never to see their homes in Haifa again. The adult male members of the Datodi family who were interned at the time were Franz, Alfredo, Ottavio, Aldo and Remo. After an overnight stay in the Haifa gaol they were quickly transferred to the Acre Prison, which is situated on the coast about 20 kilometres north of Haifa.

Remo remembers the food at the jail being awful and how grateful he was that Edwin Simes wife, Pansy, brought hampers of food to the jail for him. They remained there for a few weeks during which time Italy started bombing Haifa and Jaffa. My family remember the bombings going on for several days and the night sky being lit up as if it was day. The death toll from the bombings was later confirmed to be at least 200 people. The prison was close to an oil refinery and there was real concern the internees were in danger of their lives. The Red Cross intervened due to the danger, as well as the concern that civilian internees were housed with common criminals.

Eventually arrangements were made for the men to be moved to an internment camp, which had been set up at Jaffa. The camp was situated in an arid area near the coast, about 80 kilometres south of Haifa. The men lived in communal barracks and my uncle Remo remembers having the darkest tan of his life, due to the very hot conditions and lots of spare time to play outdoor sports and sun bake. For the first month, after the men were imprisoned, the women and children were allowed to remain in their homes. Mum and my brother Ray, who was only 15 months at the time, moved into my grandparent's home with the other Datodi women. There must have been restrictions on their movements, as at no time did they visit the men in Acre jail. Aunty Lily took on the unpleasant job of killing the rabbits and chooks that were kept in the back yard, to use as food. When the women were forewarned that they were soon to be interned, Lily let all of Dad's pet birds out of their cages. It must have been an incredibly emotional and stressful time for the women. There was war raging around them and they did not know how they would cope and what the future held for the men in prison, nor for the children or them.

On the 9 July 1940, the women and children were also interned and brought to an old convent in Bethlehem called Casa Nova, where they were to spend the next 12 months. Bethlehem is situated about 100 km southeast of

Haifa. At least the women were given some notice and were allowed a suitcase of personal effects. Perhaps due to his age, Grandpa, who was 58 at the time, was not sent to Jaffa but transferred to the convent in Bethlehem to be with his wife. The women and children's group comprised of Anna Datodi (my grandmother), Giovanna (Grandma's sister), Lily (my aunty), Costanza (my mother), Ray (my brother) and Yolanda (my cousin), who was seven months pregnant with Mario at the time. The Italian Consul in Haifa had assured the Italians that the conflict would be very short lived and the war would be over within a few months. This may explain why the women in a photo taken at the convent look relaxed and relatively cheerful. However, after this incorrect advice the Consul and his staff all departed for Italy, leaving the Italians in internment.

Figure 6.4: The interned Italian women and children, Bethlehem convent, Palestine, late 1940.

Transported

On the morning of 31 July 1941, with absolutely no idea of where they were being taken, the Palestinian internees started on a journey that would eventually bring them to the other side of the world. The women and children made the 50 kilometre journey, travelling by bus, from Bethlehem to the rail terminal at Lydda (now Lod), situated about 10 kilometres southeast of Jaffa. My grandmother was with this group even though she had begged to be left behind. She had been feeling unwell for some time and simply couldn't bear the thought of the physical and emotional strain of a journey into the unknown. The men from the Jaffa camp joined them on the train, but were made to travel in separate compartments. They travelled south through Palestine, west across the top of the Sinai Desert in Egypt, and eventually arrived at the ferry crossing at Kantara, on the east side of the Suez Canal. This was the first time the families were able to reunite after about a year's separation. It must have been an overwhelmingly emotional event.

Carrying their own luggage, they crossed the Canal by ferry, they boarded another train, and once more headed south. I can imagine what emotions this would have stirred in my mother as the train passed through her hometown of Ismailia and continued south without stopping. The trip was a nightmare. It was the middle of summer and stiflingly hot. They were sweltering in the heat, dusty and packed into small compartments all day without water or food. Lily gave a flask to a British soldier and begged for some water for the children only to have the flask stolen. One wonders what sort of human would do such a thing. After travelling for two days over a total distance of approximately 400 kilometres the train arrived outside Suez in the evening. They were made to sleep on the train that night. The next morning all the internees had to walk about eight kilometres, from the train to the pier carrying their luggage under the blazing sun. My grandmother, Anna Datodi found the walk extremely difficult and tiring because she was so sick and frail. Our family recalled with horror that at the end of the walk Grandma Anna had blood running down her legs either from chafing, internal bleeding, or a combination of both. When some mothers asked for water during the long walk for their children, the guards, who were British police, were heard to say: "If you want a drink, scoop the water from the gutters!" Such was their cruelty toward the elderly, the women, and children.

Still with no indication of where they were going they were ferried to a huge ocean liner. It was the *SS Queen Elizabeth*, which was anchored far out to sea. Bad enough they had been imprisoned but an ocean liner meant they were being moved to another country. Or did their minds race to imagine an even worse fate?

The ship was fitted out as a troop carrier to bring Allied troops to the war zone in North Africa. It had been given the code name 'Transport BB' and could carry over 2000 passengers. It weighed 83 000 ton and was the largest ship in the world when it was launched in 1938. They departed from Suez on 2 August 1941, heading south into the Red Sea. On board ship, families were crowded into cabins without fresh air. The weather was hot and humid and with restrictions on opening portholes, conditions in the cabins were very uncomfortable. Single men and women were housed in dormitories in their own separate quarters. They were allowed to mix with the families twice a day. The trip was very boring with nothing much to do to while away the daytime hours, other than walking around the deck in groups. To make things worse the entire perimeter of the ship had a canvas barrier erected that totally obscured the view of the ocean. Food was not of good quality and was served up army-style in the massive dining room. It was eaten at trestle tables, sitting on wooden benches.

They first docked at Trincomalee, in Ceylon but they were not allowed ashore. On departing, the ship turned southeast into the Indian Ocean. Spirits soared at the guess that they were heading for Australia, a country they hoped that would not blame civilians or their children for the war. They were greatly relieved to be away from the main war zone where there were minefields and the Germans had sunk many Allied ships. They docked at Fremantle in Western Australia to take on board much needed fresh supplies. Once again, the internees were not allowed ashore. Sailing through Bass Straight was particularly rough and many of them experienced severe seasickness. After three weeks at sea they arrived at Sydney Harbour on 23 August 1941.

Tatura Internment Camp

The next morning the 170 Italian and 665 German internees were taken by ferry to the railway station. The ferry journey took them under the famous Sydney Harbour Bridge. Once ashore, they noticed an enormous improvement in their treatment as the British escort handed the internees over to the Australian military forces. While waiting for the train they were allowed to rest in comfortable surroundings where good, wholesome food, including fresh fruit and milk was provided in abundance. The train was clean and comfortable and everyone was given a seat. The guards were helpful, friendly, and particularly nice to the children. What a difference! They were greatly relieved. On the train trip to the new internment camp known as 'Tatura 3', the internees changed trains at Albury on the Murray River, which was on the boarder of New South Wales and Victoria. There was a stop at Shepparton where the detainees were given a hot and wholesome winter meal. They were transferred to buses for the final leg of the journey to Tatura. They had finally arrived at Tatura Internment Camp No. 3A. It was late afternoon on a cold and windy day – 25 August 1941. August is midwinter in Victoria and the weather was cold and miserable. The camps were huge, constructed on dry arid farmland, surrounded by high barbed wire fences, with large draughty tin sheds for housing. The

"The Hard Life at Tatura One Day Will End"

Figure 6.5: Datodi family interned at Tatura Camp 3A: (back left to right) Alfredo, Giovanna, Francesco (Franz), Anna, Ottavio (Otto); (front left to right): Matilda (Lily), Iolanda Balestrieri (nee Datodi) with her son Mario Balestrieri, Renato (Ray) Datodi with his mother Costanza Datodi (nee Platone), Tatura, Victoria, 1943 (courtesy AWM).

internees were horrified at what confronted them. They were prisoners again.

Internees had their details recorded on several forms. Then came the humiliation of being fingerprinted and having photos taken with their internment number hung around their neck, just like common criminals. On the other hand, Tatura Camp 3 was a family camp and as such, the internees were treated quite well in comparison to some other camps. The barracks had cubicles for privacy rather than dormitory bedrooms. The families were together and their overall treatment was relatively good, for an internment camp. However, the barbed wire and armed guards with loaded rifles, mounted bayonets, live machine guns on the watch towers facing towards the interned families 24 hours, 365 days and unrelenting night-time spotlights were a constant reminder that they were in prison.

Each compound had ten accommodation huts and these were partitioned with Masonite, into twelve, 2.5 metres by 3 metre rooms, each designed to accommodate two people. A single electric light globe hanging from the ceiling provided at least some light. The huts were externally clad with corrugated iron sheeting with no internal cladding on walls or ceiling, making them unbearably hot in summer and freezing cold and draughty in winter. There was no facility for fires or heating of any type in the huts and as a result, internees spent much of their time in the mess hall during winter. Women, children and most of our group were issued with kapok-filled mattresses but men had to make do with much harder and rougher straw-filled Hessian bags. Grey army blankets were provided for warmth, as were the heavy, red-dyed army coats that were much appreciated during the winter months. Each of the four compounds had a kitchen and mess hall, which had a large open wood fire that provided much welcomed warmth. There were shower, toilet, and laundry blocks. Hot water was provided to the showers all day. Men's toilet and shower facilities were communal, but the women's were divided into cubicles.

When compared with the treatment by the British guards, the family was pleasantly surprised with how courteous the Australian soldiers were towards the families. For example, at the Bethlehem convent the British police would regularly barge into the women's living quarters without knocking to carry out the daily rollcall, not caring if they were dressed or not. In Australia, soldiers would always knock and politely wait until they were allowed in. This difference made a huge impression on the family, particularly my grandfather, and endeared the Australian guards to them.

The internees quickly settled into an organised life style. Ludovico Casati from Haifa was elected compound leader of internees in Tatura Camp 3A. They had rosters for all necessary jobs like cleaning, cooking, wood chopping, etc. My father's rostered job was slicing the bread and on one occasion, he cut his finger so badly he needed medical attention. Overall, amenities for the internees were good for a prison camp and soon a school for the children was established. Mass was celebrated by the interned Italian priests in the mess hall on Sundays. Most of the Italians would attend, including all the women from our family group who were regular attendees.

However, on one occasion, an Australian army priest celebrated mass and during the sermon told the internee congregation that they should "... *pray for your dead* ...", adding: "... *and we will pray for ours* ...". Casati informed the army priest that: *"We believe that once a person is dead, their soul has no nationality and we pray for all souls. So you had better not come back to this camp again!"* He didn't.

Confinement

To help alleviate boredom, various sport and entertainment groups organised activities for those who wanted to participate. Uncle Remo was a keen participant and was involved in soccer, tennis, table tennis, and athletics. They played card games and even had a few pet cats. Daily radio broadcasting censored news bulletins were played over speakers situated in the hall. In this way, at least to some degree, internees were kept abreast of the war's progress. Meals were prepared in a communal kitchen and eaten in the mess hall. The group in Camp 3A were fortunate to have Carlo Fasola, the head chef from the King David Hotel in Jerusalem, interned with them. He and three of his cooks took over the responsibility for menus and cooking. At first, the internees were supplied with a huge quantity and a great variety of food choices but as the war continued the range and quantity of supplies was somewhat reduced. Even though by the end of their internment, they found the food a bit boring, it was always wholesome and plentiful. We did not know who paid for the supply of good food. Internees were instructed to develop vegetable gardens and as a result, they produced a good range of fresh vegetables for the army's table and themselves. In addition, they grew strawberries and watermelon, which made a welcomed addition to their diet. For a short while, Uncle Remo scored the rather cushy job of valet to Major Patterson who was the Camp Commandant. Remo's primary duties entailed ironing clothes and shining shoes but usually only a few days a week. For this, he was rewarded with good quality cigarettes and was even allowed out for a swim in the local canal when the weather was hot. Unfortunately for Remo, the Major was soon transferred and Remo's job and the privileges were lost.

One of the Italian internees, Antonio Ribone, had experience at making alcohol so he surreptitiously dug a chamber under the hut's floor and constructed a distillery. The internees would bring him their ration of grapes and he would convert them to grappa, which the Italians particularly enjoyed. It is hard to believe the guards were not awake to this activity but perhaps they turned a blind eye because it was causing no harm and was no real security risk. Civilian internees were allowed to wear normal clothing in camp. My father was seldom seen in anything other than a favourite pair of overalls. However, if they left the compound for any reason like picking up supplies or to work on a farm, they had to wear burgundy-red army issued clothes with the black letters 'P.O.W.' boldly placed across the back.

The single men

Adult, single male internees from Camp 3 were moved to the Loveday Internment Camp 10A, near Renmark in South Australia, 600 kilometres from Tatura, on 10 February 1943. This was about 18 months after our arrival in Australia. This splitting up of the family was very distressing, particularly to my grandparents as they were concerned about their two youngest sons, Aldo and Remo. The popular belief for the move was that a relationship between a married internee and a young single woman in the German compound had resulted in a pregnancy.

"The Hard Life at Tatura One Day Will End"

The apparent reason for the move seemed unfair on the single men, as there was a strong sense within the camp that they had done nothing wrong.

Uncle Remo told us how conditions at Loveday were very different from those at Tatura. There, the inmates were treated much more like prisoners than at Tatura. The Loveday group of camps was huge, consisting of Camps 9, 10A, 10B and 14A, 14B, 14C and 14D. At its peak, the three camps held more than 5,500 men. The environment was arid, very hot in summer, very cold at night, windy and subject to sand storms. The men slept in dormitories on wooden bunks with coarse, straw-filled Hessian bags as mattresses. There were no sheets, only two grey woollen army blankets. There was a complete lack of privacy with both showers and toilets being communal. Another difference from Tatura was that the men were regularly taken on long walks (route marches) outside the camp and naturally, they were guarded all the way by heavily armed soldiers. Even so, it was a relief for them to be out in the open and away from the accursed barbed wire fences. My uncles felt incredibly isolated and missed the security and support of their family enormously. Uncle Remo vividly recalled his rage and frustration at the injustice. Whilst standing at the towering perimeter fence, with another two barbed wire fences enveloping the internal enclosure, he violently shook it in utter exasperation. The pressure of internment led to many escape bids, not to mention several suicides at the different camps over the years.

After about 18 months at Loveday, on 24 August 1944, my uncles were returned to Tatura, Camp 2A. This camp had previously housed merchant seamen but by then they had been moved elsewhere. My two young uncles were only a few kilometres away from their family but visiting between camps was strictly forbidden. Occasional censored letters was the only allowed form of communication. Army censors would cut out any words or sentences they considered inappropriate, resulting in many letters being tattered and almost shredded.

An internee is born

The news that my mother had become pregnant, whilst in the uncertain environment of an internment camp, was met with mixed emotions. Uncertainty about the future and my mother's poor health were of great concern. Doctor Costero the Italian doctor in our camp had warned her that because of her heart condition, she should not have any more children. The family greatly respected Doctor Costero and were very worried about what might happen. However, the Australian army doctor was much more optimistic and encouraged Mum to go through with the birth. My parents had made it clear they were very keen to have a daughter and this on top of the doctor's encouragement was obviously enough to sway them. My father was terrified at the thought of anything happening to Mum and was immensely relieved when I was born without incident. They didn't get their little girl but Mum was safe and well. I was born at the Waranga Hospital in Rushworth on 4 May 1944. The hospital was some distance from the camp and Dad had to be escorted by a guard every time he visited. We stayed at the hospital for 13 days, returning to camp on the 17 May. I spent the first 11 months of my life in the internment camp, behind barbed wire, where the four of us shared one small 7.5 square metre cabin.

By 1943, the tide of war was turning with both the German and Japanese advances being checked by the Allies. By June 1943, Mussolini was removed from power and Italy surrendered, signing the Armistice in September the same year. The Axis forces in Europe surrendered on 8 May 1945. America dropped atomic bombs on Hiroshima and Nagasaki forcing the Japanese surrender on the 15 August 1945. Some historians have estimated that during almost 6 years of WWII, 20 million soldiers and 40 million civilians lost their lives.

Released

After the end of the war, the internees who had been living in Australia pre-war were released to return to their homes in Australia. The POWs (soldiers) were returned to their homeland in 1946 and 1947. The civilian internees from overseas including our family were given the choice of staying in Australia or repatriation to their country of origin. (I think at the Italian government's expense). In our case, this meant Italy as a first stop and then making our way back to Haifa at our own expense. The Datodi family was unsure of how things would be back home, as the British government had handed over Palestine to Jewish control. As far as the Palestinian German refugees were concerned, it was made very clear that Germans were not welcomed in the new nation of Israel. My father was very keen to stay in Victoria and get involved in farming. Furthermore, Grandma Datodi was considered too frail to travel. We had lost our possessions and home in Haifa so there was virtually nothing for our family to return to. The decision was made to stay in Australia. Before internees could be released from the camp, it was necessary for them to have found employment and accommodation. For this reason, our family groups split up and left the internment camp at different times.

My immediate family was the first of our group to leave, as Dad had found work on a potato farm in Toolangi. After a total of nearly five years of imprisonment, including three years and eight months at the Tatura camp, we were released on 10 April 1945. This was just a few weeks before my first birthday. My Uncles Remo and Aldo were released on the 17 April 1945 to work under close military supervision in the Civil Aliens Corps as woodcutters at Wandong in Victoria. Unfortunately, this turned out to be too gruelling, particularly for Aldo, as they were unable to cut enough wood to cover the cost of basic bush accommodation and meals. After about a month, they were transferred to a forest plantation at Creswick to plant and trim pine trees. The decision to leave the relatively easy life in camp and trade it in for hard manual work was regretted by Aldo who was a little frail due to a serious childhood illness. This caused Remo to feel quite guilty for having talked his brother into it. Nonetheless, the decision had been made and the period of hard manual work did relieve the tedium of camp life. My grandparents and Aunty Lily, as well as Uncle Alfred's group, remained at the camp for approximately another year before they eventually joined us in Melbourne in about August 1946.

Toolangi

The potato farm where Dad got his first job was in Toolangi, which is situated about 80 kilometres northeast of Melbourne and 15 kilometres from Healesville. After the cost of food and lodging, Dad's pay was £4.50 per month. The owner of the farm was a tall, typical Australian bushman, named John Campbell. It seems the farm was not at all profitable and most of the income was derived from logging. Dad loved the outdoor life and became quite good at working the draft horses to pull the huge fallen logs through the forest to the roads. The horses were affectionately known as Dolly and Monster. The one called Monster was huge, and half of its head was white, giving it a mysterious, ugly look. Stumps were blown out of the ground using dynamite, which was bravely (or stupidly) lit by a match – by live-flame. My brother and I sometimes accompanied the men to the logging sites where there was always some adventure to be found. On one of our forays into the bush, Ray and I came across a large snake, which we nearly stood on. Ray recalls pulling me by the arm as we ran scrambling home through the bush, with both of us hysterical and screaming.

Mum worked as the housekeeper at John Campbell's house making beds, and cleaning and cooking for all the men. There were several bedrooms in the house. Our family shared one large room and Campbell was in another. The other farmhands slept in an outhouse. John

Campbell didn't pay Mum and Dad for the eight months that they worked, and over time it became clear he would never pay, so they decided to move to Melbourne. Mum was the main instigator of the 'escape' as she hated the work, the isolation, and the lifestyle. Dad had befriended a kind and generous couple named Bill and Stella Young who worked a nearby farm. They loaned Dad £2, which was enough money to get to Melbourne by train and rent a room for a few days.

North Melbourne

We arrived in Melbourne by train in November 1945 and rented a room at the Gladstone House, a shabby old hotel in Victoria St, North Melbourne. Within a matter of days, we moved to another shabby place on the second floor in Capel St North Melbourne. It was an unfurnished room except for a stove in the corner and a mattress on the floor. With nothing to do, Mum, Ray, and I, spent our days looking out the window, waiting for Dad to get home. Uncle Remo and Aldo, travelling by train from Creswick arrived in Melbourne soon after us and at first rented a room at the Gladstone House. They remembered there was an old man that also lived at that hotel who would remove his false teeth and leave them beside him at the table while he ate his breakfast. (Lovely!) The government was making land available to people who were prepared to clear and work it. My father tried to talk the family into taking advantage of this offer and settle in the country. Mum and my uncles, Remo and Aldo, were well and truly sick of the bush, as a result Dad was decisively out-voted. So our family remained in Melbourne.

Thankfully, we were only at the shabby Chapel St room for a matter of weeks. My father's first job was with the local council, but soon after he found work with The Australian Block and Chain Company in West Footscray. Uncle Remo and Aldo also got jobs at the same place and with the three brothers working, we were soon able to move into the rented two-story terrace house at 199 Peel Street in

North Melbourne. At first, the owner lived down stairs in the front room but eventually moved out when the rest of the family arrived from the camp. My grandparents and Lily were released on 27 August 1946. Then Uncle Alfred, Aunty (*Tante*) Jeanne, Yolanda, and Mario followed a few days later, when they were released on 3 September 1946. The house, which had a kitchen, a bathroom, and three bedrooms, was terribly crowded. The toilet was outside and there was no running hot water, so having a wash or a bath involved carrying boiling water from the kitchen. The family lived like this for some months. During this time my brother Ray, started at St Mary's primary school, which was only about a 10-minute walk from home.

Eventually my grandparents, Lily, Aldo, and Remo moved to a dwelling above a shop in Errol St, North Melbourne. Shopping was very difficult for Lily and my grandmother as neither could speak English. In the meantime, Dad and Aldo changed jobs and worked at Porta Brothers pouring plaster statue moulds. Once more they found better jobs and went to Homecrafts working as storemen. Aldo eventually moved to Radio Parts where he spent the rest of his working life as a counter salesman selling electrical components and parts. Uncle Ray, who was working as a waiter at the time, wasted no time finding himself a wife, and married Patricia (Pat) Horsley in November 1946, and went to live with Aunty Pat and her mum in Brunswick. After we moved out of Peel St, Uncle Alfred bought the house for £400 and lived there with his family for a short time.

Our own home in Moonee Ponds

In late 1947, my immediate family moved into a neat little weatherboard house that we rented in Vine Street Moonee Ponds. After eight years of fear, frustration, insecurity, intolerable crowding and lack of privacy, we had our own home. It is hard to imagine the relief and pleasure that my parents must have felt at last. Back in Palestine, Uncle Jack (who was British) was able to sell

"The Hard Life at Tatura One Day Will End"

Figure 6.6: Datodi family: (back left to right) Francesco Datodi Ottavio Datodi, Costanza Datodi, Iolanda Balestrieri (nee Datodi), Alfredo Datodi, Aldo Datodi, (front left to right): Mario Balestrieri, Giovanna, Renato (Ray), Anna, Enrico (Rick), Patricia holding baby Carole Datodi, Remo Datodi; Front Matilda Datodi (Lily), Moonee Ponds, Victoria, 1947.

some furniture for us that my parents had left in storage with the Catholic Church in Haifa at the time of their internment. The sale realised about 220 lire, which with the money my parents had managed to save, was enough for a deposit for the house. After having rented the place for a year or so, my parents arranged to purchase it, and signed the mortgage documents on the 23 December 1949.

My grandmother, Anna, had been unwell for many years and after having come through such hardship her death in 1948 was an enormous blow to the entire family, just at the time when things were starting to pick up.

When reflecting on the family's experiences from the early 1900s to 1940, Grandpa Datodi and his family lived in three different homes in Haifa at different times. They were situated in the international sector of Haifa at the foot of Mt Carmel. It is a sad truth that each of the homes was eventually lost or sold for a pittance due to wars. Every Italian family that had lived in Palestine lost their properties and business to the Germans in WWI and then again to the British in WWII. But, that was not all that would befall Haifa.

Mum contracted rheumatic fever in Haifa in about late 1939 or early 1940, sometime after Renato was born but before she was interned. She was 24 years old and didn't seem very sick at the time. The family recalls her symptoms were similar to having the flu. Rheumatic fever is a bacterial infection and manifests itself as an inflammatory disease often affecting the heart and heart valves. We have no doubts that the repeated and ongoing traumas of the forced internment, coercion by the British guards to carry my baby brother for many miles in torturous heat to the ship in Port Said, followed by deportation to Australia and the years in Tatura Internment Camp in harsh imprisonment conditions, all contributed to worsening her condition. For Mum, the direct result of the illness was the malfunctioning of her heart valves, which progressively got worse over the next 21 years culminating in her death in 1961 when she was only 45 and I was 17.

My mother had written the beautiful four-line poem at the start of this story to her close friend Phyllis Marsella while they were in the Tatura internment camp. Both women were fairly recently married and had young children who were born in detention. These few words express the strength of their friendship and the deep feelings of despair and helplessness in being imprisoned behind barbed wire for so long, for no good reason other than their nationality.

A strong sense of Italianness

Italian was the language spoken at home, as was the food we ate, the customs that were followed, and the general mentality of all the family. Considering my mother was born in Egypt (to Southern Italian parents) and my father was born in Haifa, Palestine, and a grandmother born in Izmir Turkey, one might think that the Italian-ness would have been diminished, but this is not so. As I grew up, there was a strong sense of pride in our Italian culture permeating through the entire family. Even now, I have the same feeling and I am very grateful for my Italian heritage.

As I write this family story, I reflect on the many experiences of my grandparents, parents, uncles, and aunties, who were interned and have now all passed away. I marvel at how resilient and uncomplaining they all were. I also contemplate how we, the youngsters in the camp, were so protected from traumatic events, physical hardships, ordeals of imprisonment, and the uncertainty of what the future held. There is no doubt that our parents and family made a valiant attempt to protect us from the distress of camp life. However, there remain emotional scars, perhaps subconscious, that have a profound effect on the lives of all that have experienced incarceration in an internment camp. The interned Datodi families settled in Australia and their offspring are now spread far and wide. They have survived and thrived in spite of the family's difficult start. Our family's internment experience of the war years now mainly remain in our memories as stories told by the oldies. What happened after the war is another story and continues as I write the next chapter…

– Rick Datodi

Hidden Lives

Figure 7.1 : *RMS Queen Mary*, passenger ship postcard, 1940.

Claudia's Story

In April 2012, I took a group of musicians and parents from my school to London, Paris, and the Western Front. In London we gave a performance in St Margaret's Westminster Abbey, which was one of the highlights of my career as a music teacher at Kooweerup Secondary College. How does a country high school teacher from West Gippsland get to perform at Westminster Abbey? To answer that, I have to go back to the beginning.

My father Cosimo Marsella was born in 1906 at home in Oria, a tiny medieval town in the South of Italy. He trained as a hairdresser, served in the Italian Army and then, amid lean economic times in Italy, set off for China where he worked in what was known as the International Settlements in Tientsin. Young Cosimo made the most of being in his 20s in the 1920s. Photos of the time reveal him to be young and handsome at high society social functions. Always immaculately dressed with a carnation in his lapel, he mixed with whoever had the best party and was regularly photographed with a beautiful woman by his side.

In the mid-1930s, the Japanese began their expansion into China and Cosimo left there in good time. He arrived in Penang, Malaya in about 1935 and set up his hairdressing salon in Light Street. It was in the salon that he met the much younger Phyllis, the daughter of an affluent Portuguese-Goan doctor, Eduardo de Cruz. Again, various photos show Cosimo in a dashing white suit at dinner parties usually with the expatriate English set and in the company of Phyllis and members of her family. Cosimo sometimes made the trip to Singapore, where his favourite hotel was Raffles. There, he would continue to pursue an idyllic lifestyle. In the 1930s Singapore was a small luxurious island that everyone thought was far enough away from the troubles in Europe.

It was unthinkable that Singapore could ever be in a war. But things can change very quickly.

In 1939 Hitler invaded Poland and England declared war on Germany. The following year Mussolini declared war on Britain and France and my father went from living the society high life to becoming an enemy alien having been arrested in Penang on June 11, 1940. Churchill was determined not to allow foreign nationals to become security risks so he gave the order: "Collar the lot!" Germans, Austrians, and Italians were arrested and imprisoned in the now infamous Changi prison in Singapore. It is ironic that many of these prisoners had actually fled to Singapore to escape Hitler and Mussolini. In September 1940 Cosimo married Phyllis.

Recently, I had the task of looking for documents to enable two of my sons, James and Daniel to obtain Italian passports. I was warned that it would be impossible to obtain a marriage certificate from Singapore. At the boys' insistence I persevered and was amazed when the certificate duly arrived and divulged that Cosimo and Phyllis married in the Church of the Good Shepherd, St John's Island, Singapore on September 6, 1940.

The marriage would have caused considerable angst in the de Cruz household in Penang, as somehow Phyllis must have made the trip to Singapore on her own. Three days after the wedding Cosimo wrote to her (I still have the letter) which indicates that they were still not together. Of special interest on the marriage certificate is that one of the witnesses was Augusto Martelli, a well-known sculptor in Singapore at the time – but more about him later.

Phyllis' family was of Portuguese descent from Goa. Although she was a British subject, she immediately lost her British citizenship when she married Cosimo. She was now an Italian by marriage and was detained as an enemy alien. In Cosimo's letter to Phyllis he apologises for its lack of romance – understandable due to their unbelievable predicament. He had no idea as to where they would be transported. He advises that they might be going to a place where "the clime is a little cold in winter" and suggests that Phyllis get or make a good overcoat. Given the tropical nature of the retail offerings in Singapore and the imminent timing of their departure, it would seem unlikely that either suggestion could have been acted upon. Along with about 270 Europeans, they were transported as civilian prisoners of war to Australia on the British liner, the *SS Queen Mary*, which had been fitted out as a troop ship for war duties.

When the detainees disembarked in Sydney their sartorial elegance was described by a September 28, 1940 press report: "... young men in spotless white suits, women in fashionably tailored costumes with the latest hair-dos ..." However there was also a more sinister headline: "The prisoners were fifth columnists ... Australia will keep these dangerous aliens until the end of the war ... ." The article concludes that the internees had behaved themselves on the voyage, and that the disembarkation was supervised by "... more than 100 soldiers, 25 police, and naval officers."

The British Government had requested that Australia take and house 'prisoners of war'. In Victoria the internment camp established at Tatura became the home for enemy alien civilians who were deemed a security risk even though they had no adverse political records. The situation then was similar to the situation now when interned men, women, and children are held in barbed wired compounds in inaccessible areas of Australia. Then, as now the camps provided few facilities.

My parents rarely spoke about their six years behind barbed wire. Perhaps an insight can be gleaned from an entry in Phyllis' autograph diary. There is an entry by her dear friend, Costanza (Lola) Datodi dated November 11, 1942:

> La vita dura di Tatura
> un giorno finira`
> pure seperandoci la nostra amicizia
> per sempre durera`
> Life is hard at Tatura

> but one day it will end
> even if we will be separated
> our friendship will endure (translation)

In Tatura, the inmates realised the importance of organisation, routine, and keeping everyone busy. They proceeded to appoint their own group leaders. They moved to ensure that the children received an all-round education and the adults were kept usefully engaged. Amongst the internees was some of the cream of Europe's artistic society. Despite the primitive living conditions, the lack of freedom and the barbed wire, they managed to establish a cultural and intellectual atmosphere. I understand that inmates could attend concerts, which were held in other compounds, exposing them to a cultural richness, which would have been hard to match elsewhere in Australia at the time.

Many inmates produced lasting masterpieces and went on to make a significant contribution to Australia after the war. Although not in the Italian compound, Karl Duldig, the Austrian sculptor, Felix Werder, the German-born composer and the 'tingle-tangle' musician from Vienna, Hans Blau, are examples of artists who have been a significant influence in my career. Due to my parents' reluctance to speak about their life in the camp, some gaps in my story have been filled by the curators of the Tatura Wartime Museum, Lurline and Arthur Knee who managed to track me down in 1990. Lurline affectionately refers to me as "one of our children" – one of the children born in the camp. She has taken a keen interest in my musical pursuits.

In 1945, at the end of the war my father rejected an offer to return to Italy and decided to remain in Australia. Father Arthur Owens, the Army Chaplain, obtained him work as a gardener at the Convent of Mercy, Mornington in Southern Victoria. Initially he took my brother Riccardo, who was the first baby to be born in the camp and they lived in a tiny room in the Convent grounds whilst my mother awaited my birth in the Tatura camp hospital.

Life in Mornington immediately after the war was very hard, maybe even harder than in the camp. My mother never really adjusted to the Victorian climate and to leaving her life of luxury in Penang. In the Tatura camp she had been supported by the Italian families and had learned to cook and speak Italian. In Mornington, she had a family of four to care for and initially no permanent home. She later told us of her collapse in the street whilst looking for accommodation. Eventually, the family was offered a house in Little Waterloo Place, which was owned by Frank Arter, the Surveyor General. However, the condition was that we moved out every holiday for the owners to take up residence. One of my earliest memories is of my parents, my brother, and me, crammed into a tiny bungalow in the bottom of a neighbour's garden.

Having grown up before the war in an affluent family in Malaya, my mother always had domestic helpers. She now found herself with no idea of how to shop for a family of four. She later told me that once released, she would wait in the Mornington butcher shop to see what others would order and then she would order the same. When she washed her first sheet she excitedly wrote home to her father to give him the news. I later discovered that as internees, we had no sheets on the rudimentary wooden beds in the Tatura internment camp.

After a few years, things started to improve. My father had opened a 'fish and chip' shop and was able to purchase the house in Little Waterloo Place. Riccardo, who had always been a fixture at the Convent since arriving there at three years of age began classes at Padua House, as it was called in those days, in Tanti Avenue and my father purchased a piano. And so began our childhood growing up in Mornington – growing up in paradise. In those days you could walk down the main street and every shopkeeper knew you by name. The beaches, the cliffs, the pier, the rocks all became our playground.

In a short time, the town's only fish and chip shop flourished. A vivid memory for me would be accompanying my father to the Melbourne Fish market in a 1948 blue 'Morris 8' which was later replaced by a 1951 'Morris Cowley Ute'. We would bring home crates of live crayfish, which would be delivered to our bathtub for drowning. My mother would then cook them up in the family copper and prepare them for sale. In those days crayfish were poor man's fare and could be enjoyed by all.

However the fish shop was not my father's only business. In those days there was no Totalisator Agency Board (TAB) so to bet legally you had to actually attend a race meeting. This opened a huge window of opportunity for my father – he became an illegal starting price bookmaker. In Mornington, everyone, including the police, knew the local bookie. Every so often, the police would mount a 'raid', but my father would always know when they were coming – somehow. I would watch in innocence as the police came in the front door and my father headed out the back door. With his portable office safely relocated to the woodshed, my father would then conduct a grand tour of the house where there was not a betting slip in sight! Along the way my father attempted to resurrect his old profession of hair dressing and actually sat exams so he could become registered to practice. Despite his talent and the possibility of an Italian salon in town, his English was not considered good enough to pass the written exams and his applications failed.

In the 50s in Mornington, very few young people learned a musical instrument and we often resented the time we had to devote to practising but our father gave us no option. The first thing he would ask my mother when he returned from work was "Has Claudia practiced?" This discipline has persisted to the present and I do not like to miss too many days without some form of practice. My sister, Iolanda learned the violin from Leila Steedman, who had been the conductor of the Mornington Peninsula Orchestra whilst I studied piano with the nuns. My parents always took great pride in my piano playing and I would be trotted out to play for visitors who would politely listen, oblivious of the fact that the performance was only

Claudia's Story

Figure 7.2: Phyllis with infants son Ricardo in pram, possibly borrowed, Tatura Interment Camp 3A, c. 1942.

taking place on the promise of a two-shilling payment.

My music lessons originally took place in the old convent, 'Shelbourne House'. Over the main gates to this building was an arch of wrought iron containing the name 'College of Our Lady of the Sea'. In front of the building and situated in the middle of a circular lawn was a beautiful sculpture of Our Lady. The statue had been made at the Tatura internment camp reportedly by moonlight and with material collected locally. The sculptor was Augusto Martelli, who was the witness for my parents' marriage in Singapore in 1940. Augusto, his wife Alma and daughter Marisa had been interned with my parents. How and why the statue was transferred from Tatura in central Victoria to Mornington, an hour south of Melbourne is a mystery. From time to time my piano teacher Mother Gertrude would extol the beauty of the statue's hands, which apparently had international acclamation. Sometimes, on my way to a lesson, I would pause to check them out but could never quite fathom what the fuss was about.

Hidden Lives

A constant fear for me during the lesson would be the sound of the Angelus Bell at midday. It would then be necessary for me to stand and recite the Angelus from memory. This would prove to be more daunting than giving a musical performance but I would always obey out of fear of Mother Gertrude's wrath rather than to obtain any spirituality. My own reward came when I passed my first Australian Music Examination Board exam when barely five years old.

Padua College in Tanti Avenue was known as 'a college by the sea'. Listed on the many things that the Sisters of Mercy had us pray for was a reduction in the 'enormous' debt of £80,000 incurred by their splendid new building, which included a new convent and classroom.

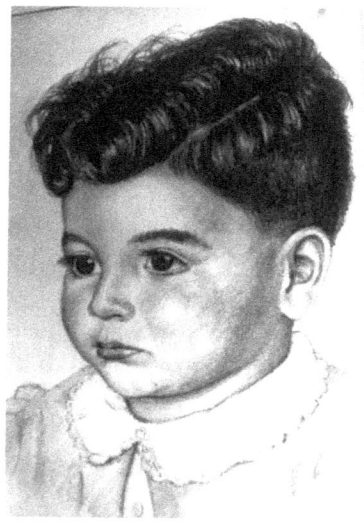

Figure 7.3 : Sketch of Riccardo Marsella by interned artist Augusto Martelli, Tatura Camp 3A, 1943.

Archbishop Mannix opened it in 1953. Every year we would work tirelessly at the annual fete to reduce the mortgage. My father was a great spruiker on the spinning wheel and his and the efforts of others, would have contributed to the equity the Sisters eventually had in the property, which they later sold to developers. It has now been converted to apartments and people pay millions of dollars for the view that we took for granted every day. We also prayed that the Democratic Labour Party would win the election and that Bob Santamaria would be Prime Minister. My father decided that his only son might be better off with a more secular education. He took the bold step of removing Riccardo and sending him to the local state school. However after two years, the nuns managed to convince my father that excommunication was looming and Riccardo was subsequently packed off to St Patrick's College, Ballarat, in those days a 4-hour journey in the back of the Morris Ute.

Another prominent memory of growing up Italian in Mornington was my rejection of my Italian heritage, which reflected the discrimination I was experiencing at school and beyond. Determined not to acknowledge my Italian identity, I refused to speak Italian at home, which was a great disappointment to my father. I would refuse to eat the Italian dishes that my mother had learned to prepare in the camp and many an evening was spent with me locked in the bathroom trying to force a plate full of spaghetti down the plughole. The fact that my parents' Australian friends would come around for lessons in how to successfully roll the gnocchi mixture or prepare minestrone meant little to someone who just wanted to be the same as her peers. Salami or 'melanzani' (eggplant) sandwiches that my father would carefully pack for our lunches were treated with similar disdain.

Figure 7.4: Phyllis and step-sister Louise, Penang, 1930s.

First Communion Day was a disaster as my mother had made me a long dress in the Italian tradition. It didn't matter that all the other girls wore short dresses, my mother was determined to have acceptable photos to send to my grandparents, Anna and Giacomino, who lived in Oria in Puglia, Italy. When I tripped over the long skirt whilst running to the communion breakfast, one of the nuns scolded that it served me right for being different. Some time later, in an effort to gain acceptance, I took a black scarf to school, which I had found in a drawer at home. The nuns couldn't send me home with it quickly enough. The scarf was emblazoned with a speech and

Figure 7.5 : Tatura Camp 3A interned families: (back left to right): G. B. Reginato; Cosimo Marsella; G. Hreglich; G. Hreglich. (front left to right): O. Reginato; E. Reginato; Felicia (Phyllis) Marsella; Riccardo Marsella; A. Hreglich; V. Reginato; C. Hreglich. Created by C. T. Halmarick, Tatura, Victoria, 13 February, 1943 (courtesy AWM).

signature of none other than Il Duce himself – Benito Mussolini!

Cosimo died in 1965, aged 59. A heavy smoker, he had developed lung cancer. The tragedy was that the light of his life, my baby sister Derinda, was only 5 years old and has only fleeting memories of her father. Cosimo is buried at the Mornington Cemetery. When I visited Oria for the first time in the late nineties I was surprised to see that the Marsella family had also 'buried' him. His plaque and all his details rest alongside other members of his family in the family crypt.

Phyllis had never enjoyed good health after the trauma of the internment camp and hardships in Mornington. Yes, the internees were treated well enough considering it was wartime, but there was always the reality of the barbed wire imprisonment. No one knew who would eventually 'win' the war and take control. Cosimo had a brother in the Italian army and family in Italy, and Phyllis had a brother (killed as a result of the Japanese invasion of Malaya) as well as family in Penang. Not having any 'outside news' subjected internees to enormous stress. In addition, Cosimo was a difficult man – very Italian in his ways. After years of doing as he had pleased he was confined for six years in the internment camp where he worked as a gardener for five shillings a week. He then started a new life in Mornington with a young family and

Figure 7.6: Cosimo Marsella, early 1930s.

absolutely nothing. There was also the shame of having been interned – after all he was 'the enemy'. So Cosimo developed an insatiable appetite for gambling. Although he worked long hours in the fish and chip shop he had little to show for it in the end. The little old house in Mornington slowly deteriorated and would have further contributed to Phyllis' poor health as she sank into depression.

In the 1950s depression was not understood to the extent it is today. We kids didn't understand our mother's illness and wished she would just get on with it. Alcohol provided temporary relief but combined with her medication had disastrous effects. Most days we would walk home from school wondering what sort of night was in store for all of us. In the end, the Mornington doctors, who would be telephoned at all hours of the night, found her a place in a Warburton sanatorium. This led to electro-shock therapy in Kew. In the 1950s shock treatment was one of the available methods for treating mental illness.

Nowadays, it is administered under general anaesthesia but in those days the patient would be wide-awake and it would be a harrowing experience. At the time we kids knew none of this. We just felt relief from the terrible nights, which we all endured when she was home. In any case the treatment did little to improve Phyllis' situation and the depression continued.

Despite having retained some good friends from the camp and making a few friends in Mornington Phyllis never really adjusted to her new life. I can remember people commenting that by coming from Malaya she should be able to cope with the Victorian climate. She would be indignant with her reply: "But it's a different sort of heat!" She would recall the magnificent Malayan climate and the huge ceiling fans operated by houseboys. As time drifted on she became more insular. She had no middle-aged friends that she could talk to. She certainly didn't have the valuable female friendships that her daughters have experienced. Our mother died in 1986, aged 67 in Mornington a few days before Derinda's wedding in San Francisco.

Figure 7.7: The Marsella Family: (left to right) Riccardo, Cosimo, Phyllis, (centre front) Claudia, Mornington, Victoria, c. 1948.

And so what am I to make of internment? If my parents had not been expelled from Singapore my father may have been repatriated to Italy and conscripted into Mussolini's army. Despite the hardships, Tatura was a viable solution during a terrible war. At its conclusion my father, fortunately for his family, made the decision to settle in Mornington. Despite their difficulties, both parents imbued in their children a rich cultural upbringing.

The wartime bond continues with the 20-year association I have established with the magnificent 39th Battalion. This unit fought in the Battle of Kokoda and helped prevent a Japanese invasion of Australia in 1942. In a tribute to the ANZAC spirit ex-students join with the Kooweerup Secondary College Marching Band. We continue to lead the surviving 39th veterans in the Melbourne March to the Shrine of Remembrance every ANZAC day. My one regret is that my parents did not live to see the end result of what they started. Their gift will stay with me for the rest of my life.

– Claudia Barker

Figure 8.1: Cosimo and Anna Caminiti, Mourylean, Qld, 1930s.

There Are So Many Questions I Wish I Had Asked…

Family background

When I was approached to write a story about Mum and Dad's early years, especially around the time Dad was interned during the war, and how that event had changed and affected our lives, I had never given it much thought. I debated whether I would do it, and as the subject was never talked about in our family, I had no idea where to start. With a limited amount of research and discussions with my two older sisters Phyllis (Filippa) and Frances (Francesca), I decided: "Yes, I would give it a go!" Our family's wartime story starts with my father Cosimo Caminiti.

Cosimo Caminiti was born in 1902 in Calatabiano, Sicily, and was the eldest of five children. I don't think poverty would have been the reason he migrated to Australia, as his family was more financially well off than most of the locals. They owned their own home, a horse, and a cart that was used to deliver goods to surrounding villages. The ground floor of the building was a barn and was used by passing travellers, who would house and rest their horses and leave the carts overnight. The men probably slept there, too. When I asked my sister Phyllis if she knew anything about dad's younger years in Sicily, she recalled that dad had mentioned that his father, Francesco, would travel to a nearby village to buy grain and then he would distribute it to nearby villages. During the almond, walnut and chestnut season, again, he would buy the nuts and then sell them at the weekly markets around the area. She had no idea what else they may have carted. At an early age, Dad began accompanying his father on his trips, and to keep my dad awake, his father would give him cigarettes to smoke. Dad was nine years old when he started smoking, a bad habit he kept till the end. In his later years, when Dad was advised to stop smoking because of ill health, he would sneak out to the garage and have a few puffs, later coming indoors looking guilty and smelling of tobacco smoke!

Dad did twelve months of compulsory national service in the Italian Cavalry division and in 1925, at the age of 23, Dad left his hometown and migrated to Australia on the steam ship named the *SS Palermo*. The passenger list had his 'occupation or calling' as a 'mine-labourer'. Maybe that was a requirement to enter Australia? We will never know why my father decided to migrate. His decision may have been made because of someone he met whilst doing his military service, or it could have been his cousins' influence as two were already cutting cane in northern Queensland. My sisters and I don't know how Dad spent his first ten years in Australia, apart from being a cane cutter as well as cooking for the cane-cutting gangs. He and the gang would move from one farm to another in the nearby districts. He was apparently full of life and loved the task of breaking in horses, which he did from time to time.

My mother, Anna Russo, born in 1913, came from Giardini Naxos, a beautiful seaside-fishing village in northern Sicily. Mum was one of eight girls and three boys. Her father, a fisherman, had died when Mum was nine years old, so there was much poverty in her family. Soon after her father's death, Mum was sent out to work. She mentioned that she worked in a 'fabbrica' (factory) that would extract spirits and oils out of the lemon peels. I know Mum did a bit of schooling. She would always say that because of Mussolini's free education policy for all Italian children, she learnt to read and write. She also learnt 'ricamo' (ornamental needlework), which she developed with the nuns who ran the orphanage, Orfanatrofio di San Antonio, in Giardini Naxos.

There Are So Many Questions I Wished I Had Asked...

Figure 8.2: (left to right) Anna Caminiti holding Frances, Cosimo Caminiti, (front centre) Phyllis Caminiti, Grazia Neri, Nancy Neri (front) and Leonardo Neri, Etty Bay, Queensland, 1940.

A new life

By 1934 at the age of 32, Dad mentioned to his friend Leonardo Sorbello that he thought it was time he should settle down. Leonardo's wife Agata had a number of unmarried sisters back home in Sicily, and wrote to her mother if one of them would be interested in coming to Australia. I don't know if Mum was happy about the proposition, but as she was the eldest unmarried sister, the decision was probably made for her. Aunty Agata sent a photo of dad and I am sure she would have spoken well of him. Mum thought Dad was very good looking, he was tall, very slim, and fair-skinned with beautiful blue-green eyes. That was how the marriage was arranged. Because of tradition, Mum could not come out to Australia as an unmarried young woman. She had to leave the family home as a married woman. Cosimo and Anna were married by 'proxy' (marriage at a distance) that same year. I remember Mum mentioning that her father-in-law walked her to the church. I don't know if any of her family went with her. I don't remember Mum ever mentioning a wedding gown.

Not long after, Mum's sister Grazia married Dad's friend Leonardo Neri, also by proxy. Grazia was two years younger than Mum. They always had a special bond; a bond that lasted through thick and thin. Years later, when they spoke on the telephone, I could hear laughter one minute and see Mum in tears the next. I never knew what their conversations were about. If I asked, she would just say "Gioia (darling), we are talking about things that happened a long time ago". They had experienced a hard life during their early years, the war years and also the years in Shepparton. They must have been mentally and emotionally strong women to keep it all together during those hard times. When Grazia came out to Australia, she brought a wedding gown with her. She may have always dreamed of having a wedding photograph. I can remember always seeing the photo hanging from the wall.

Figure 8.3: The Caminiti and Vaccaro families picnicking at Etty Bay, Queensland, 1940.

"C'e` peggio ..."

It would have been very distressing for the women to leave their family and friends in search of a better life and to meet up with a husband they did not know. I'm sure that if they had known how harsh the living conditions in northern Queensland would be they would have never left. Once here, there was no turning back and they made the best of it. I never heard mum complain. She would always say "sempre c'e` peggio", which means there is always worse. During the cane-cutting season life was difficult for the men. By the end of the day, they had sore backs and blistered hands and would be grateful snakes or rats had not bitten them. When the cane season was over, they spent many hours with family and friends and often go for picnics to Etty Bay, near Mourilyan. When there was no cane to cut from June to November, Dad would sell fruit and vegetables transported from Stanthorpe in Southern Queensland by train to the Boogan Station. He collected the produce and then travel to farms and houses in the proximity selling his goods in his ute, a T-model Ford. Dad had made Mum a fishing line and she would fish in the South Johnstone River, where there probably would have been snakes and crocodiles, but Mum never mentioned these. Her greatest fears were rats and mice. They also grew vegetables on the riverbanks, which together with some of the fish mum had caught, would be exchanged for groceries. By this stage, Mum and Dad had bought a house. The ute and house were not in our family's name, because as foreigners, Italians were unable to own property in Australia until they became Naturalised British Subjects.

Under master warrant

In 1939, war was declared against Germany by the British Commonwealth. Europe and Germany seemed so far away from our family and relatives in Mourilyan in northern Queensland. The men continued cane cutting as usual, but in June 1940 everything changed for Italian families when Mussolini declared war against the British Commonwealth. We became enemy aliens. In 1940 and 1941, the cane cutters kept working in the cane fields as they were considered essential farm workers. But family life was disrupted in April 1942. Dad was arrested 'Under Master Warrant'. He and hundreds of other men were ordered to meet at the Innisfail Showgrounds. Just before being arrested, Dad had been involved in a big accident. His ute had been written off and he had sustained injuries to his arm and hands. His arm was still in a sling when he was arrested. That day of his arrest was very traumatic for everyone. My sister Frances, who was three years old at that time, started running towards Dad crying. She was too young to understand what was happening to her dad. A soldier suddenly pointed a bayonet to her head. My mother and aunt screamed in horror and Dad collapsed in shock. He must have thought they would shoot his little daughter. Fortunately, the men around him held him up as they were escorted to the rail station. Phyllis recalls that only Mum and a few women close by noticed what had happened, most of the other women were too distressed worrying about their own men being taken away to notice what was going on around them.

The men were loaded onto a train, which then took them to an internment camp at Gaythorne. We can't imagine what went through their minds. Once there, papers were processed and were then sent to the different camps. Dad, together with his brother-in-law Leonardo Neri, was sent to Cowra. Luckily, he was interned for only eight months. Many were interned for up to five years. The majority of these men should never have been arrested. They were hard working, easy-going cane cutters and wouldn't have known the full extent of the war. They had no radios and the men who could read would only buy the Italian newspaper when they went to town, which wasn't often. According to the official documents we found in the National Archives, when Dad was taken away, in his possession he had two suitcases, two blankets, a pillow, and a small amount of cash. It would have been devastating for the internees not knowing where they were being taken and also not knowing for how long. Their biggest worry would have been what would happen to their families and how they would manage to survive without the breadwinner.

Taken away

Soon after the men were taken away, Mum and Aunty Grazia moved into a tin hut, which was on Aunty Agata's farm. My Uncle Leonardo Sorbello, was not interned as he was naturalised. The shed had previously been divided into two small bedrooms and a small kitchen. Mum and Aunty cleaned it up and made it quite liveable. They probably made that move so the three sisters could be close together during those unknown times. Phyllis does not know what happened to our home. Mum may have sold it. Phyllis recalled that she had to change schools, but as a six-year-old life was the same to her. She missed Dad not being around as she was very close to him. Phyllis and my cousin Nancy remember seeing Army trucks driving past where they were living; it was a dirt road that led to Mount Basilisk that is just near Boogan. Nancy said there was an American Army base there. Apparently the soldiers were stationed there and used the mountain as a lookout. From that point, Mourilyan Harbour was visible. They were watching out for Japanese boats. The girls both said it didn't seem to worry the adults. Maybe seeing the army trucks go by made them feel safer.

From what I've read, the men had enough to eat while in the Cowra Internment Camp. It may not have been to their liking but it was edible. On one occasion, my cousin Frances commented that her father could not tolerate the smell of lamb as it reminded him of the mutton stews in Cowra. Dad did not have a problem eating lamb, and I remember all our family enjoying a lamb roast. I guess they had their fair share of mutton whilst there. I never heard Dad complain about anything, actually, I never heard him speak about his internment days. During the

Figure 8.4: The Caminiti family: (left to right) Cosimo and Anna with baby Josie, Frances and Phyllis, Shepparton, Victoria, 1945.

men's stay at Cowra, the women would bake biscuits to send to them. Mum would tell us that she and many of her friends would send "S" shaped biscuits. If they went hard, they still tasted good dunked in tea or coffee. As it was cold at Cowra, the women would knit socks and balaclavas to send to the interned men. Mum knitted all these items not only for dad, but also for other internees as not all the women could knit. I had a good laugh with my cousin Frances as she recalled her mother telling her that one woman wrote to her husband telling him that she would send a 'passamontagna'. But, all internees' letters were scrutinised and censored. When the army censor came across the word 'passamontagna', he informed the authorities that some of the internees were planning an escape! The word passamontagna literally translates: "to cross the mountain". It is in fact a balaclava; a knitted head-cap that covers the head and neck like a glove. He obviously thought that they were using some form of secret code. Whatever words the interpreter didn't understand, would be blocked out, especially if some of the words were written in dialect, resulting in most of the letter being unreadable. As Dad was a smoker, Mum would send tobacco and cigarette papers. It was quite an expense. On top of buying whatever else was being sent, there was also the cost of the postage. Phyllis remembers Mum going to the Post Office to collect the ten shillings per week the Government gave some families and remembers her using the coupons to purchase tea, sugar, and flour.

Stawell

On 30 December 1942, fifty-one men were released from Cowra and sent to Stawell to work for the Forestry Commission at Glynwylln. After being released on parole from the internment camps the men were required to work for the Manpower for as long as required. Dad, with Leonardo, his brother-in-law, and a number of their cane cutting friends were amongst those sent to Stawell in central Victoria. On a recent trip to Stawell, I visited the Stawell Historical Society. Whilst there, I was handed a copy of a booklet written by J. D. Gillespie – Former Divisional Forester-Horsham – "Wartime wood trail" 1942–1945 – Italian Internees – Glynwylln Forest. I found it very interesting as I learned why the internees were sent to cut wood. The wood sent mainly to Melbourne was used for fuel. Gillespie states:

> Forty men arrived here to cut wood. We were Lucky, we got 40 fellows from Queensland, most of whom were used to hard work and the hot climate. In camps in some parts of the state, people in charge of the Forest District finished up with 30 to 40 greengrocers, and grocers etc. out of Melbourne and you can imagine they didn't cut much wood but they had to do it. Originally the arrangement was that the men at Glynwylln cut wood at six shillings per day – the same as our men were paid in the army. They didn't cut much wood for six shillings per day and the aim of the exercise was to produce wood for Melbourne so it became a question of payment by result.

Hidden Lives

Figure 8.5: Cosimo Caminiti, woodcutting, Stawell, Victoria, 1944.

He further stated:

> It would be great if I could say the Italians here cut so many tons of wood. I know of no records that survive that would enable that to be said ... Once the camps were established and the men were in full operation and the whole scheme was flowing, a major part of the wood supply to Melbourne was provided by the Internees. For the three years from mid-1942 to mid-1945, total production across the State from all emergency services meant that the Forests Commission handled and sold 1,106,700 tonne of wood. Internee labour played a major part in this.

While the men were sent to Victoria, the women were still struggling on their own in Queensland. By the beginning of 1943, Mum was feeling unwell. It would have been so stressful as Dad was not there with her. Luckily Mum had Aunty to help her. A doctor from Innisfail advised her to see a specialist in Sydney. Numerous letters were written to the National Security Division, asking permission to travel to Sydney. It was not possible to travel without the proper government authority's permission. It was so unfair that she had to practically beg to go see a doctor. Finally in June 1943, Mum was given permission to travel to Sydney. That same month, Dad sent a letter to the Allied Works Council, asking permission to bring his family to live in Stawell. He also stated that he had a comfortable home for them and was in a position to bear the cost of their transfer. At the end of August 1943, Mum and my two sisters, Aunty Grazia with her two children, Nancy and Joe, and a number of other women and children, were finally leaving Queensland. It would have been difficult knowing what to pack. How many suitcases could a woman with two small children manage to take?

The journey

The trip was very long, tiring and unpleasant. Phyllis recalls that it was a five-day journey, with numerous train changes. There were no beds to sleep on. How did they manage to get any sleep? At some train stations a few of the women would hop off and buy food. The families were travelling on the same train as a group of Australian soldiers on leave. They were drinking heavily and in no time they were verbally abusing the Italian women. They kept on saying "Drink, you bloody dagoes!" The women were scared for their safety and if it were not for the children, they had seriously considered jumping off the train. Fortunately, a group of American soldiers of Italian background boarded the train and made sure the women were safe. They gave the children biscuits and chocolates to eat. Happily, the drunken soldiers left the train at Townsville and the Italian families were able to continue their journeys in peace. At the end of their travels, the families were finally reunited with their loved ones.

It was a completely different life for the women in Stawell. Since arriving in Australia, there had been no need or possibility to learn the English language. The older children who had started school knew enough of the language to interpret for their mums. Phyllis recalls her first day of school as being frightening. Apparently, the children had been informed new children would be starting at the school. As Italians were the enemies, the children were eyed suspiciously. Mum had dressed Phyllis in an embroidered skirt she had made and soon the girls were touching the skirt and telling her how pretty the skirt was. By the end of the day they were all on friendly terms. At the start of our stay in Stawell, the Australian women were wary of the Italian women but in no time they became friends. Phyllis remembers that on numerous occasions, on returning home from school, Mum would be seated around the table teaching a group of women how to crochet and do embroidery. In return they would bring scones and cakes for afternoon tea. So our neighbours had their first taste of Italian coffee!

The accident

On 8 June 1944, while still working for the Forest Commission, Dad had an accident. A big log fell on his feet. I have copies of medical reports stating dad was unfit for work. Another document, dated 11 October 1944 states: "I have a request from Caminiti C requesting a transfer back to work wood cutting on piece rates..." We will never know if Dad worked during those four months or if he was paid sick leave. I don't know whether Dad returned to woodcutting as on the 9 November 1944, as he was given travelling instructions to travel to Kinglake "... to report to cook, in view of his experience as a cook and in view of dissatisfaction with present cooking arrangements at Kinglake....' On 18 November 1944, Dad applied for ten days leave as I was due to be born. I was born the next day and dad was in Stawell for my birth. I don't know how long he was home. He was so excited at having another daughter that on telling Aunty Grazia, they had had another girl, she didn't believe him. Mum didn't know if it had been a difficult birth as in that era, just before giving birth, the women were given ether to put them to sleep. They would awaken after the baby was born.

Kinglake

Dad went back to Kinglake and on the 7 December 1944, obtained another leave pass to travel from Kinglake to Melbourne, where he visited a doctor. I have a copy of a medical certificate stating "definite disability." Dad was released from the Civil Aliens Corps and could return to Queensland for "employment in the sugar industry". However in February 1945, Dad relinquished his rights to return to Queensland on medical grounds, he stated he wished to remain in Victoria. He vowed he would never return to Queensland. Dad didn't want to go back north because he was upset with the Queensland government for what they did to their Italians during the war. Almost 3000 cane cutters were interned, while in comparison, Victoria only interned no more than 100 men with a similar Italian migrant population to that in Queensland. Even if our family had returned to Queensland, Dad would never have been able to go back to cane cutting again due to his age and poor health.

In early 1945, we moved to Melbourne. I guess we travelled by train. It would have been a four-hour trip. I would have been about four months by that stage. Once again Mum would have had to decide what to pack. I wonder why we didn't remain in Stawell as it was a nice town and the women seemed quite settled there. Maybe there was no work available. Dad had a position as a kitchen hand at the renowned Australia Hotel in Exhibition Street. The Civil Aliens Corps may have arranged that position, after Dad had been injured working in the wood cutting industry. The family recalls that Dad enjoyed working there. During that time, we were living in an upstairs apartment in a terrace house in Drummond Street, Carlton. It was comfortable enough but there was no running water upstairs and whatever water was needed, Mum would have to carry it upstairs and then bring it down again. The owner of the building lived downstairs. Unfortunately his wife had mental problems. She had taken an instant dislike to Frances and would slap her when she thought no one was looking! From time to time, she would be taken away for short periods. Moving elsewhere was not an option as accommodation was difficult to find. Life would have been fine in Melbourne if not for the owner's wife. Dad was working, Phyllis and Frances were at school, and Mum was sewing beading on frocks for a dressmaker.

Shepparton

By chance, Dad met a man he knew from the Cowra internment camp, and mentioned he was 'share farming' in Shepparton in central Victoria. Because of our poor living conditions, Dad obviously thought Shepparton would be a better place for us to live. Another move! We were becoming nomads, yet again! Most likely, we would have travelled by train again. It would have been a three-hour journey. But moving to Shepparton was possibly the biggest mistake Dad could have made. Not knowing anything about farming, everything seemed to go wrong: floods, dry spells, grubs in the tomatoes, and when the season was good, the prices were low. Life was harder than ever. Aunty Grazia, Uncle Leonardo, and children, Nancy, Joe and Frances joined us in Shepparton, as Uncle, like Dad, was no longer fit to cut cane. After years of backbreaking work in the cane fields and cutting wood while being interned, all the hard work had taken its toll on the men's health. Our parents worked very hard, and they were bad times but we lived as one big family and supported each other. But there was always the occasional picnic. We all lived together until each family bought our own respective farms. These times were stressful but years later when we recalled certain events we would see the funny side to it.

At the beginning of our time on the farm, Dad would

use his horse and cart to get to town, but later on he bought a car. Mum and Dad grew peas, beans, and tomatoes. Dad's back always ached from his cane cutting years and his feet were bad because of the accident at Stawell. Mum worked just as hard beside Dad, and at the end of the day had to face the housework with the help of my sisters. Most Saturday mornings, Dad would go to town to buy whatever was needed for the farm, food and household goods, picked up the Italian newspaper "La Fiamma" and always bought violet crumble for my sisters and myself. That was our treat! During the cooler months, Dad would buy small amounts of meat to make soup and spaghetti sauce, it was impossible to store meats in the hot weather as we had no electricity and only had an ice chest. As

Figure 8.6: Caminiti and Neri families and friends on their way to a picnic, Shepparton, Victoria, 1950s.

we had our own chickens, eggs were plentiful. As long as Mum had eggs and vegetables, she could cook up a feast. When the chooks stopped laying eggs they would be killed, and once again soup and spaghetti sauce would be made. For special occasions a tender chicken would be roasted, Dad would make rice stuffing for it. The killing was left to Mum as Dad couldn't kill anything, and I enjoyed plucking the feathers off the chicken.

We had a dairy farm close by and Mum would buy fresh milk to make junkets, sago and rice puddings and baked custards. She may have learned these recipes from the Stawell women. Camp pie (tinned meat) was always a handy food staple. Mum would slice and crumb it and we would have it in place of schnitzels. Dad's rainbow cake must have been a recipe he learned at the hotel. As we didn't have cake too often, it was always special. It was probably just a plain cake with a bit of cocoa and red food colouring thrown in, but I will always remember it being the best cake ever! During the winter months, mum knitted jumpers for the whole family and socks for Dad. Whatever she made for us girls always had a bit of embroidery on it. I don't know where she found the time or energy to do what she did. Dad would play a few Italian card games 'Briscola' and 'Scopa' with two of his friends who also were share farming nearby. As they needed a fourth player, I was taught to play cards. I felt so important playing cards with the men. I would have been about four at that stage. My older sisters were busy cleaning, so I really liked being the youngest as I got to do fun things. I still love playing cards but I am a very sore loser.

From Melbourne to Adelaide

I started school when I was four, but not because I was smart; it was so that my sister Phyllis would not miss so much school. She would have to stay home to mind me while Mum and Dad went to work in the fields. Phyllis left school at an early age, much to her sadness and the teacher's disappointment, as she thought my sister was a bright student and would do well. To this day she still regrets not having had the opportunity to stay at school longer. By 1952, after seven years of struggling to make ends meet, Mum and Dad decided to sell the farm.

We moved back to Melbourne. I remember this move, as I was eight years old. All our belongings were loaded on the back of uncle's truck, with us included. Talk about the Beverly Hillbillies! Dad obtained a job mowing lawns for the Post Master General Department, and life became much easier for everyone, especially Mum. The English language was still a problem for her but she soon picked up enough to manage with everyday living. Whilst living in Melbourne, Mum and Dad met up with a few of their Queensland friends, who were also living in Melbourne. I don't know whether they had returned to Queensland after being released. Those friendships lasted a lifetime, as they became more like family than friends. In 1963, after much pressure from Mum, we moved to Adelaide. This was our last big move! This time, we hired a removalist and Mum, Dad and myself travelled by train. Phyllis had married and was living in Adelaide. Mum wanted to keep the family together, so Dad obtained a transfer and worked as a cleaner in the Post Master General building in central Adelaide. Frances had also married, so they decided to move to Adelaide as well. A number of Mum and Dad's cane cutting friends had moved to Adelaide after the war. These friendships once again took off where it had ended in Queensland many years previously. Why didn't the subject of the war or the internment camps ever come into our conversations? Or why was our family's move from Queensland never explained? I don't remember anyone in our family or friendship networks ever mentioning anything about the war – not a word. When Dad retired at the age of 65 he had difficulty walking because of his badly deformed feet. He was also showing signs of dementia.

Later years

Dad died in 1977 at the age of 75. He left behind three daughters and ten grandchildren. I feel sad not to have experienced the way Dad was in his carefree days. Phyllis and Frances remember him as being full of life and fun. To me, he always seemed very tired and old, not much life in him. But I never heard Dad raise his voice, he was always gentle and when he was emotional, his chin would quiver. After Dad died, Mum moved in with our family, my husband Ennio and two daughters Lisa and Vanessa. She lived with us for 22 years until she died in the year 2000 at the age of 86. At the time of her death, Mum had ten grandchildren and five great grandchildren and another five were born after Mum's death.

Mum never complained about the hard life she had lived. She was always very positive and would focus on the good times. She wanted the family to understand that happy times outweighed the hardships. She did not dwell on negative experiences. This was her way of dealing with life. We will never know whether being interned broke Dad's spirit or whether he would have aged that way naturally. Life may have been different if we had stayed in Stawell, Melbourne or had returned to Queensland. I guess if Dad had not been interned, I may have been a Queenslander instead of a Victorian. Mum had a few sayings to get her through hard times. The ones she used most were thank God (for whatever the occasion was) or 'it is God's will'. Mum had a lot of faith in God and prayed frequently to the Madonna and Saint Anthony. Our parents gave us the opportunity to have a happy and normal life, always surrounded by family and friends even though they had experienced so much stress, hardship and suffering as a result of Dad being interned. Somehow they managed to put it all behind them and moved on. I am sure times were so much worse than I have made them sound, maybe I have looked at things through rose-coloured glasses. Then again, I think that is the way my parents would want us to remember things. As Mum would always say: "…that happened a long time ago…" I think what she meant was, "Stop thinking about the bad times, remember the good times and focus on the future."

– Josie Verbis

A Kafkaesque Experience

The internment of Italians in Australia during World War II

One of the most representative novels of the 20th century is *The Trial,* by the Jewish Czech writer Franz Kafka. The protagonist Joseph K wakes one morning into a nightmare, having been arrested without charge. So begins a bizarre trial by ordeal of persecution by an irrational authority. The novel was amongst the literature burnt by the Nazis in 1933. It is ironic then that during World War II, when Australian troops were fighting against that authoritarian regime, back home the Australian military was administering a Kafkaesque regime of preventive deterrent internment of some 8000 enemy nationals and Australians of foreign, mostly Italian, extraction. These people were classified in the language of the day as 'enemy aliens'.[115] To understand how and why this happened is to take a journey back to an older Australia, before we became a multicultural country. There to be 'British to the boot-heels' was to be presumed to be loyal to this country. Doubts were entertained about others seen as strangers in our midst. The very concept of Australian citizenship had yet to come into being.[116] Another dimension of the historical significance of this episode of penal Commonwealth national security legislation is its current parallel in the controversial policy of preventative mandatory detention of refugees.[117]

---

[115] Mia Spizzica, "On the Wrong Side of the Law (War): Italian Civilian Internment in Australia during World War Two", *International Journal of the Humanities,* vol. 9, issue 11, 2012, 121.

[116] The Australian Citizenship Act 1948 gazetted the following year brought Australian citizenship into effect: see Ilma Martinuzzi O'Brien, "Citizenship, Rights & Emergency Powers in Second World War Australia", *Australian Journal of Politics & History,* vol. 53, no. 2, 2007, 208.

[117] The historical nexus between the two policies which I assert here has been argued by A. Bashford & Carolyn Strange, "Asylum

This chapter will describe the political psychology and legislative framework of wartime preventive deterrent detention, the overarching structure of the psychological experience of trauma to which detainees were condemned indefinitely without trial.

The fundamental foundation of internment policy was primeval ethnocentricity, not to say racism. Since European settlement in 1788, Australia had been an outpost of the British Empire in the antipodes. The Commonwealth Constitution that came into effect in 1901 was an Act of the British parliament. Although conceived by Australians it studiously avoided any reference to Australians as citizens, designating them as British subjects. Well into the 20th century, many Australians considered themselves Australian Britons, tied by the crimson thread of kinship to the old mother country. The horrendous Great War of 1914-18 had traumatised Australian society, reforging old links. The blood of 60,000 war dead had reinforced conservative bonds to Great Britain in this Dominion of the British Empire. Critics of those links and that war effort had mustered sufficient votes in a majority of States to veto plebiscites in 1916 and 1917 to reinforce the volunteer Australian Imperial Forces with conscripts. But the criticism of conscription and the conduct of the war effort split the country and the Labor Party. As a result, government remained in conservative Nationalist hands federally until 1941, except for a brief, tumultuous hiatus under Labor during the Great Depression. During that profound trauma, national indebtedness to principally British creditors was queried on the centre-left. This occasioned right wing dalliance with subversion.[118] Ultimately, the Labor Party again split under the strain and conservatives reorganized themselves as the United Australia Party under the press patronage of Keith (later

---

Seekers and National Histories of Detention", *Australian Journal of Politics & History*, vol. 48, no. 4, 2002, 509-527.

[118] See Michael Cathcart, *Defending the National Tuckshop: Australia's Secret Army Intrigue of 1931* (Melbourne: Penguin Australia, 1988).

A Kafkaesque Experience

Figure 9.1: Lamberto Yonna, artwork, 'Long Bay Prison', Long Bay, New South Wales, 1940. (courtesy AWM)

Sir Keith) Murdoch[119] and the parliamentary leadership of financially orthodox former Labor Treasurer Joseph Lyons, ostensibly to raise fiscal issues above the political hurly-burley. By contrast, critics of the banks and deflationary economic policy and the high unemployment that went with it were generally critics of the British connection. Inchoate antagonism to the old country as 'the auld enemy' reached a peak in popular culture with the 'Bodyline' Ashes cricket Test series of 1932-1933. Ethnic, economic and defence ties with Britain thus remained very much live issues politically between the wars, and very much the touchstone of 'sound' conservative thinking. This remained the case despite the passage by the imperial parliament of the Statute of Westminster in 1931. This Statute legislated parity between Westminster and the

---

[119] See Tom D.C., *Roberts Before Rupert: Keith Murdoch & the Birth of a Dynasty* (St Lucia: UQP, 2015), 175-205.

Dominion parliaments. Looked upon by antipodean conservatives as an unwelcome separation, the Statute was not ratified by them even after war broke out in Europe in September 1939. Not until the advent of total war in 1942 did a Labor government bring in an Adoption Act to give effect to the Statute.

By that time Australia had been at war as a British Dominion for three years. We had entered the fighting, as Prime Minister Menzies had announced to the country, primarily because Britain was at war with Germany. Only with Hitler's onslaught against the Soviet Union in the northern summer of 1941 and Japan's blitzkrieg in the Pacific in December of that year was the mortal contest between the Third Reich on the one hand and the imperial powers of Britain and France on the other expanded into a world war against fascism. Until then the presuppositions of the contest had been nationalistic rather than philosophical: the viscerally anti-socialist aristocratic maverick and British Prime Minister Churchill remained an admirer of Mussolini for example even during and again after the war, hailing the dictator as 'the Italian law giver'.[120] Nothing demonstrated the nationalistic presuppositions, which were the keynote of the twentieth century globally and in this country as the impact upon the Italian community in Australia of Mussolini's opportunistic entry into the war alongside Hitler in June 1940. The Fall of France in May left Britain isolated and mauled at Dunkirk. Australian leaders were panic-stricken at the dire tidings from Europe, which included alarming Whitehall circulars about the danger of Axis Fifth Column subversion.[121]

---

[120] See Winston Churchill, *The Second World War*, vol. 5: Closing the Ring, (London: Cassell, 1952), 48. See also his *Great Contemporaries* (London: Thornton Butterworth, 1939) 261f. For extended argument to these contentions see Robert Rhodes James *Churchill: A Study in Failure 1900-39* (London: Penguin, 1973).

[121] See Margaret Bevege *Behind Barbed Wire: Internment in Australia during World War II*, (St. Lucia: University of Queensland Press, 1993), 1; and Bruce Muirden *The Puzzled Patriots: The Story of the*

Australian authorities addressed the prospect of war in 1939 with the best of intentions towards the nation's ethnic minorities. Practical precedents were not however encouraging. During the Great War demonisation of the German Australian community had envisaged the destruction of this, the nation's largest ethnic group of non-British extraction and the liquidation of trade with what was then Australia's second largest trading partner.[122] Regulations under the draconian War Precautions Act of 1914 were successively broadened until they provided for the internment of anyone who could be defined by authority as 'of hostile origin or association'.[123] By war's end in 1918 nearly 7000 individuals had been interned from Asia, the Pacific and Australia. Approximately 4500 of these persons were Australian residents, of whom 700 were naturalised British subjects; 70 of these were Australian born. Leading religious, medical and business figures were interned to decapitate the community.[124] It was to this notorious episode that Prime Minister Menzies alluded in speaking to the debate in the House of Representatives in 1939 on the National Security Bill when he stated that he was

> well aware that we have, perhaps, not been without experience in the past of some want of understanding, by rigid minds closed with authority, of the rights and privileges of ordinary people.[125]

Australia First Movement (Melbourne: Melbourne University Press, 1968), 96. On the British circular of October 1940 to the Dominions regarding Fifth Column Activities see Gianfranco Cresciani, "The Bogey of the Italian Fifth Column..." in Richard Bosworth and Romano Ugolini, editors, *War, Internment & Mass Migration: The Italo-Australian Experience 1940-90* (Roma: Gruppo editoriale internazionale, 1992) 12-13.

[122] See Ilma Martinuzzi O'Brien "The Enemy Within: Wartime Internment of Enemy Aliens" in Martin Crotty & David Roberts *The Great Mistakes of Australian History* (Sydney : UNSWP, 2006), 140-41.
[123] Cited by O'Brien, 141-2.
[124] Ibid., 142.
[125] Ibid., 145.

However, alongside such gracious and authoritative sentiments, lurked deeper racial antagonisms. Speaking likewise with cognizance of the unfortunate Great War precedents on 10 May 1939 in the Second Reading debate on the 'Aliens Registration Bill' in the House, the Labor Member for Denison GW Mahoney declared

> It is only right that migrants who come out here should be supervised, but in the event of trouble arising with other nations, they should not be treated as criminals…In the event of war breaking out aliens should not be indiscriminately be placed in concentration camps. Such things should not be done in a democratic country.

But Mahoney was only an Opposition MHR, and Lane from the government interjected darkly in reply 'It is well to keep an eye on them.'[126] Lane was hot under the collar about racial issues. He had previously in the same debate tackled the Italian Australian ALP Member for Werriwa Bert Lazzarini for defending the good character of alien immigrants, including recent political refugees. Lazzarini reminded honourable members for good measure that British ancestry was no guarantee of good conduct. At this Lane bridled, interjecting

> Let the honourable member stick to his own nationality, and not take liberties in his criticism of British nationals.

Lazzarini replied stoutly

> I am an Australian, and I am not ashamed of the stock from which I come. If the honourable gentleman has sprung from as good a stock he has nothing to be ashamed of either.

At this, Lane became rowdy and had to be recalled to

---

[126] Commonwealth of Australia Parliamentary Debates, 1st Session, 15th Parliament, 3rd Period, 294.

order by the Speaker.[127] Subsequently in June when the Independent Labor MP and lawyer Maurice Blackburn protested that an amendment to the Bill moved by Archie Cameron would enable a Minister to arbitrarily deport aliens in a week, Cameron replied 'That is exactly what I intend.' The amendment was passed along party lines.[128] It fell also to the individualistic Blackburn, who was a genuine socialist internationalist and antifascist who had denounced Mussolini's police state,[129] to state the principle that the nation at war ought to be true to its best libertarian inspirations:

> I should say that the most important thing is that the people of this country shall believe that in this struggle they are preserving as much of their freedom, as much of their constitutional rights as can possibly be preserved for them; that those rights are not taken from them; that they are not losing those rights in the struggle which this nation is waging.[130]

These parliamentary tensions surrounded the definition of the national security regime out of which internment arose in 1939 and developed in the crises of ensuing years. Regulations authorized under these laws restricted the possession of firearms, cameras, radios and the use of motor vehicles by aliens. These draconian measures were all designed to limit the scope for subversive activities. All aliens were obliged to register with local police and official permission was required to change address. Alongside these legislative arrangements went the keeping in readiness of administrative measures

---

[127] Ibid., 158.
[128] Ibid., 20-23.
[129] On his political career see Susan Blackburn "Maurice Blackburn & the ALP 1934-43", Australian Society for the Study of Labour History, 1969.
[130] Cited in Kay Saunders and Helen Taylor "The Enemy Within? The Process of Internment of Enemy Aliens in Queensland 1939-45", *Australian Journal of Politics & History*, vol. 34, no. 1, 1988, 16.

such as the Department of Defence *War Book*, a manual closely modelled on its British counterpart and designed to co-ordinate military and police measures between the Commonwealth and the States should hostilities approach. Chapter XII of the *War Book* laid down general internment policy, whose guiding principle was supposed to be that the internment of resident enemy aliens should be kept to 'the narrowest limits consistent with public safety and public sentiment.'[131] As to public safety, it is important to stress that no one was ever interned based on a conviction for acting against the war effort.[132] Internment of enemy aliens was a measure taken against individuals under suspicion that they might represent a threat to the national interest because of assumed ethnic patriotism. As such internment placed the national interest as embodied in National Security Regulations over individual rights. It thus effectively reversed the onus of proof against the suspect in violation of centuries of common law guarantees.[133]

Internment was deemed a precautionary wartime measure and not punitive in nature, which was little comfort to those affected.[134] The public sentiment test was equally vague and insidious, especially for the Italian community. From the outbreak of war in 1939 the government was deluged with correspondence

---

[131] Ibid.
[132] Noted by Kay Saunders and Helen Taylor `The Impact of Total War Upon Policing: The Queensland Experience' in Mark Finnane *Policing in Australia: Historical Perspectives* (Sydney: New South Wales University Press, 1987), 150 and reiterated by Saunders in "'Taken Away to be Shot?': The Process of Incarceration in Australia in World War II" in Kay Saunders and Roger Daniels, editors, *Alien Justice: Wartime Internment in Australia & North America* (St Lucia: University of Queensland Press, 2000), 166.
[133] That this was the case is deduced from commentary on internment offered by Paul Hasluck in his *The Government & the People 1939-41* (Canberra: Australian War Memorial, 1952), 593-4.
[134] See the official policy statements cited in Saunders & Taylor "The Enemy Within?...", 16-18. See also O`Brien "The Enemy Within:...", cit., 154.

demanding the mass detention of all enemy aliens and Italians in particular.[135] This public outpouring in favour of wholesale internment of all enemy aliens featured ex-service associations, conservative lobbies such as the National Defence League and anti-catholic Loyal Orange lodges, local government leaders and both the Housewives Association and the Feminist Club of NSW.[136] A Mary M Williamson of the Nursing Staff, General Hospital, Brisbane, wrote to Prime Minister Curtin on 15 March 1942 protesting that

> It is vastly misleading to the American people to tell them that we have no Fifth Column [of traitors] in Australia, when in North Queensland [there] are thousands of uninterned Italians who openly boast of their anti-British feeling.[137]

Williamson touched on a raw nerve. Since the Great War, when Italy had been a British ally, Italian immigration to Australia had increased significantly, to the point where the Italian community had superseded the German as the most numerous non-British enclaves in the nation. It was localised mainly in North Queensland.[138] The creation of a tropical little Italy had been a cause for official concern about racial 'purity' as early as the Queensland Ferry Royal Commission of 1925, with Italians and especially Southern Italians being viewed as a lesser breed liable to constitute 'alien groups... anti-British in sympathy and outlook'.[139] In subsequent years Italian success in obtaining work and property in the sugar industry occasioned resentment, leading to attempts to reserve

---

[135] See National Archives of Australia Vic MP508/1; 115/703/516, 543, 553, 560 & 568.
[136] Ilma Martinuzzi O'Brien, "Citizenship, Rights & Emergency Powers in Second World War Australia", *Australian Journal of Politics & History*, vol. 53, no. 2, 2007, 211.
[137] NAA Vic MP508/1; 115/703/468.
[138] O'Brien `The Enemy Within...', cit., 143-4.
[139] Saunders and Taylor, "The Enemy Within?...", cit., 20.

employment to 'British' labour.[140] Now with Australian personnel engaged against Italians in the Mediterranean theatre, antagonism excited by Italy's entry into the war as an enemy reached new heights.

This was the socioeconomic context in which official internment policy slid under the impact of the adverse course of the early years of the war from the initial doctrine of 'narrow limits' to an ever less discriminating dragnet, approximating the sad experience of the Great War. By November 1940, when limited appeal provisions against internment were instituted over conservative protests,[141] 2376 enemy aliens had been detained; 650 Germans and 1726 Italians. Of the latter, 951 were from Western Australia. This reflected the fact that the local military command to which internment decisions were delegated had sought 'right from the outbreak of war with Italy to break up the large Italian communities for purposes of general security.'[142] Around this time Acting Prime Minister Fadden was receiving a letter from J. J. MacDonald of the Northern Country Party protesting the restricted number of internments of Italians in North Queensland and advising that 'it would be better to intern hundreds of innocent people than to be lenient [with]... these scum.'[143] On January 21 1941 Northern Command advised that 'although the war against Italy has been in operation for...6 months there has been no evidence of attempt at sabotage traceable to Italians in Queensland'. It

---

[140] See William A. Douglass, *From Italy to Ingham* (St. Lucia: University of Queensland Press, 1995), 168f.

[141] Saunders and Taylor "The Enemy Within?...", cit., 22 and Hasluck *The Government & the People 1939-41*, cit., 594; See also O'Brien "The Enemy Within:...", cit., 149-50. 594.

[142] Official statistics cited by Saunders & Taylor `The Enemy Within?...', cit., 18, and NAA Vic. MP508/1; 115/703/371 Western Command-Military Board 23 July 1941, in which it was noted that the initial internment of Italians in WA was so comprehensive that supplementary sweeps would not be necessary.

[143] Letter dated 22 November 1940 in NAA Vic. MP508/1; 115/703/296 Internment Policy – Italians in Queensland.

discounted the representations by MacDonald that discord and dissatisfaction at the low level of internment in North Queensland were alarming as 'an exaggeration from the military point of view.' Nevertheless, by 17 February 1941, well before the military disasters in Greece and the Pacific, plans were being drawn up for the internment of a further 4500 Queensland aliens and 'naturalised subjects of enemy origin' suspected of surreptitious subversion.[144] Fundamental to this planning was a 1940 Security Service report entitled *Italian Penetration*, focussing on Italian settlement in North Queensland. It began

> Consequent upon frequent complaints evidencing strong Australian public feeling in areas to which Italians had gravitated, by reason of Italian preponderance in certain industries and the commonly insolent demeanour of such enemy aliens, a careful survey has been made of the relative effect upon the economic life of the affected districts as also upon public morale...[145]

This structural context of racist, anti-Italian prejudice was inherited from the interwar years. It incorporated subsidiary wartime aims of encouraging informing against Italians, deterring presumed disloyalty and thereby encouraging AIF recruitment.[146] It was the prime motivation of mass internment of Italians in North Queensland, starting in February 1942 after the disasters suffered at Pearl Harbor, Singapore and Darwin.

The consequences for the Italian community in the region and the impact on its war effort were catastrophic.

---

[144] NAA Vic MP508/1; 115/703/296.

[145] NAA MP729/6; 65/401/133.

[146] On the motivation of mass internment in North Queensland see the undated memoir Deterrent Detention in NAA Vic. MP508/1; 115/703/371. Consult also O'Brien's discussion of the document entitled Italian Penetration in "Ubi bene, ibi patria..." in Beaumont et al., editors, *Under Suspicion: Citizenship & Internment in Australia during the Second World War* (Canberra: National Museum of Australia, 2008), 21.

In the Innisfail district 501 persons were interned of whom 406 were Italian by birth, representing a quarter of the Italian population of the district, notwithstanding the high degree of assimilation there. At the 1933 Census, 51% of Innisfail's Italians were already naturalised British subjects, with Italians representing 12% of the district population.[147] Perhaps the most assimilated victim in the district was the pioneering Veneto Italian settler and hotelier Charlie Dalla Vecchia, 51 years an Australian resident and 41 years a British subject.[148] As he wrote to Prime Minister Curtin in 1943 'I have been interned, dishonoured [and] damaged morally and materially... under your government.'[149] The local sugar industry staggered under the blow to its workforce. The tonnage of cane produced and its value fell to a wartime low in 1943 and did not recover until the internees returned to the cane fields in 1946. Italian mass internment on the Sugar Coast was a clamorous own goal: worse than a crime, it was a blunder.[150] Mass internment was the single most adverse social event experienced in the history of the Italian community in Australia, and 'a sorry chapter in Australia's history of immigration, citizenship and civil liberty', not to mention a public policy snafu of the highest order and an object lesson for future generations in how not to conduct communal relations.[151]

Nor was it without tragic absurdity. Most of its victims were not politicised at all, and love of Italy was not universal among them. Some looked on Italy as a stepmother which had denied them bread and liberty, and adopted the classical motto 'Ubi bene, ibi patria'

---

[147] See O'Brien "Ubi bene, ibi patria...", cit., 23 and O'Brien, "The Enemy Within:...", cit., 144.
[148] For a profile of Dalla Vecchia and the uncorroborated evidence as to his fascist sympathies see O'Brien "Ubi bene, ibi patria", cit., 28.
[149] Ibid., 29.
[150] See Don Dignan, "The Internment of Italians in Queensland" in Richard Bosworth & Romano Ugolini, editors, *War, Internment & Mass Migration: The Italo-Australian Experience 1940-90*, cit., 61.
[151] O'Brien, "The Enemy Within:...", cit., 152-3.

out of loyalty to the adopted country which had given them a stake in life. Thus along with a small minority of convinced fascists and fellow travellers, including some Italian physicians handpicked by the Partito Nazionale Fascista during the years of the regime,[152] were interned an even smaller but substantial number of qualitatively significant antifascist refugees. It was not uncommon for the politically naïve local Queensland police to denounce North Queensland aliens simultaneously for esoteric fascist and antifascist opinions, so foreign did they find their heterodoxy.[153] Pre-eminent amongst these anti-fascist internees were the anarchists Luigi Danesi, prominent with his brother Costante in the Innisfail Mourilyan Italian Progressive Club, the epicentre of pre-war resistance to discrimination against Italian labour. Francesco Giovanni Fantin, a Danesi brother associate, known throughout the cane fields for his anti-fascist activism since his arrival in the tropics in 1925, after escaping fascist and police attention in Italy. Interned at Edmonton near Cairns on 19 February 1942, as a communist fascist of anti-British persuasion, Fantin was later detained at Loveday in the South Australian Riverland. There he became embroiled in a battle for the hearts and minds of the internees in Compound 14A, with a fascist clique that ended the conflict by assassinating him on 16 November 1942 shortly after the Battle of El Alamein.

This crime was carried out by an executioner with a blunt instrument and probably masterminded by the

---

[152] See David Brown's PhD thesis, *Before Everything, Remain Italian: Fascism & the Italian Population of Queensland 1910-45*, University of Queensland, 2008, 114-15.

[153] See Kay Saunders, "'Taken Away to be Shot?': The Process of Incarceration in Australia in World War II" in Kay Saunders and Roger Daniels, editors, *Alien Justice:...*, 155. See for example the description of Luigi Danesi's politics given by the Innisfail police according to O'Brien "Ubi bene, ibi patria...", 27; Kay Saunders "'Inspired by Patriotic Hysteria?' Internment Policy towards Enemy Aliens in Australia during the Second World War" in Panikos Panayi, editor, *Minorities in Wartime* (Oxford: Berg, 1993), 300.

antagonistic fascist camp leader and Italian medico Dr Francesco Piscitelli.[154] At its very worst, internment killed at least one of its victims. The positive aspect on this singular tragedy if there was one was that it shocked Evatt's Director General of Security Brigadier WB Simpson, who had been in the process, not without resistance from his Queensland Deputy Director JC MacFarlane, of having Fantin released. A number of Fantin's associates in Loveday Compound 14A were expeditiously released to forestall fascist reprisals. Security Service review of all internees' dossiers with a view to release to labour conscription with the Civil Aliens' Corp was accelerated.[155] In all some 2300 Queensland Italians were interned, including 1631 of the estimated 2764 registered Italian aliens in the State. Of the 5559 naturalized Italians in Queensland 666 were detained.[156] For most of these their experience of internment was not one of terror such as Fantin and Danesi experienced at the hands of antagonists committed to political violence. Nevertheless they were subjected to the trauma and humiliation of maddening injustice such as Kafka described. For them 'the whole experience was one of disbelief, shock, humiliation, anger and enduring bitterness.'[157]

[154] Iconographic evidence of Fantin's Danesi links dated 1927 can be seen in a photo of the Mourilyan Italian Progressive Club in Ilma Martinuzzi O'Brien *Australia's Italians 1788-1988* (Melbourne: The Italian Historical Society & the State Library of Victoria, 1988), 80-81. Documentary evidence can be found in his Italian secret police dossier, dated 20 April 1927 Regio Consolato Brisbane –Direzione Generale di Pubblica Sicurezza in Archivio Generale dello Stato Roma Ministero Interni DGPS CPC busta 1948 fascicolo 20852.
[155] Reported by Dignan, 61; G. Cresciani *Fascismo, antifascismo e gli italiani in Australia 1922-45* (Roma: Bonacci editori, 1979), 158-9.
[156] 1942 statistical return cited by Dignan, 63; see O'Brien "The Internment of Australian Born & Naturalized British Subjects of Italian Origin" in Bosworth & Ugolini *War, Internment & Mass Migration - 1940-90*, cit., 89f.
[157] Saunders '"Taken Away to be Shot?': The Process of Incarceration in Australia in World War II' in Saunders & Daniels *Alien Justice: Wartime Internment in Australia & North America* (St. Lucia: UQP, 2000), 153.

A Kafkaesque Experience

Figure 9.3: Francesco Giovanni Fantin, textile worker, cane cutter & political activist; born 20/1/1901 San Vito de Leguzzano, Vicenza, Italy, assassinated Loveday Camp 14A on 16/11/1942.

One test of historical significance is contemporary significance, the degree to which a precedent holds lessons for subsequent eras. Certainly during the Cold War Evatt had come to understand the perils represented by the situation presented to him when he had come into office as Curtin's Attorney General in 1941. Speaking in 1955 on a debate on security issues in the House of Representatives when the risk to civil liberty from government was very real he said:

> When I became Attorney General… I found that 7000 persons had been interned in this country by military intelligence. Thousands of these people should not have been interned. Mr Curtin, together with Mr Mackay, who was the civilian security director at that time, and I appointed

> the then Deputy Leader of the Opposition… Harrison…to a committee to go through those cases, and after exhaustive enquiries extending over a period of 12 months the number of cases was reduced to 700.[158]

Today the risk of wholesale internment of ethnic minorities is slight, but the price of liberty nevertheless remains eternal vigilance. Legislation such as the Commonwealth Anti-Terrorism Bill (No. 2) 2005 presents political opportunities for the demonisation of ethnic communities and political minorities and the targeting of individuals through the arbitrary violation of civil rights.[159] As noted in the introduction, the present regime of deterrent mandatory detention of refugees presents disturbing parallels, not without racial undertones, to the episode discussed here, both as to suspension of civil liberties and the infliction of psychological trauma on its victims. With no Bill of Rights to provide protection, the precedents of the Great War and the Second World War remain unsettling.

– David Faber (peer reviewed)

---

[158] Cited by Brian Fitzpatrick in his *The Australian Commonwealth* (Melbourne: Cheshire, 1956), 281.
[159] O'Brien "The Enemy Within:…", cit., 153-4.

The Life and Death of Raffaele Musitano

Family Testimonies

Raffaele

Raffaele Musitano was born 2 September 1911 in Delianuova, a town in the province of Calabria in Southern Italy to parents Domenico and Caterina. At the age of fifteen and a half, sponsored by Rocco Colella, he migrated to Australia and arrived at the Fremantle Port in Western Australia on 23 March 1927 on board the steam ship *Orama*. He returned to Italy in April 1929 and then returned again to Australia in April 1930. He became a Naturalized British Subject in September 1933. Raffaele purchased a 14-acre property in Caversham Western Australia in August 1935. The property consisted of 11 acres of vineyard, one and a half acres of orchard and the remaining was made up of the horse paddock, residence and sheds. In October 1936, Raffaele submitted an application and was successful in sponsoring his older brother, Giuseppe, for admission into Australia. He worked in his orchard and vineyard upon his arrival then moved further south.

On 24 December 1936 Raffaele married Domenica Frisina by proxy, with Raffaele in Australia and Domenica in Italy. She remained in Delianuova at the same time as Raffaele worked and saved to pay for the property and her passage to Australia in 1938. Their first son Domenico was born 1939, followed by Giovanni in 1940 and Giuseppe in 1942. Caterina was born in 1943. Raffaele would not have known that he was to be a father again when he was arrested in 1942. The Second World War raged in Europe, with Britain and its allies in bloody conflict with Nazi Germany from 1939 and Fascist Italy from 1940. As a Naturalized British Subject, Raffaele was not

Hidden Lives

Figure 10.1: Raffaele Musitano, 1930s.

initially interned as an Italian enemy alien. However, his membership of an Italian club and his continued links with his Italian origins was held against him once the Japanese attacked Australia in early 1942.

Raffaele was taken away from his home and young family in Caversham on the 12 October 1942 and interned, even though he was a Naturalized British Subject, and transferred to Parkinson internment camp near Kalgoorlie. In November, he attended a tribunal with the advisory committee to appeal his internment. These appeals were rejected and he was ordered to remain interned in the detention barracks in Fremantle, which were a part of the Fremantle goal. To date, no documentation of the tribunal hearings have been found. While in internment, Raffaele withdrew money to pay the full amount due on the property to enable him to have freehold of the land. On 19 December 1942, he was transferred from Fremantle to Loveday Internment camp in South Australia via train. The train bound for South Australia consisted of four German prisoners of war and 21 Italian civilian internees. On the fourth day of the journey, Raffaele's behaviour was reported by the army to have become erratic. We do not know if this is true or fabricated to justify the events that led to Raffaele's death. The statements of the events leading up to Raffaele's death were only submitted by army personnel witnesses and are contradictory; fellow internees submitted none. We do not know if they were asked to make eyewitness statements. It's interesting as coronial reports on internee deaths usually included testimonies by internees.

In the Coronial Report, Lieutenant Hogg stated that Raffaele hadn't eaten all day and that at 11.45 pm his behaviour had become erratic and was held down by two army personnel and two internees. He was then placed on a seat and his hands and feet were tied with blankets secured by Red Cross bandages. It was reported that at 1 am, an injection of 'half grain' morphine (32 mg) was administered by a doctor. A second injection of quarter grain (16 mg) was administered at 1:45 am. The second injection took effect after about half an hour and he became quiet and was released from the restraints. The report states that an Australian army medical corps orderly was in constant attendance and requested a doctor's presence at 3:30 am as his condition appeared unsatisfactory. Raffaele had become unconscious and had stopped breathing and artificial respiration was applied on the train and after sometime he regained consciousness. Artificial respiration was applied until 5:30 am, and his condition appeared to improve. The military doctor, who happened to be travelling on the train, contacted Doctor Thompson in Port Augusta. We are not sure how this was done.

Twenty minutes before the train arrived in Port Augusta, he became comatose. The military authorities were very anxious that Raffaele be taken to the Port Pirie military camp. But, Doctor Thompson, who attended to Raffaele at the railway station upon arrival of the train, conducted a thorough examination and advised immediate removal from the station to the hospital. He stated that it was essential that he remain in Port Augusta. He was then taken to the Port Augusta hospital. When the doctors examined Raffaele he was cyanosed and unconscious. The pupils of his eyes were small and he was sweating and breathing with difficulty. The report goes on to say that the medical officer advised that he had been given an injection of morphine followed by another shortly afterwards. The statement given by the army doctor on the train said that they had no medical equipment on the train other than morphine and considered that he was suffering from morphine poisoning following the injections.

Doctor Thompson contacted the hospital and treatment was commenced upon arrival at the hospital at 8:10 am where Raffaele was given two injections of Cardiazol, which is a respiratory stimulant, and also an injection of Atropine Sulphate and Strychine Sulphate that are used to block or reverse the adverse side effects caused by some medicines. Artificial respiration was applied and his stomach was washed out. The treatment was to no avail. The doctor saw Raffaele again around 9 am and his condition had worsened. Doctor Thompson was with him until he passed away just after 9:30 am. Just before death, his breathing ceased but his heart continued to beat for 10 minutes. The doctor's opinion was that the cause of death was morphine poisoning, as the quantity he was injected was in fact excessive. But morphine is used as an analgesic not a sedative. So, it is inexplicable why a trained military medical doctor would have administered such a large dose of a potentially lethal opiate.

To the present, there have been no records to show that Raffaele was ever admitted to the Port Augusta Hospital, even though his death certificate states Port Augusta hospital as the place of his death. Raffaele was buried 24 December at the Port Augusta Cemetery on what was his and Domenica's sixth wedding anniversary. The family was not notified of his death. In 1943, Raffaele was exhumed and reburied at the Port Augusta Cemetery whereby all cultures were to be buried together. The family was not informed. In 1948, due to unexplained reasons, Raffaele was again exhumed and reburied at the Barmera War Cemetery, near the location of the Loveday Internment Camp in South Australia. The family was not informed. In 1968, Raffaele was exhumed and reburied once again at the Murchison Cemetery in Victoria, which was to be his final resting place. A letter was sent to the family on 10 March 1943 to advise Raffaele that his naturalisation was to be revoked. He had passed away over two months *prior* to the letter being sent. The family was never notified of any of the burials and none of his personal effects were ever returned to them. What can be made of this? Six members from three generations of the Musitano family offer their personal testimonies on Raffaele's life and untimely death.

The testimony of Nicole Musitano, Raffaele's Granddaughter

Growing up we always knew that our Nonno had passed away of a morphine overdose after being injected on a train bound for Loveday Internment camp in South Australia. The exact details of his death were not known until 2012 when the family received information outlining the details of how his life had come to a tragic end. Imagine being taken away from your property, your loving wife and three small children aged three, two and six months and not knowing where you were or where you were going and if or when you were coming back. Nonna had also had no contact with Nonno or the authorities since he was taken away. She was not even advised of his death. The news was sent via a neighbour. She was at home when the neighbour's son came over and told her that his mother wanted to see her. Upon arrival at the neighbour's home, she was advised of her husband's death. The shock was unbelievable, especially as she was pregnant with their fourth child. As the authorities had collected Nonno's ration book when he was taken away she relied on the assistance and generosity of her Italian friends and neighbours to get by.

Nonna always spoke so lovingly of Nonno and through her, he lived in our hearts. She would always tell me how other families in Italy where they lived would try to get Nonno to marry their daughters and he would always decline and tell them "No, I only want to marry Domenica!" Nonna said he was very good to her and looked after her and their children very well. She also said that they were very happy and that he was a

Hidden Lives

Figures 10.2 & 3: Domenica and Raffaele Musitano and Raffaele with infant son Domenico at Perth Zoo, Western Australia, 1939.

loving, beautiful man, hard-working and used to tend to his own vineyard as well as others. He'd regularly climb through the fence of the neighbouring property to work at Valencia's vineyard and orchard. We would get the photos out and she would show me the ones of Nonno in his vineyard. Her favourite photo was of them both at the zoo when she was pregnant with Uncle Domenic. She would also tell me how devastated she was when she found out that Nonno had died. Nonna revealed how she had to sell the vineyard and then remarried and relocated to Brunswick Junction in southern Western Australia. Sadly, Nonna passed away in 2007 at 94 years of age without knowing the details of what had happened to her beloved Raffaele. Nonno has always been a part of our lives. Even though he was never physically with us, there has always been a special place in our hearts for him. My Nonno had always been so much a part of my life that in 2011, I had a tribute tattoo etched in memory of him.

In 2012, 70 years after Nonno's shocking death, our family received a call that would bring news of his final resting place. Nonno was buried in the Italian Mausoleum in Murchison in central Victoria. Our journey to Murchison began in June 2012 when we were advised of the annual Memorial for the Italian War Dead at the *'Ossario di Murchison'*, which is my Nonno's final place of rest. This was to be the first time that anyone from our family would see Nonno's resting place. For me it was a dream come true and a memory that I will cherish forever. On the second weekend of November in 2012, I boarded the plane with my Mum and Dad (Nola and John), Aunty Katie and Uncle Joe. My brother Raffaele and his wife Fleur were meeting us in Melbourne. We met a friend who was an internment researcher for the first time that evening and she briefed us on the memorial proceedings and also shared with us a lot of information on internees and our Nonno. The next morning on Sunday 11th November, we packed up our gear and headed to the Furlan Social Club in Thornbury, where we were to catch the bus to Murchison with the 'Alpini', a renowned group of retired Italian soldiers. The bus was loaded and we were on our way.

The President of the Alpini Club, Aldo Zanetta, welcomed us on the bus and there was singing and an older gentleman playing a piano accordion and a lot of chatting. A friend was telling us a lot of information on the Internment camps and the internees. Arriving in Murchison, I felt a mixture of emotions. Excited, as it was a dream come true to find my Nonno, and sad because of the emotion that I knew lay ahead. Walking through the gate of the cemetery had the same feeling of walking into a funeral. The ceremony started with the laying of wreaths, followed by many speeches and a Mass. At the conclusion of the Mass we were going into the crypt and would be able to pay our respects for the very first time. At the conclusion of the Mass we were taken into the crypt, it was an amazing feeling to be standing in front of

Nonno for the very first time. It was indescribable. It was something I had always wanted to do. My cousin David and I had always talked about finding our Nonno when we were young, and here I was standing in front of my Nonno's grave. A dream come true and a memory that I will always cherish.

Watching my Dad and Uncle Joe standing in front of their father for the first time in 70 years was very overwhelming. I could not even begin to imagine what they were feeling. We spent some time as a family in the crypt, and then we headed back to the bus, leaving Dad and Uncle Joe with their Dad. Walking away from the crypt was hard as I felt like we were leaving Nonno behind when we had only just found him. I felt a sense of closure and felt truly blessed to be part of our family's special day. My Nonna would be so proud of her boys and our family. My only wish was that she was still with us to share the special moment. I know she was watching us from above with a heart full of pride and love. The picnic was a fantastic experience, people everywhere, singing, music and a lot of stories told of loved ones that were interned. Someone in our group proposed a toast in honour of Nonno and we celebrated his life and the discovery and visit to his resting place. It was like the wake he never had. Many people approached us to share their family stories with us and considered themselves lucky as their loved ones returned home. They may have been emotionally or physically injured but they were grateful that they had come home. It was a wonderful afternoon shared with the most kind and caring strangers that welcomed us with open arms and showed us the true meaning of the Italian spirit.

On the way home Aldo made his final announcement for the day and thanked us for joining them on our journey and invited us back for the next year. He promised us that if we are unable to make it in future years that he will honour our Nonno in our absence. This was a promise that Aldo kept and in 2013 when we walked into the crypt Aldo was standing in front of Nonno paying his respects and honouring his promise to our family. It was a moment that I will never forget. It was amazing to see how the lives and deaths of the Italians who had died during the war in Australia had an impact on many people. Mum, Dad and I returned to the Murchison memorial in 2013, 2014 with Dannielle and 2016 along with Aunty Katie and Uncle Joe. It doesn't get any easier or take away the pain of our loss, but it is a nice peaceful special place where we can visit to honour and respect our loved one. A friend has guided me in the right direction when it comes to the research on my Nonno and without that guidance we would not have found some of the information that we have on him.

The testimony of John (Giovanni) Musitano, Raffaele's son

As children we were told that our father had passed away on a train after being sent to an internment camp in South Australia. Our mother was never officially advised of our father's death and heard about it from a neighbour. She never knew the details of his death other than he died after receiving an injection. Details of where he was buried were also unknown for many decades – a lifetime in fact. When we were young, our mother remarried and moved to a small farming community in southern Western Australia and had four more children. Unfortunately due to our age we have no memory of our time in Caversham or of our father. In our new family, we grew up in a happy environment where we were very well provided for and never wanted for anything. When I was a teenager a family friend took me to Perth to the markets. When we drove down West Swan Road he pointed to some chimneys that were a part of a roof tiling factory and said: "That was where your father's property was." That's all I knew of my family's life before the war.

As I was getting older I started to think of how our lives would have been if our father hadn't died, but you just can't turn back time. I worked on our family farm alongside my brothers as milk producers and potato growers until a few years after I was married. In August

Figure 10.4: Raffaele Musitano in his vineyard in Caversham, Western Australia, c. 1940.

1969 my wife Nola gave birth to our first child, a boy named Raffaele in honour of my father. My grandson Cruz also bares his great-grandfather's name as his middle name. The year 2012 became the year that we found out a lot of information on our father; how he died, confirmation of his exact burial site and we were to visit his place of rest for the very first time. We also opened my father's file at the National Archives of Australia in Perth. That's where we saw his handwriting for the very first time in the form of his signature, such a small thing that we take for granted in our everyday lives. It was very emotional for our family.

With my family beside me we made the trip to Melbourne to the annual Italian War Dead ceremony, which is always on the second Sunday of November. On that Sunday we boarded the bus to Murchison for the Memorial Day event. We watched the procession of wreath laying, speeches and Mass. At the end of the Mass we were to make our way into the crypt to see my father's resting place. Just before the end of the Mass I became quite emotional and shed a tear as finally we were to visit my father after 70 long years. Next we were standing in front of his tomb looking at his name. It was a very emotional time as I was standing in front of the Father that I never got to know. It was like a funeral and we were saying goodbye and paying our respects after all these years. A priest said a blessing for my father and then we were left to spend the time as a family and to take it all in. It was hard to walk away knowing that I had just been with him for the first time in 70 years then had to leave him again. The crypt is a very nice peaceful environment and I feel at peace knowing that my father is resting in such a lovely place.

The testimony of Nola Musitano, Raffaele's daughter-in-law

John had told me that his father had died when he was very young and that if he ever had a son he wanted to name him Raffaele. When our son was born in 1969, John came to the hospital and his first words to me were "We got our Raffaele!" I felt so proud at that moment as it meant so much to John to be able to carry on his father's name. When we went to Murchison in 2012 it was like going to the unknown: we really didn't know what to expect or how it was going to affect us. I remember standing opposite the crypt entrance watching the ceremony when it suddenly hit me that John's father was lying beyond that entrance, and that we were finally here. I was sure that he was waiting to be with his two sons, he had waited so long already, as had his sons. It brought tears to my eyes knowing we were so close to that moment. Next thing we knew we were standing in front of Raffaele's tomb, it was such a special moment, especially for John and Joe. Emotionally it affected all of us as a family but it was so special and something that we thought would never happen. The emotions we felt on that day will stay with us forever. As we walked away with sorrow we all left a piece of our hearts with him so he will never be alone again. We were so glad to be able to go to Murchison and share the journey with our children as well as with Joe and Katie. Our only wish was that

John's mother Domenica could have been with us to have shared the day. She would have been extremely proud of her boys.

The testimony of Joe (Giuseppe) Musitano, Raffaele's son

At the outbreak of WWII, all Italian men considered a threat to this country were arrested and interned by the Australian government. My father was one of such citizens that were to be interned. One night in October 1942 the military police arrived at the door of our humble dwelling and arrested our father. As they led him away, he assured my mother that she had nothing to fear and that he would be back soon. However this was not to be, as my father was put on a train with a number of internees and transported to Kalgoorlie and from there he was transported to Perth, then to South Australia and passed away in transit. I can only imagine the heartache, sorrow and fear that my mother went through after being informed of my father's death by a neighbour and being left on her own, pregnant and supporting three small boys under the age of four years old with very little income from the sale of grapes from the vineyard and no support from the government.

After the birth of her fourth child, my mother was presented with the opportunity to remarry and in the years to follow had four more children. As I was only eight months old when my father died, I have no recollection of life with him. But as the years went by I became very curious and anxious to learn more about him. My mother only spoke briefly of him saying he was a good, hard-working man and that he died on the train while being taken to South Australia but nothing of the circumstances surrounding his death. In 1968 my wife and I visited an old family friend in Perth who informed us of the treatment, and death of my father on the train. We had previously been to the Barmera cemetery in South Australia assuming we would find my father's grave but were unsuccessful. By chance I happened to meet the Catholic priest at Barmera who informed me that internees who died while being detained were buried at Loveday Internment Camp cemetery but were exhumed and were reburied but was unsure as to where it was.

As I have been married for over forty years, became a father and a grandfather my thoughts are ever present of my father who would have experienced a similar life had he not been struck down at such an early age by the callous treatment and misjudgment of the guards on that fateful train journey. Feelings of bitterness and sorrow will remain with me forever. After 70 years, a researcher, who has become a household name with our families, has, with the permission of our families, pursued my father's case, because of the mystery surrounding his death. It has been through her efforts that we were informed of the annual memorial held in Murchison in November. In 2012 my older brother John and I decided to attend the memorial with our wives and John's two children. We flew to Melbourne and boarded a coach along with about 50 other people and made the two-hour journey to Murchison. On arrival at the cemetery, I didn't know what to expect and was overwhelmed by the massive crowd in attendance. There was an Italian brass band playing during the large procession of many different Italian organisations, and dignitaries being introduced. A truly amazing spectacle.

Many sad thoughts raced through my mind to the point where I was so overcome with emotion that I unashamedly chose a spot at the rear of the crowd to shed some of the pain that rose within me. A Mass followed the procession, and we were introduced to the Italian Consulate who was in attendance. Entering the crypt and sighting my father's name on his tomb was a very emotional moment. I found it difficult to speak to the man who was filming the event and interviewing my brother and I. This experience bought me so close, yet so far away from my father and even though it had been 70 years since his death it felt like we had just attended his funeral. At the conclusion of the ceremony we headed to a nearby park for a picnic, which to me resembled a wake in respect of my father. Mingling with the many strangers that displayed their great kindness and friendliness in the Italian way, I felt I had known them for years. Boarding the coach to return to the city I had an emotional feeling as though I had deserted my father at such a lonely remote place. I have been thinking of him every single day of my life. Yet, I also had a feeling of contentment having witnessed his place of eternal rest.

The testimony of Raffaele Musitano, Raffaele's grandson

Before going to Melbourne to finally see where Nonno was laid to rest, I had a few hesitations. Did I need to know more or was I satisfied with the limited amount of information that I knew? Once I made the decision to go, I was still unsure of how I would feel. The hardest part for me seeing Nonno's resting place was actually seeing my name on the plaque. This made me very sad but at the same time extremely proud of the man I'm named after. Once I saw the look on my father's and uncle's faces it gave me a sense of closure, as we finally knew where our Nonno was. I am very proud and honoured to have Raffaele as my name. In 2001 my son Cruz Raffaele was born. As Cruz gets older and learns the story of his great grandfather and where his middle name has come from I hope he will feel the same pride and honour that I feel.

The testimony of Dannielle Musitano, Raffaele's great-granddaughter, age 24

When I first saw the plaque 'Raffaele Musitano' I felt no emotion. To me, it was just a name that my family had spoken about and the man that my father was named after. I knew only of the tragic and horrific event that had taken him and had left my Nonno fatherless and without any closure.

It wasn't until I saw the men marching down the white pebble path, at the Italian Mausoleum in Murchison, with their heads held high and how proud they were, that I realized that it wasn't whether or not I felt anything towards a man that I never knew. It was about who Raffaele Musitano was, where my family came from and where I came from. Even though he never returned, Raffaele was never forgotten and now found at peace, he will always be loved and remembered. He will always be a part of my life and I will cherish every story I am told about him. He will continue to live on in our hearts and never be forgotten from one generation to the next.

Figure 10.5: Raffaele Musitano's grave in the Italian Mausoleum at Murchison, Victoria.

Raffaele's legacy

No one can ever be sure what may happen to a person once they are in custody of the police or the army. During wars terrible things happen. But there is no good reason why Raffaele Musitano should have been injected with morphine on the train. His family has suffered for more than seven decades because he had died needlessly. A few people have even said that Raffaele was murdered. But no one investigated his treatment and his death. No one in the army seemed to care. Raffaele's wife Domenica never stopped grieving for him to her dying day. His children still grieve. The family's pain has never diminished or will their grief ever cease. The manner in which Raffaele Musitano died has left his family with a very deep sense of unnecessary loss and many decades of wondering how their lives would have been had he returned home after the war. The story of his life and death will always be a part of the Musitano family history from generation to generation. Raffaele Musitano currently has 39 direct descendants and still rising.

– Nicole Musitano

Memories of Port Pirie and the War

Looking back

Last spring, I took a trip back to my hometown Port Pirie, located on the eastern coast of the Spencer Gulf, 230 kilometres north of Adelaide in South Australia. Approaching the town, I silently reflected on how my family had arrived in Port Pirie in the 1890s from Molfetta in Italy. These migrants introduced their Catholic tradition of celebrating the feast of the Madonna Dei Martiri – Our Lady of Martyrs. To the present day, the statue of the Madonna is part of a yearly procession on Main Road near the Port Pirie boat-ramp, in Adelaide and in previous years, Sydney.

Figure 11.1: The Caputo family, Port Pirie, South Australia, 1920s.

As I walked down the main street, I could see the lovely beach where I would go swimming on hot days as a child. Further along was the Savoy Soccer Club, which had been established by the Port Pirie Italians before WWII. It is still a social club for the entire Port Pirie community today. The Migrant Memorial Stone was my next stop. This memorial was a combined effort by the Molfettese Community and the Port Pirie City Council. It was erected as a monument in honour of the early pioneers who had migrated from Molfetta, a large fishing town located on the Adriatic coast and part of the Puglia region of Italy. Standing in front of the monument which houses all the names of the first Italian settlers, I searched for the names of my father, Gioacchino Salvemini, my grandfather Onofrio Caputo and other family members. It is amazing to think that Mum's Dad came to Australia in 1898 and my own Dad in 1926. And how can I forget my Nonna (grandmother) Francesca whom I was named after. She migrated to Australia in 1913.

Figure 11.2: Gioachino Salvemini, Port Pirie, South Australia, 1930s.

The wharf nearby seemed quiet compared to the years just before the Second World War, when it was full of small fishing boats. As the older generation have passed on, their children have chosen to seek different career paths, not in the fishing trade as their Molfettese forbearers. They have moved to Adelaide for work with the hope of giving their children better opportunities for the future. The dear old home is still looking as good as ever. Our next-door neighbours on one side were the Amato family. They were Uncle Sergio (Sam) and Aunty Beatrice and their children, Francesco

(Frank) and Onofrio (Ron). On the other side lived the De Gioia family. Further down, lived the Mezzino and Valente families. Some of these families now live in the city, in Adelaide. Going past my grandparents' home on King Street affected me the most as I had spent so much of my younger years there. On either side of my grandparents lived another Caputo family and the Altamura family. It brought a lump to my throat knowing that it no longer belongs to our family and there are now strangers living there. I have such beautiful childhood memories growing up in that house with my grandparents. I was too young to understand how difficult the years must have been for my grandmother and mother with both their husbands being interned in a prison camp during the Second World War. Before returning to Adelaide, we drove past our second home, a large stone house in Queen Street Port Pirie, the one we moved to after the war, to accommodate our larger family. I reflected back to when our history in Port Pirie all began.

Arriving in Port Pirie

My grandfather Onofrio (Nonno) came to Australia in 1898 at the age of fourteen on the sailing ship the *SS Oronsay*. He immediately went fishing with his four brothers on their individual boats based at Port Pirie. Like most of the fishermen in the village they only spoke their Molfettese dialect. Consequently, they did not learn to speak or write English or even Italian. For them, living amongst the Molfettese community in Port Pirie was a home away from home. In 1910, Nonno became a Naturalised British Subject in Melbourne and soon after he returned to Italy marrying Francesca Capurso in 1911. He later returned to Australia, leaving his new bride behind with their baby son. Two years later, my Nonna Francesca, together with their 17-month-old son Salvatore, travelled on the sail ship *Otway* to Australia to join her husband. Like all ship travel at that time, the journey took three months to arrive in Australia.

Figure 11.3: Maria Antonia Caputo, Port Pirie, South Australia, 1930s.

Nonna was a refined seamstress. When I was a young girl, she would tell me that after putting her children to bed, she would stay up late making clothes for them. People were amazed at how she found the time to sew for all her children - Salvatore, Beatrice, Maria Antonia, Francesco, Pasqualina, and Leonardo. She told me how she was initially disappointed when she arrived in Port Pirie. It was so different to her hometown of Molfetta, which was a bustling, internationally well-connected coastal town. In comparison, Port Pirie was a village, isolated from big cities and on the farthest continent from Europe. Nevertheless, there were some modern comforts in Port Pirie. There was a woodshed for storing wood used in the stove in the kitchen. I remember Nonna roasting chestnuts and almonds in the oven. There was a copper in the yard, which was used for heating water for bathing, washing clothes, and dishes. As the children went off to school, they soon began to mix English with their Italian conversations at home and this helped their parents learn their new language. I used to enjoy visiting my nonna. She had an old gramophone, which she would wind up to play '78' records for us. I enjoyed listening to both Italian and English songs. When the family got together, we would play 'tombola', a game that is similar to bingo. In summer, we would all gather at Nonna's house and make our yearly quota of tomato sauce for pasta, under a large pergola covered with grape vines. Nonna was always making homemade pasta, and 'taralli' a savoury Italian biscuit.

Nonno Onofrio had become a member of the Fascist group in Port Pirie in 1929. Being an Italian and having love for his country of origin, he looked upon this as a means of maintaining his ethnic identity and a way of participating in social gatherings with other Italians. He did not understand the political implications of being part of that political group as there was no indication of conflict with the British in the 1920s and 1930s. Besides, Italy was on the side of the British in the First World War and even a few Australian Prime Ministers were partial towards Mussolini before any trouble began. But this changed as political circumstances changed.

The records show that my father's older brother Gennaro came to Australia in 1913. My father Gioacchino was born in 1913 one month after Gennaro had migrated to Australia. In 1926 at the age of 13, together with a relative, my father ventured to migrate to Australia to join his brother. He came on a steam ship named the *Osterley* that disembarked in Melbourne. They travelled to Adelaide by train and then headed out to Port Pirie because there was a large Molfettese community already settled there. On his arrival, Dad began fishing with his brother. After a few years Gennaro decided to return to Molfetta. Dad liked his new adopted surroundings and refused to go back with him. He continued with his fishing. By this stage Dad had met Mum, Maria Antonia Caputo, a local young woman. That could have been the reason he remained in Port Pirie. They married in 1936.

A fisherman's life

At times, the working life of a fisherman is very hard and quite dangerous. Dad had to wait until the weather was calm enough to go out to sea in his small boat. He also had to mend nets to ensure good catches and repair the boat to be certain that it was always seaworthy and reliable. Should the boat break down he would have to row the boat back to shore perhaps in poor weather conditions. Mum also did her part in sewing and patch up smaller sails called 'jibs'.

Dad would go to sea with enough food supplies, as quite often he would be out at sea for many days at a time. There would be a number of other boats out at sea with dad. The price of fish was very cheap in those days and with a bit of luck, Dad would be able to make a big enough catch to make a living and ably support his family. The local fish merchant, Sergio Amato, who was Dad's brother-in-law, would buy the fish from him. In winter, bad weather conditions made it impossible to go out to sea in his small boat and thus making an income was much harder. If the men were out at sea and the weather turned bad, it caused great anxiety for the women waiting for their husbands to return home safely. Some nights when the weather turned very rough, I remember lying in bed with the rain pounding on our iron roof, and saying a prayer for Dad's safe return.

Figure 11.4: Francesca, Sofia and Maria Antonia Salvemini, 1940s.

My mother Maria Antonia was born in Port Pirie on 8 April 1918, the fourth child of Onofrio and Francesca Caputo. Mum attended St. Mark's Catholic School until year seven. She left school to help her mother with the home duties until the age of eighteen when she married Dad at St Mark's Catholic Church in Port Pirie in 1936. On 8 September 1937, my sister Sofia was born and I came next on the 10 July 1939. The war against Germany started in the same year. But in mid-1940, everything changed for Italians. Italy's Benito Mussolini decided to join Germany in the Second World War against Britain and therefore also Australia. Things were not looking good for Italians but the fishermen still were allowed to continue working. By early 1942, Japan had attacked Darwin as part of the Axis with Germany and Italy. The Australian authorities changed their attitude towards the Italian migrants.

Removed from home

On 20 March 1942, Nonno Onofrio and many of his compatriots from Port Pirie were rounded up and sent to Camp Loveday near Barmera where they were interned. At the same time, his son-in-law Gioacchino Salvemini (my dad) was also interned. Dad was arrested by police even though he was a Naturalised British Subject in the early hours of the morning, and taken away in an army truck. Mum was left to take care of the family on her own. I have no idea how she managed financially. I remember being happy having my big sister's clothes being handed down to me as times were tough. Fortunately, Mum had some support from her mother, Francesca Caputo.

The authorities confiscated Dad's fishing boat. This was due to the fact there was a strict surveillance of all types of sea vessels. The Italian fishermen were hard-working men trying to make a living using their boats to catch fish. Even though they had sympathy for their country of birth, helping its war effort was the furthest thing from their minds. Because of their membership with the Fascist Party, they were not treated as Australians but as aliens and were looked upon as the enemy of the country. I was not quite three years old when all this occurred. I felt in some way that things were different, no Dad or Nonno around, sometimes Mum and Nonna would be crying, and if they wanted to speak about things they didn't want us to hear, they would send my sister and myself outside to play. I suppose they didn't want us to see them upset. We spent quite a lot of time at Nonna's home, which I loved doing.

Internment

In the camp, because of his age and good behaviour, Dad was assigned to work in the gardens. I was a toddler when mum took me to see Dad at Camp Loveday via Adelaide so he could see me. Mum recalled the guard saying: "No touching! No kissing!" It must have been very distressing for my father not being able to make any physical contact with Mum and myself. I have no recollection of this event, but I remember Mum mentioning it to me. During his time in camp, Dad made many objects out of wood, including a lovely sailing boat in a bottle with my name on the flag. I also treasure a card with koalas on it, which was posted via Red Cross International. My father made many applications to be released but to no avail.

On 16 May 1943, he stated to the captain in charge that he was prepared to accept work in any state of the Commonwealth, under any conditions in preference to being interned. That was the day when Mussolini was removed from governing Italy. It was finally considered that apart from his political leanings, he was a good type of person and on 10 November 1943, he was released from Loveday and sent to Manpower authorities for employment in Adelaide for the South Australian Railways.

On the 10 November 1943, again because of his good behaviour, and not being able to read, write, or speak English, Nonno was released from Loveday and sent to work for the South Australian Railways at Mile End, Adelaide. In 1944, Nonno wanted to return to his fishing and re-applied for his fishing permit, but was rejected. We cannot understand why because he was quite old and yearned to return to a job he could do. Instead, Nonno was then directed to work at Vacuum Oil Company at Port Pirie and he was allowed to reside at home with his family. On the 19 April 1944, Nonno was finally released from Man Power duties at the age of sixty.

Returning Home

My father's restrictions were revoked on 2 May 1945. In all, Dad was away from home for five years because he was an Italian. When Dad returned home, he walked into our kitchen and mum said to Sofia and me that this was our Dad. Of course there was an abundance of hugs, kisses and tears of joy! Soon after Dad returned home, he started to rebuild his family life and managed to go back to fishing. We do not know what happened to the boat that had been confiscated. I guess Dad had to buy a new boat to return to fishing. A few years later, there were two more additions to our family. Another daughter Rosa and a son Ignazio were born. Having three brothers-in-law and two sisters-in-law and their families, there were many happy occasions spent together at Easter, Christmas, and New Year when everyone in Port Pirie would be so happy enjoying the festive season. It brought the small Italian community even closer together. On New Year's Eve, if there were ships in the dock, at midnight they would blow their horns aloud to welcome in the New Year. For family gatherings we would usually meet at Nonna's home. The men would play card games such as Briscola and Scopa and the women and children would play tombola. They were great days with the family finally united again.

Years pass

Many years after Nonno Onofrio passed away Nonna went back to Italy with friends, Mr and Mrs G. De Giglio. She was amazed that the voyage only took one month by ship there compared with the sailboat, which took three months to get to Australia many years before. She mentioned that her native Molfetta had grown into a big city. Some of her relatives had passed on and she in no time began to miss her immediate family back in Port Pirie. She couldn't wait to return to Australia! Nonna made me promise to go to Italy, to see Molfetta, and to trace my roots. I kept my promise, and in 1996 went with my husband Francesco (Frank). Italy was so beautiful that we returned a second time.

I can still remember in later years, Dad telling me a story that one day while fishing, he felt the boat rocking and when he looked over the side of his boat, he saw an enormous shark, which he thought looked pregnant. It really frightened him. I can still remember the day we went out in Dad's boat, it was a boat picnic. My uncle and family were with us. All of us children were given fishing lines to help pass the time of day. That was my first experience of feeling the fish pulling on the line. It was such a happy and enjoyable day. But, I still think the best day was when Dad returned home after being interned. We were so happy hugging each other. I didn't let him out of my sight!

From the day he arrived back after being interned, we always tried to spend as much time as possible with Dad. We were always a very close family. I regret that we never spoke about the years he was interned and what life must have been like for him. I can imagine how unhappy and stressed he would have been worrying about his family, as he had always been a hard worker, and wanted to give his family a good life. He would have missed us tremendously. Dad died at the age of sixty-four in 1977 and Mum died in 1998 at the age of eighty. I can't help but wonder how no one ever spoke about those years. Did the men speak of it amongst themselves? Did Mum and Dad speak behind closed doors just in case it would upset us children? Up until recently, I had never given the internment years much thought, but now the more I look into it the more curious I become. I know I will never know what my parents, grandparents, and other families in the same situation went through. I am certain they all made sure their children were happy and didn't go without even though the war was raging away outside. I will always be grateful.

– Francie Puccini (*nee* Salvemini)

Hidden Lives

Figure 12.1: Italian internees, Loveday Internment Camp, 1943.
(photo: Hedley Keith Cullen, courtesy AWM).

With a Suitcase and a Mandolin

In 1959, Giuseppe (Joe) Cali` was Secretary and Treasurer of the committee that erected the marble Sugar Industry Pioneers Monument, more commonly known as the Canecutter Monument in Innisfail. Funds were collected, mostly from the Italian community throughout the district. As a Queensland Centenary gift to the town of Innisfail, the committee had commissioned the monument to honour the early pioneers of the sugar industry and to create a bridge of harmony between the Italian and Australian communities in the district. The memorial was sculpted in Carrara, Italy and carries the inscription – "Ubi bene, ubi patria" which means: "Where life is good, there is your homeland". At the unveiling of the monument, Joe said, "In ten years from now the only cane cutter around here will be this one in marble!" His words resonated as machinery slowly took over the cane cutters' work in the fields. He had seen many changes in far northern Queensland in the previous 30 years. Joe and his family had experienced many twists and turns, and highs and lows, especially during the Second World War. His successful settlement in Innisfail was the product of decades of hard work, personal sacrifices, a supportive family, and luck. His story begins in Sicily just before World War One.

Leaving home

Giuseppe (Joe) Calì was born in 1912 in Zafferana Etneo, in Sicily. He was the third child of parents Rosario Calì and Rosaria Calì and he had four siblings, Gaetano, Maria, Alfina, and Leonardo. They all grew up in Giarre, Sicily. He left school when he was ten years old to learn the cabinet making and French polishing trade, training under master tradesman Orazio Campione in Giarre. This important skill would later prove to be very valuable to Joe in hard times. At 16 years of age, Joe left his hometown to migrate to Australia, where his older brother Gaetano already lived. He boarded the ship Citta` di Genova at the Sicilian port of Messina in May 1928. One could imagine how heart-wrenching an occasion this departure would have been for him and his parents; this was to be the last time he saw them alive. He disembarked in the port of Brisbane on 4 July 1928. With a suitcase, a mandolin, and very little money, he took a northbound train. Joe's destination was the tiny railway station of Boogan, south of Innisfail, Far North Queensland. He settled in the nearby township of Mourilyan, a busy coastal town, which was home to many Southern Italian migrants, who mostly worked as cane cutters or farm labourers. Being entrepreneurial by nature, he bought a driver's license and commenced work for Innisfail Stores, a grocery shop, as a truck driver delivering groceries to the gangs of cane cutters working in the district. It was through his contact with the English-speaking gangs that Joe learnt to speak the language.

The 1930s

By 1932, Joe had saved up enough money to be able to repay his father for his voyage to Australia and to buy himself a car to use as a taxi. At 20 years of age, he had established himself in the passenger transport business. He later traded in his first car and bought two new taxis. He was very pleased with his new business and life was getting better as time passed. However, in those days the local mafia gang, known, as the 'Black Hand' was active in northern Queensland. In 1933 they tried to demand money from Joe. He refused. So, one night they bombed his taxis and destroyed them. But they didn't expect to encounter Joe's strong will and tenacity to overcome misfortune. With the help of friends, Joe bought another taxi to continue his taxi business. Joe was determined to defy the Black Hand, which was made up of a handful of lawless men. Authorities eventually caught them. With more hard work and long hours, life soon progressed well once again for Joe. He became a Naturalised British Subject in April 1934 and by 1935, he had made an application to commence a bus route from Cowley to Innisfail. Some years later, Joe was operating a number of bus services (later called the Cream and Green Buses) in the Innisfail district and the Mourilyan Taxi Company.

In his spare time, he hand-built his first bus and started a Calì tradition of giving names to all the buses. Two of his early buses were called the 'Cleopatra' and the 'Lady Godiva', which became the region's most esteemed transports. During those early years, Joe lived in a small room attached to his garage and workshop in Mill Street, Mourilyan. Life was good even if it was packed with a lot of hard work and very long hours. His aim and desire was to reunite the entire family to make a better future for them than in Sicily.

By 1937, this plan was slowly taking shape when Joe's younger sister Alfina and 16-year-old brother Leonardo (Len), a mechanic by trade, migrated to Australia. Joe always prepared to help anyone especially his siblings, offered Len employment in his business. During 1938 and 1939, Joe made two attempts to sponsor his older sister Maria, her husband, and her two young daughters to Australia. But, on the grounds of job shortages, the authorities refused both of his applications, even though Joe was prepared to offer work to his brother-in-law in his now thriving transport business. These two requests had been the last opportunities for the extended Calì family to be reunited in Australia before their lives were to be forever changed.

Harbour Road

Germany and Italy declared war in 1939 and 1940 respectively. As a Naturalised British Subject, Joe was able to buy a house in 1940 on Harbour Road in Mourilyan. It was a short distance away from his bus workshop, and next door to the Mourilyan Police Station. At this time, all Italians in northern Queensland, many of whom were Naturalised British Subjects, were under observation by the authorities to see if there was anyone showing any disloyalty to Australia (NAA), because Italy had sided with Germany against Britain. With a new home and a thriving business, the time was right for Joe to establish his own family. In January 1941, Joe married Anna Rinaudo at the Mourilyan Catholic Church. They moved into the Harbour Road house, along with Anna's widowed mother Maria and her two young brothers aged eight and six years old. Joe became the father figure for the two boys and ensured that they had good schooling, later encouraging their interest in music and singing as well as careers in the trades. His brother Len also lived with the extended family for a time before he married.

The family was of central importance to Joe and Anna. So in April 1941, they applied to buy some land in Mourilyan, to build a house for Joe's mother-in-law and two growing boys. But the application was refused. This was because at the time, the local Australian public had resentment towards Italians buying more land and believed that they were trying to control the transport in the district as they were buying and operating trucks, even though there was a lack of work for these vehicles. In fact, resentment and suspicion of these 'foreigners' was so high in the community that it reached the point of some members of the public fabricating the truth by making false statements to the police of "supposed wrong doings" by the Italians, just to have them investigated.

Detained

As the war with Italy progressed from 1940 to 1941, the police had subjected Joe to many house searches. They were looking for items such as cameras, binoculars, radios,

Figure 12.2: Joe Calì (left) with taxis, c. 1934.

or anything that might be considered as 'suspicious'. Things went from bad to worse. Shortly after Japan bombed Darwin, in January 1942, panic swept the nation. On 21 February, during yet another house search, Joe was taken into custody by the police under 'Master Warrant' and held in the Innisfail Police Station watch house along with other Italians, before being sent to the internment camps down south. The authorities did not know what to do with the situation of the Italians living in Australia, so the solution was to detain them in internment camps. The government at that time considered these people could be a threat to Australian security while Australia was at war.

Joe's wife, Anna said that the anti-Italian sentiment amongst a lot of the Australian public was very strong and 'lively'. An example of this sentiment took place on the day that the Italians internees were being loaded onto the southbound train at the Innisfail Railway Station. One woman, who ran a store where these Italians had been customers for some time, was heard shouting, "Shoot the bastards! Shoot the bastards!" How could such negative sentiments have resulted in such outbursts of rage and hatred when Italian migrants had done nothing wrong?

Figure 12.3: "Cleopatra" bus built by Joe Cali, c. 1934-5.

South to Barmera

Joe and along with hundreds of other Italians were initially sent by train to Gaythorne prison in Brisbane. Within days they were transported to an internment camp in South Australia named Loveday Camp No. 14A. It was situated near Barmera in the Riverland area. With Joe confined to a prison camp, his wife Anna was left with the huge responsibility of keeping the bus and taxi businesses operating. However, she was faced with one immediate problem. She had never driven a vehicle before. So, Joe's brother Len had just enough time to teach Anna how to drive the taxi and get her driver's license before he was also arrested and sent to the same internment camp, not long after his brother.

During the next two years while Joe was interned, Anna kept the business going. With the help of good friends and the few loyal staff who had not been interned, she managed to salvage the company, although she had many problems in procuring parts to keep the vehicles running. But this was not the least of her worries. As a 20-year-old woman, to feel more secure when driving the taxi, she would take along her eldest little brother, especially when taking male passengers to their destinations. These were very difficult times for her, but somehow she managed. Anna always said that one of the biggest regrets she had was that the authorities had taken two years of married life away from Joe and her, for no reason other than his place of birth.

Internment

While in the internment camp, Joe made a number of attempts to appeal against his imprisonment so that he could return to his businesses, but these appeals were always rejected. Medical certificates written during his internment showed that he was beginning to have some significant health problems. He was healthy when he was arrested, so it is unclear why Joe became so ill whilst interned. Joe's health had dramatically declined by the time he returned home, possibly because of the internment conditions and poor diet that was high in fatty mutton. In 1948, a few years after his return home, he had emergency surgery to remove one of his kidneys due to a complete renal failure. During his internment Joe spent his time doing woodwork, examples of which are still in his family's possession. A surviving fellow internee, named Carmelo Lo Giudice, mentioned that one particularly beautiful piece of woodwork caught the camp commander's eye. He asked Joe if he would part with it, but Joe said he was keeping it as a memento of his internment camp days. Joe also spent his time playing music, as he was quite an accomplished musician. He played the mandolin and the guitar to keep morale high behind the barbed wire fences. However, we don't have stories to retell about his time behind barbed wire.

Although Joe always said that the Australian guards in the camp treated the internees reasonably well, he never spoke too much about his time in the camp. Perhaps it was through disgust and disappointment at his unfair detainment through no fault of his that he didn't? After all, just like most of his fellow Italians, he came to Australia long before WWII to seek a better life for himself. He had become a Naturalised British Subject and had contributed to Australia's economy. He had paid taxes just like every other Australian citizen and had been accepted into the local community as a businessperson of good integrity. He wasn't a criminal. He had not taken up arms against this country so he wasn't a military Prisoner of War. He was like the other Italians who were just hard working civilians, businesspersons and farmers. No one had committed or wanted to commit sabotage or crimes against this country. Why? It was their new homeland. They were taken away from their families, their businesses, and farms and held in indefinite detention a long way from home. Above all, he had great concerns for the welfare of his wife and her family back in North Queensland as they did not have protection. The Japanese forces were advancing closer to the northern part of Australia, having started with the bombing of Darwin 14 days before his arrest. There were also many American and Australian troops in the area and Anna was a vulnerable 20-year-old woman living with her mother and two very young boys. This all played heavily on his mind and was a constant source of mental stress and worry for him, and indeed for all internees in similar circumstances. Time passes very slowly behind barbed wire.

The Mighty Atom

It was during the two years spent in internment camp that Joe had an idea to build a special style of bus to add to his fleet. Together with Len, they planned towards constructing a bus that would become renowned throughout the transport industry. Always planning for a better future and positive outcomes was part of Joe's way of viewing life. Designing a new bus would take his mind off worries and poor health, if only for a short time. He was eventually released from the internment camp on 29 December 1943, arriving back home in Mourilyan in January 1944. For some time after his release, Joe had to

With a Suitcase and a Mandolin

Figure 12.4: Joe and Anna Calì.

report to the local Police Station (next door!) each month where the Officer-in-Charge would complete a report stating that: Joe was conducting himself and his business in a respectable and trustworthy manner. Good news came in the same year. In October 1944, Joe and Anna's first son Rosario (Ross) was born.

Now back in the Mourilyan workshop, Joe and his brother Len returned to building buses for the fleet. In 1946, the new bus that they had designed whilst imprisoned in Camp 14A at Loveday was built. It was called the 'Mighty Atom'. Joe fashioned and built the curved timber framework of the bus using sturdy local timbers and did all the upholstery for the seats, while his brother Len did the mechanicals and curved metal panel work. It was simply stunning! People were intrigued by the name the 'Mighty Atom'. It was named after the atomic bomb, which was used to force Japan to surrender.

Connections with England

News of this bus reached Stevenage, in England where George Manning read about the 'Mighty Atom' bus in the press. He was so impressed by the story that he started corresponding with Joe and they became 'pen pals'. A close friendship grew between the two families and still exists today. It's amazing how something good can come out of war's bad consequences. As things were grim in England after the war, Joe and Anna would often send 'food parcels' to George and his family. They all eventually met face to face for the very first time in 1955 during an overseas trip to England. Not long after the war, George sent a book to Joe, because what caught George's attention in this book was that Joe and Len were mentioned in it. The book titled, *We went to Australia*, was written by David Walker. He wrote about an English journalist's account of Australian life in the early post-war period. While visiting Italians in North Queensland, this journalist was conscious of the fact that Joe and Len stood to attention while he spoke to them. He was reminded by one of his party that like many other Italians, the two brothers had been interned during the war. Under military prison conditions and rules, this meant standing to attention when spoken to by military guards and officers. This was the after-effect that stressful life in internment camp had on Joe and Len! Some years later, Joe was to be the sponsor for George's eldest son and daughter-in-law when the young couple decided to immigrate to Australia.

A better future

Over the following years, Joe and Len hand built ten buses in Joe's Mourilyan workshop. In December 1949, Joe and Anna's second son Giovanni (John) was born. By 1950, Joe was operating most bus services in the Innisfail district and incorporated them and his taxi business into his company named the Johnstone River Transport Company, with Joe, Anna, and their two sons as the sole owners. In 1952, Joe received a 'Certificate of Merit' from the Italian President, in recognition for his achievements in a foreign country. In 1955, Joe took Anna and their two young sons to Sicily to his hometown of Giarre. This was quite an emotional visit for him. He visited his older sister

Maria, her family, and the graves of his father and mother who he last saw alive back in 1928 when he migrated to Queensland as a 16-year-old boy. This occasion was to be the one and only time that Joe was ever able to visit Sicily due to his business commitments. Back in Australia, life was becoming busier and the family began to slowly thrive once again, but not without many long days, much hard work, creativity, teamwork and much luck.

Transporting sugar

In 1960, Joe saw an opportunity for expansion and this time, to help give his younger brother Len a start in business. He and Len went into a partnership in a new trucking company for transportation of bulk sugar initially from two far north sugar mills to Mourilyan Harbour terminal. To help start this new venture, Joe was prepared to sacrifice everything he had worked for and achieved in this country. He mortgaged his entire livelihood and he stood to lose heavily if this venture was not successful. This was Joe's commitment to helping family. Creating a successful business was the way that family would secure a good future. From that year onwards, this company progressively grew to the extent of transporting sugar and molasses produced by all sugar mills between Townsville and Mossman in North Queensland to port terminals at Cairns, Mourilyan Harbour and Townsville. This company was sold in 1998 after many years of successful operation

Figure 12.5: Joe and Len Calì's "Mighty Atom", c. 1946.

under the management of the founders and then their sons. But life was not always smooth sailing for Joe and his family. In 1970 due to ill health, Joe sold his bus business to his brother-in-law Sam Rinaudo. In December 1970, Joe tragically lost both his sister Alfina and her husband in a motor vehicle accident. After continuing health problems and suffering a stroke, Joe passed away at 62 years of age in 1974. His brother Len, after retiring from the business, moved to Brisbane in 1982. He passed away in 1993. Joe's wife Anna passed away in 2004.

Final words

Giuseppe and Anna Calì were strivers and achievers, like so many other immigrants of the 1920s and 1930s era. They possessed a determination to carry on against all odds. With much hard work, teamwork and luck, their story has been one of overcoming the very difficult early years of settlement as migrants and surmounting the adversities of WWII. They have given much to Australia, even though they were treated so cold-heartedly during wartime. They are remembered for their dedication to their work, to their family and to their friends and to their new hometown of Innisfail.

– Ross Calì

Beyond the Barbed Wire

Some families' experiences of coping on the outside

The entry of Italy into the Second World War on 10 June 1940 brought considerable disruption to the over thirty thousand strong Italian Australian community whose presence was seen by the Australian authorities as a serious potential threat to national security. Australian Italians, whether naturalised or not and whether born in Italy or in Australia, were classified as "enemy aliens" (along with Germans, nationals of other Axis-linked countries, some Australians who were members of the Communist Party and, after Pearl Harbour, Japanese) and were subject to a number of restrictions. Under the provisions of the *National Security Act* of 1939-1940 the Federal Government could intern any person whose loyalty was suspect although much of the detail of this process was delegated to the military authorities and to state police forces. Italian community leaders in the sugar cane districts of North Queensland were among the first to be interned regardless of whether their loyalty was proven or not. Internees were stripped of their rights, their dignity, their liberty, and their family. In total about 4700 nearly all male Italian Australians were incarcerated in internment camps while those not interned were subject to restrictions.

The wives, siblings, and children of the internees were left to fend for themselves in a highly hostile and restrictive environment. They also lost their livelihood and personal security and were faced with the task of sometimes single-handedly looking after farms and businesses. The stories of most families who had to negotiate the difficulties of wartime Australia outside the internment camps are yet to be documented. This paper proposes to examine the experiences of a few families, particularly the children, as expressed in their written and oral accounts.

For those who had become naturalised British subjects or had been born in Australia, the denial of citizenship rights because of ethnicity could not be seen only as a phenomenon that arose in the crisis of war. It was also part of a much deeper racist attitude towards Italians, which had increased since the first groups of Italian workers arrived in Australia. The small Italian Australian communities comprised mainly of middle class professionals and businesspersons that formed in Australia in the last decades of the 1800s were tolerantly perceived by the host society. Such tolerance however was not extended when the first consistent groups of Italian workers, mainly of *contadino* origin, began to arrive towards the end of the 1800s. They had been recruited to replace the Micronesian Kanaka indented labourers on the North Queensland sugar cane plantations as a result of the impending implementation of the White Australia Policy.

A series of articles published by the radical labour newspaper *The Boomerang* stated, among other things, that the Kanaka, despite being cannibals, were to be considered "harmless compared to the mafia or the camorra".[160] It added that the peaceful towns of Queensland would fall prey to the terror created by these criminals who were used to settle differences by easily resorting to use of the knife.[161] Although progressive in its outlook, the magazine *The Bulletin* displayed anything but a progressive attitude towards these Italian immigrants characterizing them as "crass, dirty dago pests, a greasy flood of Mediterranean scum that seems to defile our country"[162] and were quite

---

[160] *The Boomerang* cited in Douglass, William A., *From Italy to Ingham: Italians in North Queensland* (St. Lucia [Qld]: University of Queensland Press, 1995) 49.

[161] *The Boomerang* cited in Ray Evans, Kay Saunders and Kathryn Cronin, *Exclusion, Eploitation and Extermination: Race Relations in Colonial Queensland* (Sydney: Australia and New Zealand Book Company, 1975, 5.

[162] Karen Agutter, "Transplanted identity: the continuing North/South divide experienced by Italian emigrants," *La Questione Meridionale / The Southern Question I*, no. 1 (February 2009): 94-95.

willing to belong to criminal organisations.

This tendency to articulate negative stereotypes was constantly present throughout the first half of the 20th century. In the years before the First World War the Australian press continuously gave prominence to the strikes by miners in Western Australia and the anti-Italian riots at the Gwalia and Leonora mines against the employment of Italians on the grounds that they were perceived as eroding wages and working conditions. In 1925, a Royal Commission set up by the government of Queensland to examine the economic and social impact of the growing numbers of "aliens" (mainly Italians) in North Queensland came to the conclusion that Southern Italians constituted a potential menace to the integrity of the Australian social fabric. This was allegedly because of their tendency to live in close-knit communities and to follow their own traditions and customs, including mafia-type activities. When in 1934–1935 a few homicides and other criminal acts occurred as a result of a quarrels between a few Southern Italian families in north Queensland, the Australian press was quick to claim that these isolated incidents clearly indicated the existence of the *Mano Nera*, (Black Hand) an Italian Australian criminal organisation involved in extortion, kidnapping and murder.

It was this uneasy background of relations between Italian Australians and wider Australian society, which was to prove one of the important factors in determining events when Italy entered the war on the side of Germany. About four-fifths of Italian Australian families paid the price of war with Italy through their classification as enemy aliens, even though they had left Italy and its politics behind to start afresh in the Antipodes.

At the outbreak of the Second World War Italian Australians were the largest non-Anglo-Celtic group in Australia and were thus a highly visible minority group. They soon felt the deep-seated hostility of Australian locals, particularly in North Queensland. It was believed that some of these Italians were responsible for fifth-column espionage activities including the use of secret radio transmitters. Many Italian Australians were confused, bewildered, and dismayed at the hostility shown towards them. This feeling was articulated particularly well by Peter Dalseno (who migrated from Padua to Australia with his mother as a baby in the 1920s and grew up in the North Queensland sugar belt) when he states that Australian friends became very quickly circumspect and kept their distance.[163] Dalseno was interned for a time then sent to work on war-related projects.

For those left on the outside the changed relationships with Australian friends, neighbours and in the school environment, in many cases leading to ostracisation and hostility, was felt in a particularly acute and at times traumatic manner that impacted on their everyday lives. Women and children who had remained in Italy also suffered substantially since they could no longer receive money or direct news of what was happening to their husbands and fathers. Silvana recalls that her father migrated to Australia in 1938, but war broke out before they could join him there in 1948. Her father was interned, together with his brother who had a photo of Mussolini in his car window, and could not send money. However, he found that he could communicate with his family by sending letters to an uncle in America who would send them on to Italy. Her mother had to support the family working as a day labourer picking olives and oranges.[164] Italian Australian men who were not interned or drafted into the various labour organisations found that they had to face a number of difficulties and restrictions. These included the closure of their businesses, forced relocation, open hostility and discrimination from neighbours and in the workplace. Experiences in the workplace seemed to vary widely. Although Giuseppe was not interned he found, like many other Italian Australian workers,

---

[163] Peter Dalseno, *Sugar, Tears and Eyeties* (Brisbane: Boolarong Publications, 1994), 180.

[164] Morag Loh, *With Courage in their Cases* (Melbourne: FILEF 1980), 36.

that it was extremely difficult to get work in Melbourne because Australian employers and unions did not want "Dagos" and he spent much of the war unemployed. Ottavio, who worked at Myers Department Store in Melbourne, reported that he experienced no interference and maintained his job throughout the war.[165]

However, Italian Australian women faced the greatest difficulties. Very few women were interned, as Military Intelligence did not consider them a security risk. Some Italian Australian families, who had become destitute due to the internment of their breadwinner, were interned at the Tatura Internment camp in Victoria. Nevertheless, most women remained at home to look after their families, carry on the economic activities of the household, and bear the brunt of hostility towards Italians expressed by Australians. Many women remember the war years as times of fear and great hardship while some suffered from malnutrition, sickness, and depression.

Shortly after her husband's arrest Egle Bonutto encountered severe financial difficulties when the Australian Taxation Department confiscated the proceeds of tobacco sales and other money deposited in her husband's account and the licensee of their Texas hotel stopped paying rent on the grounds that the local population was boycotting the hotel because it belonged to an enemy alien.[166] Cosimo Caminiti, from Catania in Sicily, was a canecutter from Mourilyan in Northern Queensland. He had arrived in Australia in the 1920s and had worked hard to build a life for his family. When he was interned, his young wife and two very young children were left destitute and were forced to move into a farm shed for more than a year as they had lost their home due to the lack of Cosimo's income.[167] Maria

---

[165] Loh, *With Courage*, 38.
[166] Osvaldo Bonutto, *A Migrant's Story. The Struggle and Success of an Italian Australian, 1920s-1960s* (St Lucia [Qld]: University of Queensland Press, 1994), 74.
[167] Josie Verbis, "There Are So Many Questions I Wish I Had Asked..." in this book; and Mia Spizzica, "Interned Lives," in Il

Figure 13.1: Italian internees, Loveday Internment Camp, 1943
Maker: Hedley Keith Cullen. (courtesy AWM)

Paoloni[168] relates how she and her baby were left to fend for themselves when her husband Gino was arrested shortly after the outbreak of war and eventually interned at Loveday. Customers stopped coming to their shop in Balmain (Sydney), others who owed money did not pay, and vandals broke windows and caused other damage thus compounding her difficulties. Amidst such violent racism Maria feared for her children. Unable to sell the business, she was forced to close the shop and to travel in search of work and a place to stay. Eventually she went to went to live and work on a poultry farm on the outskirts of Sydney, facing isolation, monotony and hard times. There she worked hard for very little and only by soliciting the help of Catholic authorities was she able to speed up the release of her husband, which brought economic and emotional relief.

While most of the Italian Australian women who were subject to these hardships were born in Italy and had

---

Globo, 17 August 2011, 19, http://www.academia.edu, accessed 20/9/2016.
[168] Anna Maria Kahan-Guidi, and Elizabeth Weiss, eds., *Forza e Coraggio Give me strength. Italian Australian Women Speak* (Sydney: Women's Redress Press, 1989), 70-73.

migrated to Australia, their children were, in the main, born in Australia or had come out at a very young age. They had been brought up in Australia and felt much more Australian than Italian. To their great dismay many found that their school friends, neighbours, and other Australians who knew them no longer treated them as "equals". Years later, some of these children would write or speak about their experiences of growing up in wartime Australia.

A substantial part of Wilma Watkins' transparently autobiographical novel[169] based on her experiences as a child growing up in Australia deals with the internment of her father, Roberto De Conti, and of the various vicissitudes her mother and she faced as a result. Roberto De Conti had migrated to Australia in 1927 and over time had become a successful tobacco farmer well established in the local community. He was arrested in Mareeba (North Queensland) on 22 October 1940 although Watkins claims that his only link with Fascism seemed to be that one of his daughter's godfathers was a fascist activist. De Conti had applied for and obtained naturalisation in 1934 but was told that under the provisions of the National Security Act this could be revoked. He was taken to Gaythorne and subsequently to Loveday. It was a far from pleasant prospect for someone who as a young man had already gone through the traumatic experience of being interned by the Austrians for the duration of the First World War.[170] As a result of Roberto's internment Wilma's mother, Carolena, found herself completely ostracised and isolated on the family tobacco farm at Pukunja (North Queensland), which she had to work on her own. She had to report fortnightly to the police and had to support herself and her children on a government subsidy of 17 shillings and 6 pence per fortnight. The

---

[169] Vilma Watkins, *Pukunja* (Hurstville [NSW]: Parker Pattinson Publishing, 1999).
[170] Watkins, *Pukunja*, 10, 14, 71-72.

worry and the cruel spartan life caused depression and insomnia, but when she requested to be interned with her husband she was rejected because internments were only made for security reasons. Wilma herself, although born in Australia, was given a hard time at primary school by her Australian schoolmates who called her "dago", bullied and beat her.[171]

Young Bill Della Vedova found that he had to take full responsibility for the family potato and cattle farm near Pemberton (Western Australia) after his father, Domenico, was interned until June 1944 initially at Harvey Internment Camp then (from April 1942) at Loveday. The family was under too much pressure just surviving to appeal for Domenico's release although they had no idea why he was interned since, according to his daughter Josephine, Domenico "didn't give tuppence for Mussolini."[172]

There are other examples of torment from across the nation. Lou who found life in a secondary school in an inner Melbourne suburb an extremely difficult experience since he was regularly beaten up by his Australian school mates two or three times a week until he managed to learn enough English to communicate with them.[173] Life in rural Victoria was hard for Bianca's family after the internment of her father, who was a committed fascist. They had to survive without him by producing their own food and doing all sorts of odd jobs, from washing and ironing, to selling rabbits to the local freezing works, in a social climate where some of the local Australians discriminated against the family while others helped.[174] Angela Wayne and her two younger sisters were left to fend for themselves in the streets of Fremantle when both

---

[171] Ibid., 185, 213, 226.
[172] Bill Bunbury, *Rabbits & Spaghetti: Captives and Comrades, Australians, Italians and the War 1939-1945* (South Fremantle [WA]: Fremantle Arts Centre Press, 1995), 33.
[173] Loh, *With Courage*, 40-41.
[174] Ibid., 39.

Figure 13.2: Italian internees, being moved from Loveday Camp 9 to Camp 14, Loveday, South Australia, 1943. (courtesy AWM)

their parents were interned.[175] Frances Ianello recalls that after her father was interned, there was no money in the house and food was in short supply. In 1940, her father was working as a barman for the Casa degli Italiani in Fremantle.[176] Since he was well known and popular, the authorities thought he might have something to do with giving information to the enemy.[177] Clearly, no two families went through exactly the same experiences. The following account helps to provide a more detailed picture of what life was like for Italian Australians on the "outside" during the war years.[178]

---

[175] Richard Bosworth and Romano Ugolini, eds., *War, Internment and Mass Migration: The Italo-Australian Experience 1940-1990* (Rome: Gruppo Editoriale Internazionale, 1992), 113.
[176] An extreme Italian Australian right wing group founded Casa degli Italiani.
[177] Bunbury, *Rabbits & spaghetti*, 19, 21.
[178] This story is compiled from an interview with Robert (full name not given for privacy reasons), Sydney, 23 January 2013, as well as records of talks with his uncle and mother in 1986 and 1987.

Robert was about seven years old when Italy entered the war. His father had arrived in Sydney in 1924 where he established himself as a highly successful tailor. is long-time fiancée joined him in 1930, when she came to Australia with her parents and the two were married. Shortly after Italy entered the way security forces raided their home. Copies of the pro-fascist newspaper *Il Corriere degli Italiani in Australia* and other items were seized. His brother-in-law had left the newspapers there. He was one of the newspaper's former editors and who had been deported to Italy by the Australian authorities when Italy entered the war. Robert's father was arrested and subsequently interned at Orange internment camp, about 260 km west of Sydney. Deprived of her husband's income, his wife was left to run the household and to fend for herself, her parents, Robert, and his two sisters.

The internment of Robert's father left the family devastated. His mother was able to visit him only once since his detention. Although she could travel to and from Orange with friends and relatives who also went to visit internees, she found the 500 km round trip exhausting and she suffered severely from car sickness. To go by train would have meant a much longer absence away from the family for which she now had prime responsibility. However, they were able to write to each other. In a letter written in Italian dated 7 July 1940, which must have somehow escaped going through the camp censor, Robert's father despondently states that a most terrible fate has struck their family, and that when looking in the mirror while shaving he notices that half his hair had turned white. His letter reveals that his anxiety was because he had lost his freedom and was locked up in an internment camp with all its accompanying discomforts, including the freezing cold of the July winter. Even the presence of a number of friends and *compaesani* did not help to relieve his anxiety. He was also anxious about how his family was coping, the stress that his wife was under and, in this particular letter, over the illness of his youngest daughter. However, he also gives practical advice about family business matters and tells his wife that she should go to the police station to find out if she is eligible for a subsidy. He adds that the only ray of hope was the thought that when he is released, perhaps he might be able to earn enough money to pay for tickets back to Italy because it was impossible to live in Australia any more.

Even today, Robert wonders how his mother managed during the time his father was interned. Life was anything but easy. Pennies and halfpennies were rare items in the household and Robert recalls that at school he quickly had to learn to fight because of the antagonism of his Australian peers. His mother did have work in her husband's tailoring business but was able to do this only part-time since she also had to look after the family, and it is not clear whether his grandfather was still receiving his small pension from Italy because of the disruption caused by the war. Family income had been drastically reduced and there were not only living expenses for a family of six but also mortgage instalments on the house. There was also the problem of paying solicitors and barristers for lodging an objection against internment, a long and costly process although it was eventually successful.

Robert missed his father and his grandfather became even more of a father figure. He would also accompany his grandfather, who's English was somewhat limited, on various errands to interpret for him. A regular twice-weekly event was their walk from Earlwood to Canterbury police station since grandfather was not allowed to travel on public transport. Prohibition from travelling on public transport and periodic reporting to the police were conditions placed on many Italians who were not interned, particularly in cases that were considered as somehow potentially detrimental to the war effort and grandfather had served many years in the Italian navy. Grandfather was quite scrupulous in adhering to the restrictions placed on him so much so that Robert remembers walking with him all the way from Earlwood to Rockdale and back when he had to visit a family there. Grandfather, although in his 70s, was a great walker.

Robert's and the other accounts reported here are a few of the many stories of the almost forgotten wartime experiences suffered by Italian families because of their ethnic and cultural origins. Their sufferings were s a result of the mistaken belief that they posed an unreasonable risk to Australia's war effort, although the vast majority of internees and their families were in fact law-abiding members of Australian society and did not pose a security threat. Indeed, many were or would become citizens of their adopted country after the war. Despite wide consensus that for most Italian Australians internment was patently unjust, official recognition took half a century in coming. The various proposals requesting a formal apology from the federal government such as the request addressed to Prime Minister Bob Hawke for a 'bipartisan agreement to acknowledge that what happened to the Italians was wrong'[179] did not receive a positive outcome until 1991 when both houses of federal parliament passed unanimous motions of regret, but did not issue an apology. Furthermore, similar recognition at state level did not begin to come until after the 1990s.[180] A recent example is the debate in the South Australian Parliament on the motion tabled by Tony Piccolo (Member for Light) on 28 July 2011, which acknowledges the situation of 'enemy aliens' interned during World War II, but similarly did not offer an apology.[181] In debating the matter of a possible apology for the hardships and injustices experienced by Italian Australians and others, only a recognition was explicitly given for "the remarkable fortitude shown by women and families within migrant communities who kept their households and children afloat in a time of terrible uncertainty, hardship and loneliness."[182]

– Gaetano Rando (peer reviewed)

[179] "Locked up – just for being Italian," *Sydney Morning Herald*, 17 June 1991, 5.
[180] Bosworth and Ugolini, *War, Internment and Mass Migration*, 105.
[181] https://www.slideshare.net/ecagd/tony-pccolo-loveday-internment-motion-published-format-3-august-2011, accessed 19 December 2012.
[182] Ibid.

Within Our Limitations

From Piedmont to far northern Queensland

'We can't boast of being successful farmers but we did what we could within our limitations.'
– Rina Scagliotti

This is a story about two hard-working migrants named Enrico and Maria Tibaldi. Both were born in the town of Conzano, Province of Alessandria in Piedmont, Italy. The chronicle retraces their life journey together from the 1880s, a few decades after Italy had become a nation, to Australia in 1912 to their final years in the 1970s. They had experienced life in Queensland through World War One, the Great Depression and the Second World War.

Italy 1887

The memories retold by Maria and Enrico clearly indicate that poverty was no stranger to them. Their families were both employed by landowners. The children were expected to contribute their labour without pay to help with care of the 'burros' (donkeys) and work in the fields, especially at harvest time – picking grapes, gathering hay, and feeding the livestock. Schooling was not compulsory, so it was common for parents to consider boys at the age of nine years, to be big and strong enough to go out to earn money to help supplement the family needs. I was horrified to learn that when my Dad was nine years old, he was already working for his father's employer, when work was available, for the equivalent of one penny per day.

As my parents grew up, they continued to live near Conzana. Both had a minimum of schooling (four years), and certainly this included broken periods when their days were spent in the fields or – in Mum's case – spent at

Hidden Lives

home to care for the children while her aunt helped with the harvest. She was taught at a very young age to cook, sew, knit, and keep house. For recreation Dad played the trombone in the village band. On Sunday afternoons the townspeople would gather in the village square, listen to the band and dance on a raised platform in the open air.

1908

Mum and Dad married in 1908. They were still very poor but very daring in that they moved from the family situation to Torino (Turin) to work in the Fiat factory making tyres. They were both employed in shift work but on different shifts. The pay was small. They rented one room, which was a bedroom and kitchen, lit only by candle. Their aim was to save the fare to get Dad to Australia and for Mum to follow when he could save her fare from there. Mum worked at the factory until she fell pregnant with my sister Fiorenzina and could no longer work due to the fumes from the rubber tyres which made her feel very ill.

Figure 14.1: Enrico Tibaldi, Tully, Queensland, 1939.

Sometime later Dad managed to get a job in Torino as a tram driver. He was very proud of this achievement. He felt like he was a 'country boy made good', and often told us of the ladies he helped on and off the trams with their extremely wide and fancy-brimmed hats, some so large they would get caught on the door. I feel he enjoyed every moment of this period of his life. As time grew near to the birth of my sister, they returned to Conzano to await her arrival and plan Dad's departure to Australia. Fiorenzia was born in September 1911 and Dad left Italy in 1912. Mum lived with her father and family waiting for her husband to strike it rich in the new country.

Australia 1912

It took my father over one month to reach Australia. His ship took him to Lucinda sugar port outside of what is now known as Ingham in Queensland. He boarded a tram, which brought bags of sugar to the port from the mills, and if passengers had arrived, planks were provided for them to sit on for their journey to Halifax, about six miles inland. When he arrived at Halifax, penniless and hungry, he called at the wine shop owned and run by Mr and Mrs. Vignolio, who were earlier arrivals from Italy and known for their lodgings and assistance to new arrivals from the 'old country'. Dad heard that work was available planting cane in Hawkins Creek on a farm belonging to Mrs. Rupert Lee, twenty miles from Halifax. Of course it meant walking the distance, but it also meant work on contract and that was all Dad was interested in hearing. Three of them left for the job, including his brother Vittorio who had arrived earlier in Halifax. The next day their few possessions were packed and they journeyed to their respective farms in readiness for the start of their contracts. Cane was cut green, not burnt, as it was in later years, so the cutters had to cut grass along with cane, and tolerate 'hairy Mary,' which is the irritating fur which grows on the leaves.

The more willing the men, the more hours they worked. By dawn they were in the paddock and no question of leaving while there was still sunlight. It was not uncommon for them to have tea, a little sleep, and on nights when the moon was full and the sky clear for them to see the work, they would cut cane by the moonlight. Usually the gang consisted of eight men and a cook. The cook's job was to cater for three meals per day, plus two 'smokos' carried into the paddock. While waiting for the men to eat, the cook was expected to pick up a cane knife and cut cane while the men finished their meal. He was paid equal share of the gang's earnings for the week. Often one of the men's wives was employed as cook. She wasn't expected to cut cane during 'smoko' but her added chore was to keep the camp clean and tidy and do the men's laundry and mending.

1913

By 1913 Dad had saved some money and was looking forward to sending the fare to Italy for his family's voyage and providing a little home to live in. At this time, Felix Bellero, who was later to become his brother-in-law, along with Felix's brother Enrico, whose wife and small son were already with him, approached Dad with a proposal. They suggested that the three men should pool their savings and buy Mr Lacaze's farm at Macknade, in what is now known as Neame's Inlet, but at the time called Anna Branch Road. The asking price was £7,000 (7,000 pounds). They were brave men. Between them they had saved £750, Felix had £500, Enrico £150 and Dad £100. Of course, the big question for Dad was would he send his saved money home for the fare to Australia, or invest it on the farm where there could be future security for his family. The choice, he felt, should be his wife's, so he wrote and gave her the details and asked her to make the decision. Mum's father, with whom she was now living, advised her to encourage her husband to take the opportunity of going into partnership with his savings, and he promised somehow to find the fare to Australia for mum and my sister. It could not be immediate of course. I believe he had to find approximately £24 for a one-way sea voyage to Queensland. This took two years to manage, but my grandfather kept his promise. With his efforts and support from his relatives, the fare was saved.

1914 – 1920

Before the end of 1914, plans were made for Mum's departure for the family's new home in Australia. By the time she was due to leave, the First World War was declared and by chance, she was booked on the last ship for four years to leave Genoa for Australia. The uncomfortable journey took 40 days. When Mum left Conzano she took my sister Fiorenzina (Fina) and fourteen-year-old Eugenio Bensi. Eugenio was her cousin whose family cared for Mum, her brother and her sister when they became orphaned. On arrival in Lucinda, the group was met by Dad, who Mum had difficulty in recognizing because he was so tanned. When she last saw him, he was of a fair skin and pink cheeks!

Figure 14.2: Maria Tibaldi, Tully, Queensland, 1939.

Mum's first source of income was to cook for the working gang that Dad was employed with as a cane cutter. The day before her duties were to commence, they loaded the dray with their needs and along with my sister, journeyed to the Herbert River. They crossed at the lowest point to Cordelia and arrived at a farm where they were to work for the first part of their contract. On arrival, Mum was shown her quarters. To her horror and disbelief, the boss led her to a grass hut. She braced the entry through the small opening to inspect the interior. It proved to be no improvement from its appearance outside. She touched the grass wall and screamed with fright as it seemed to come alive with movement of what she later found to be rats – a nest of them! Life in the rugged cane fields was a challenge for the settlers from Italian cities.

By about 1919, due to the increase of members in the families, our family now two children, and Bellero four, there was too much togetherness as everyone was living under the one roof. Four adults and six children produced tensions, which started to build up when communication broke down. A flick of a coin was used, the loser to move down the road to the 'other half'. Dad called and he lost. Temporary housing was needed while arrangements were made for Dad's half share of the house to be moved approximately 500 yards to the new site. Barracks made of corrugated iron were already on the site, which had housed the gangs, so our family moved there. A carpenter was brought to literally saw the big house in half, pull down the fences and, once the new stumps were placed ready on site, the house was moved very slowly on buggies drawn by horses. A spear was sunk into a spot where a water diviner assured them water was available.

1920 – 1925

The early '20s looked much brighter. In 1922 Dad bought his first car: a Fiat, which cost £500. Mum felt it was sheer extravagance. Dad really felt he had it made. He still owed money to the bank, but the situation was promising. I was born in 1925, nine years after my brother Federico. By this time the family was starting to enjoy more comforts and new furniture in the home. The car had to contend with very rough roads, but easily carried the family on visits to friends. Before the car, the only means of transport was horseback or buggy pulled by a horse. If there were too many passengers, as the buggy could pull two adults and a couple of children at the most, three horses were harnessed to the dray. A mattress was thrown on for comfort, and food was packed as a contribution to the house party they were to join, especially for special occasions such as Christmas, Easter, weddings, and family gatherings.

Distance and bush tracks meant little, as the pleasure of seeing and enjoying the company of friends and relations was worth the effort. These parties could go on for two to three days. The women cooked the chickens and perhaps a bullock or pig slaughtered for the occasion, news was swapped and beer consumed, which had been cooled under cover of wet hessian bags. Musicians were depended on to bring their accordions, violins, and guitars. They accompanied the singing and dancing on the verandas or concrete floors. These were happy occasions and the families made the most of each opportunity because they were few and far between.

1927

My brother was one of the first boarders of the new convent run by the Sisters of Mercy that had opened in Halifax. My parents, having had little education themselves, gladly made arrangements for their only son to have the chance of a better education. This was a great occasion. Until that time, he and my sister had attended the small state school in Macknade.

The wet season of 1927 brought torrential rains, but this was not unusual. There was no wireless to keep them informed of weather conditions so they were not aware that a severe cyclone was heading in their direction. Heavy rain had fallen over Ravenshoe and the Millaa Millaa areas, which drain into the Herbert River. This can bring floods to Ingham without any rain locally. On this occasion, river waters and heavy falls locally due to the cyclone were causing one of the biggest floods Ingham and its district had ever seen. Our family was not alarmed when waters started to reach the farmyard late in the afternoon. They had seen the river break its banks before and water lie around in low places for a few days, and then things would be back to normal. This time it was different.

The water was rising fast. By nightfall, it was over the bottom step of the home. The floor was four steps above ground level. Floodwater continued to rise until it was four and a half feet into the house. What contents were not washed away were ruined. We huddled in that ceiling for three nights, no food, or water and terrified when the force of the water drove a huge tree into a corner of the house. Movement of the current caused it to thump and make the house shudder until the adults were sure it would cause the house to break up. The cyclone continued to blow into the next day. An enamel dish was floating in the floodwater in the room below us. Dad reached it and pushed a small portion of the iron roof out in an effort to catch some rain water in the dish. A gust of wind blew it off the roof, so we never did get a drink while up there. During those three days, shots could be heard, no doubt from people trying to raise help. During the first night, our family could hear screams and cries for help. They were to learn later that then people were swept off their home at Bemerside. The house finally disintegrated on the banks of the Seymour River and all perished. Some were babies.

    The impact of this disastrous flood was far worse than I can describe. In our case, the home was intact along with the stable and sheds, but thirty-two of the horses were never to be found. Harnesses were swept away or ruined; fences were a tangled mess and had to slowly be replaced. Contents of wardrobes and linen presses were a pitiful sight: mud stains and dyes out of some materials adding to the loss. It was obvious these articles could not be replaced, as we had no money, so eventually these were laundered and placed in the sun to whiten as well as possible. My parents' first reaction was to walk away from the whole mess and cut their losses. Once the shock started to wear off, the realised they had nothing better to consider. Along with so many other people in the area, they gradually repaired their damage, cleaned up the property, and started again to try to forget this nightmare.

1929 – 1938

Another terrible loss was to fall again on the family in the next two years. My brother, who was by this time thirteen years old, was complaining of severe stomach ache. He was diagnosed as having appendicitis, which required immediate surgery. He passed away eight days after the operation. Prior setbacks in the lives of our parents were minor compared to the loss of their son. It took Mum almost five years before she appeared to take much interest in life again and Dad seldom spoke of their tragic loss. For a long time it seemed to drain them both of hopes for the future. Next, came the Depression years. I can't recall that these years affected us to a great extent because we always seemed to have more home grown vegetables as well as poultry, eggs and fruit. Even if cash was short, food was plentiful. Mum was a fantastic cook. She could make her own bread, churn butter, and always made interesting meals regardless of the ingredients available. And it was no effort for her to make clothes out of old ones.

1939 – 1941

By 1939 life on the farm had stabilised. Dad had gradually brought the farm into productivity in spite of a plague of beetles, which had covered a large area of farmlands as far as Innisfail. By this time, Dad was the proud owner of his first crawler tractor, a McCormack T20. Gradually, machines took the place of horses in the fields. Hours of manual labour were automatically reduced. Men who had worked in the fields all their working life realised that if they were no longer young enough or strong enough to be part of a gang to cut cane in the season, they moved to other areas. Many went west of Cairns to Mareeba or Dimbulah into the tobacco growing area to share farm or pick the leaf. Many settled permanently; others drifted to the cities, bought homes, or invested their savings in flats or small business.

The Herbert River area had by now its settled farmers of mixed ethnicities: Britons, Italians, Spaniards, a few Germans and Chinese and the district showed every promise of growth and future prosperity. Battery operated wireless had been introduced with overseas frequencies. I can still see the excited faces of my parents and their friends as through the crackle of the airwaves, they first heard broadcast of news items and music from Italy, the land of their birth. News from abroad was not always pleasant. Talk of war was threatening. Naturally, this worried them, as many had parents and relatives in Europe. In 1939, war did break out and eventually Italy became the enemy of the British in June 1940. This caused great concern for the Italians in Australia, as there were strong rumours that they would be interned. This soon proved to be correct.

I was born in Australia. The family's immediate worry was what would become of a seventeen-year-old and an eight-year-old during wartime. Occasionally word would spread that police had arrived unexpectedly along with army officers to farms, and confiscated tractors or near new sedan cars and told that they were required for the forces. No one dared to argue. My parents, along with many others, had been naturalised British citizens for many years, but this did not give them the security they had expected in time of war. It was rather strange and confusing. In some instances a father was interned because of Italy's involvement while his son, who was born here, had received his call-up from the forces and was fighting in New Guinea, or perhaps had volunteered and was serving in the Middle East or training in Canada to become part of an air crew.

1942

In our immediate family the inevitable happened. We received a phone call from my sister at Hawkins Creek to tell us her husband had been taken along with others in their area to the police station. Instructions were to bring his suitcase, as they did not expect he would return home for quite some time. He was later sent to Cowra in New South Wales where a huge camp had been arranged to accommodate Italians, Germans and Japanese born in Australia, while another section held the military prisoners of war (POWs) captured from the war areas and some sent to Australia. Arrangements were quickly made for my sister and her daughter to move in with us on the farm. My brother-in-law was at the time working in Hawkins Creek and living in an isolated area – no place for a young

Figure 14.3: Rina Tibaldi with Maria Tibaldi, Tully, Queensland, 1945.

mother and child to continue to live on their own. Dad's motto through life was never to keep anyone waiting. It was always a family joke that if he had an appointment he was always there one hour before the due time. This applied to people or transport. He never missed a train or bus in his life. His attitude towards a possible visit from the Government was no different. Mum was encouraged to pack a suitcase in readiness. Clothing coupons were pooled to buy necessary woollen clothing if he should be interned in Cowra or a cold area. We didn't have long to wait after my brother-in-law's detention. A week later, at 8pm we heard two cars drive onto our property. Two detectives named Donoghue and Stone from Ingham police station came into the house. There was no need to explain their presence. We were well aware of their purpose.

Mum's reaction was to be expected. She had been under strain for quite some time anticipating this moment. In trying to comfort her and Dad, we were all in tears and somewhat hysterical. The detectives were very kind and understanding. They had known Dad for some time. They kept apologising for the upset they were causing, but had no alternative. Even if personally they felt that Dad was not suspected of being disloyal to Australia in any way, it was a war precaution and orders had to be carried out. Dad, always anxious not to inconvenience in any way, explained that his suitcase was ready, just to give him a few minutes to try to console his wife. Much to our surprise, after a little chat between themselves, the two men asked if we could promise to have Dad at the police station in Halifax by 7am next morning. They would leave him to spend the night with the family. Of course this suggestion was gladly accepted. I wanted to explain this because it is important to show how Dad was a man of his word and of good reputation, for he would never have been otherwise given this privilege.

Going to bed was not even considered that night. Once we accepted the inevitable, Dad rang our immediate neighbour, Mr Roy Blackburn, to tell him of our predicament. Roy's parents had been neighbours when Dad bought his farm. They had been very helpful through all those years. Roy was no exception. We all admired and trusted him. Within minutes after the phone call he was with us. He assured Dad that he would supervise work on the farm and give the family support in his absence. To this day we have the greatest respect and admiration for this man, his wife and family. He proved to be a rare friend. He made himself available to guide us, encourage, and sort out our problems as they arose. It took much of his time and patience I'm sure. Our family could never repay him or forget his generosity.

Leaving Dad and Roy to talk over business and other arrangements, Mum had to keep herself busy so the wood stove was lit and a couple of unsuspecting chickens were snatched from the coop. Before long they were dressed and in the oven; a few tins of canned meats and fruit were packed along with freshly baked biscuits. By daybreak, Dad, the family and food were ready for the trip to the police station. True to his habit, Dad had to be there before the appointed time. We were amazed on our arrival to see about sixty more men in a roped off enclosure outside the police station. Most had been collected during the night. Police and army officers were busy filing in forms for these men, and arrangements being made for transport to the Ingham Drill Hall, which was situated in the show grounds. Trucks were brought in to load the 'prisoners'. We drove on to Ingham with hopes of seeing Dad again before they left. The scene at the Drill hall was worse than Halifax. Well over one hundred men were inside with their luggage, wives and children distressed and confused. On Dad's arrival we were permitted to spend a few minutes with him again.

Shortly after lunch, two ropes were stretched from the door of the hall to the railway line, which was a distance of about fifty feet. A train with several carriages arrived and barred windows and armed soldiers. The arrival of the train and its appearance caused near hysteria especially once the husbands, fathers, and friends appeared at the door of the hall and were escorted to the train. I will never erase this sight from my mind. To see your Dad's face at the window with bars and trying to give us a little wave as the train pulled out is not something to forget easily. At this stage no one knew where they were going. The train travelled south and we knew others had gone to Cowra so guessed that is where they were heading. We learnt later that they spend a few days in Stuart jail in Townsville. They were held there while more arrests were made in Ayr, Home Hill, Ingham, Innisfail, and areas where Italians had settled in numbers. Accommodation in the jail was overflowing. Food was in short supply and severely rationed. Bedding was their blanket if they had one in their possession and space on the ground. Mum's food parcel came in very handy. The next part of their journey was to Cowra. Here, they were placed in tents of four to six men. The fact that there were so many familiar faces there was a comfort to the new arrivals. Dad's first letter as well as brother-in-laws to my sister assured us they were well treated. Food was plentiful and we were not to worry on that score. We were to learn later that they were treated kindly, encouraged to form their sporting activities, concert groups, and their own canteen where they could purchase items such as smokes, chocolate, writing materials, soap, and shaving materials.

This concentration camp was in the form of a huge circle, divided in four parts by rolls of barbed wire as well as around it of course. Italian, German, and Japanese prisoners of war occupied particular sections, and the remaining sections were internees living in Australia. Dividing wire fences made it impossible to converse or clearly see those in adjoining camps. Listening to stories of their experience on their return, I can honestly say that they had no complaints regarding their treatment. At home, we were facing the problem of future survival; no jobs, no income if we didn't produce a crop of cane and no idea how long it would be before the internees returned home.

At home

Apart from Mum's efforts in the very early days, my sister and I had no experience whatsoever. The most we had ever done in a paddock was to supply the men with smoko or cool drinks on a hot day. It was decided that my sister should learn to drive the tractor and that I be shown how to harness the work horses that we still owned. Roy patiently made himself available for this exercise. Meanwhile, we were advised by the Canegrower's secretary that soldiers were to be released from the forces to cut the harvest that year, and that cooks would not be supplied – that would be our responsibility. Also the tractor, which had not been confiscated, had to be made available to farmers who needed it on hire, at a rate to be decided by the forces. We had to nominate the time we expected to use it so they could work out a roster. We panicked at the though of soldiers living in barracks not far from our house full of women. What's more, we had to cook for them!

Mum agreed she would take care of the meals, but in our dining room. My sister Fina and I would serve the meals and help with washing up. Mum made it clear to the Canegrower's secretary that she insisted on a few rules too. The men were expected to come to the table respectfully attired, to only be in the house for meals and retire to the barracks when finished. In spite of Mum's hopeful instructions we were very worried and were not looking forward to the arrival of these six strangers. We understood later they weren't looking forward to their new venture either. They were all from New South Wales and had never seen cane before. They had been told that they would cut cane for Italians, so expected a complete language barrier, and soon found out after a few days of cutting cane that they did not need encouragement to retire to the barracks.

Five of the men persevered with their blistered hands and sore backs, but one just couldn't cope physically and had to be replaced. The five originals turned out to be an asset and caused no problems at all, but the replacement gave us sleepless nights. He was a particularly big man with very shifty eyes. He never conversed with the other boys, and had frightened my sister and I by his obvious sneaky manner, by appearing when we least expected him and just staring at us. The remainder of the gang realised our concern and felt that we were under enough strain and pressure so went to the Canegrower's secretary to see if he could be moved. Fortunately, this was arranged. By this time we slept with a cowbell under my sister's bed and a solid piece of wood under her pillow and Mum's. The need to use them never arose but it would have been a very noisy and painful experience if anyone had molested us.

That first year, in 1942, with Roy's guidance and help from our cousin Eugenio Bensi's two sons and Sandro Novelli (their father also was interned), we managed to prepare the land and plant cane. Mum's time was fully occupied in keeping house, growing vegetables, milking cows, and cooking for the cane gang. Fina and I worked in the fields after taking weekly turns to get up at 4.30am and help Mum prepare and serve breakfast plus smoko, which they would carry with them to the paddock. In the evenings our neighbour, Mrs Maggiora, would walk in at dusk and stay the night with us. She was left alone on her farm as her husband and two sons were all born in Italy and interned in Cowra. We would lock up and then spend time sewing, reading, and writing letters to the menfolk. One night it was very windy. We didn't hear footsteps, but a loud knock on the door. We all froze with fright. A voice finally said "It's only me Mrs Tibaldi – one of the gang". He had walked home from Bemerside, a distance of about four miles with five Peter's ice cream buckets as a treat for us. Poor man, instead of showing gratitude, Mum abused him for frightening the daylight out of us. Knowing Mum, we realised she did not want to encourage familiarity. It left no question in his mind I'm sure. Our fears turned out to be unfounded because the men in the cane gang proved to be gentlemen in every sense of the word. As we got to know them better we relaxed and enjoyed their company when they came in for meals. If they saw us doing chores like chopping wood or heavy work, they would quickly offer to help. We were fortunate in having these types of men around, even if they were not initially welcome.

1943

We can't boast of being successful farmers but we did what we could within our limitations. We managed three meals a day, and had each other for company and comfort. Apart from one family friend, no women had been interned but Mum decided we should take precautions to store and hide some of our prized possessions in case she or Fina were picked up. As I said previously, in such a case Roy and his wife had offered a home to Lydia, my little sister and I. We had no doubt that promise would be kept if necessary. Mum's idea of salvage was to thoroughly clean two heavy 44-gallon drums from the shed with heavy lids and snap on rims. They were painted inside, lined with layers of paper and we packed these with embroidered linen and other treasures we valued. A large hole was dug at the back of the vegetable garden on the edge of the cane paddock and instructions were that if she and Fina had to leave, these were to be buried. This also applied if there was an invasion by Japanese. The drums were never buried but one of the cane cutters almost broke his leg when he disappeared out of sight while burning cane and fell into a ditch about 10ft by 4ft. He did think it a clever idea to have a trench in case of an air raid, but had no idea we had one handy! Poor Mr Ladbrook was never told the truth about this 'air raid shelter'.

A shilling

Dad's letters came weekly. After nine months in a camp he told us they could appeal against the government's decision to interment and he was waiting for his case to be heard. This news gave us some encouragement as were confident that Dad had never taken any interest or part in any clubs or organisations since his arrival in Australia that could lead to suspicion of being a disloyal subject. In the meantime, he had been included in work groups at camp who were driven out to collect firewood or collect other needs for camp requirements. For these chores they were paid one shilling per day. Dad and others enjoyed the outing as well as the pocket money they had earned for their trouble. With this money he would buy chocolate, PK's and other goodies from the canteen and send them home for us to enjoy. It seemed incredible that they had these luxuries available when we on the 'outside' couldn't buy them.

Eventually his case was heard. He was cleared of any suspicion of being connected in any way to groups or activities, which could be a threat during the war. He was to be released from internment camp but not permitted to return home as a 'war precautionary decision' as they didn't think it wise for large groups of Italians to form again in any town. Many of the men were released with work found and arranged for them in various parts of Australia. Dad was sent to Whyalla in South Australia, miles out of that city, again in a tent camp. The Whyalla pipeline was under construction and Dad's job was to push a wheelbarrow moving soil as ground was dug up. He was free to move about but had to report weekly to the police station. His workmates were mostly Australians, on average wage, while Dad continued to collect his one shilling per day, plus food and bed. Once Italy was defeated in the war, the men were allowed to return to their homes. My sister's husband was released from the camp and was allowed to return to Ingham. He joined us on the farm. To add to our problems we had a long dry spell that year. Cane we had planted wasn't making much progress and the matured crop wasn't very exciting or promising either. It was a hard year.

1944

On the day of Dad's return home, we had a storm that normally we would avoid driving into. As the train arrived with Dad on board, the clouds seemed to burst. I'm sure no one noticed. We were so happy to see him. We were laughing and crying at the same time. Typical emotional Italians! We felt so happy on the drive home, drenched from this driving rain in our small Fiat car. The world looked promising again. Strangely this experience did not make Dad bitter. He felt it was an arrangement that the Australian government felt necessary at the time. Financially of course, it did affect our family greatly despite the fact that Dad's son-in-law had returned home before him and worked on the farm a few months before his return. We women had been unable to keep up the production level and the farm suffered considerably. Our farm's income had dropped when Dad was interned and the bank saw it necessary to put us on a stringent budget. Every month we had to supply a list of our requirements and they decided what would be approved. Fuel and fertilizer were cut down significantly. Our food account was limited to four pounds per week. Without Mum's ability to improvise with her vegetable garden, home grown chickens and eggs, fruit and fresh milk, our physical health would have suffered.

Clever as she was with the needle, she spent hours unpicking old clothes and always managed to produce 'new clothes' for us in spite of the shortage of funds and lack of coupons necessary for food and clothing. Dad accepted his run down farm plus his worn out tractor that had been used and abused by others and gradually restored his material things. He was extremely grateful that his family were intact and had suffered nothing more serious than blisters, sunburn, and sheer frustration. The reminder, he felt in time he could handle. Unfortunately not all of the men accepted their internment as Dad did. Some were very bitter for a long time and felt that they were harshly punished for a situation not of their making or choice. Few even suspected false reports from people who had hoped to gain the White Australia policy by ridding themselves of these foreigners who they considered were gradually taking over and owning British land. A natural reaction one can expect in a period of wartime when one's property and way of life is threatened. With our menfolk back again our family life settled once more.

1945 – 1950

Financially, Dad couldn't afford to pay much in the way of wages and couldn't expect my brother-in-law to do much other than to make arrangements for himself, so with his family he moved into Ingham to seek regular work. It wasn't long before I too joined their household when I found employment in an office there. I married Savino Scagliotti in 1946. During his life he was known as Sid, but occasionally the nickname Scally was used. He was a grandson of the Vignolio family, the very first people who had met and accommodated Dad in Halifax on arrival in this country. They were the owner's of the Wine Shop in Halifax. We had one son who we named Ray Scagliotti. Most of his life he was known as *Scag*, the abbreviations are typically Australian idiom.

By 1948, the farm was producing in full peak again. Around this time the sugar industry had an influx of displaced persons from Europe whom the Government had assisted to Australia and found work for, mainly in factories or the land. They had come from all parts of Europe and were in our area, of course, to cut cane. Their language barrier was a big problem. Many still carried mental scars from the war or terrible experiences from war and concentration camps. It wasn't uncommon to hear stories of farmers or cane inspectors to be chased by an irate cutter with a cane knife when there were disagreements.

1951 – 1980

By 1951 Dad and Mum had had enough of farming with all its problems and decided it was time to change their lifestyle. By 1980, the farm to which my parents devoted so much of their life was owned by the Chinotti family. They were neighbours who had leased the farm from them for eight years and then bought it. The home Mum and Dad bought in George Street, Ingham, for their retirement, was purchased by my sister Fina. She is the only family member still living in Ingham area. My husband and I sold our farm at Warrubullen in 1973 and now live in Innisfail. We all have in some way benefited through the lives and sufferings of two loving and caring people we are proud to be our parents. Maria Tibaldi passed away aged 81 in 1971 and Enrico Tibaldi who passed away in 1972 aged 84 years. Rina Scagliotti passed away in Innisfail in 2012.

– Excerpts from Rina Scagliotti's original unpublished manuscript.

Like a Dream So Long Ago

Long ago

My story begins on 24 January 1927, the day I was born in Linguaglossa, a small town along the highway that goes to Taormina, in the Province of Catania in Sicily. My father Mariano Emmi was the youngest of six children and my mother Maria Rosa Turnaturi was the oldest of eight children. It was a tradition in Southern Italy to name children after the grandparents, so I was named Rosa after my father's mother and my younger brother was named Giuseppe after my father's father.

My parents owned property, vineyards and more. It was a wonderful childhood in my native land. There, I spent endless happy hours together with aunties, uncles and cousins on weekends and school holidays. My first recollection was at the tender age of three years old. My uncle, Francesco, dad and brother took me to the town's beautiful gardens where the church of San Rocco stood to celebrate the patron day. It was a yearly event and everything around was very colourful with balloons everywhere. I remember wearing a beautiful white dress with a ribbon in my hair. My uncle bought

Figure 15.1: Giuseppe, Maria Rosa, and Rosa Emmi, Linguaglossa, Sicily c. 1930.

me a small sweet in the shape of a nun. We walked home with my small hand in his. I remember my baby brother in his pram at the door. I gave him the tiny gift.

The grape harvest in Linguaglossa was something I will never forget. I can still remember with a smile the women with baskets full of grapes on their heads. They were bringing them to the men waiting in a large room to pelt the grapes with their feet, until the juice fell into a large cistern. In the afternoon the juice was taken in the town where we had big caskets in a canteen where the wine was kept. All these are fond memories of my childhood years.

When I was five, we moved in with my sick grandmother, so that my mother could look after her. We returned home when I was six years old, after my grandmother had passed away. My uncle Francesco was now alone in the house, as he had never married. The home was three storeys high with a beautiful terrace where I spent many sunny days. I will never forget this wonderful time, as it is still in my memory. I also recall fondly the many hours and days I spent with my mum's parents, Nonna (grandma) Carmela Vecchio and Nonno (grandpa) Sebasitiano Turnaturi. One of my aunties was three years older than me, one of my uncles was two years younger. We used to go down the road leading to the farms. On the walls we would pick berries. As I write this I have that nostalgic feeling that brings tears in my eyes. I want to be there again. My home was in a beautiful part of town, Via Trieste: two doors up from Via Roma, the principal throughway that led out to other towns.

Opposite our home was the big building of the Police Station in Via Roma. All we children would gather to play outside the Police Station with the police officers watching over us. The boys made a cart and we would have rides on it. Some of the boys that made the cart later migrated to Australia in the 1950s to make their homes and raise their families in a new land. When they came to

Sydney, we used to meet and have long, long talks about our childhood. These happy memories are still with me.

Queensland

My father Mariano Emmi was fifteen years old when his father passed away. He migrated to Australia in 1922 where he went to Ingham Queensland to cut cane, and then loaded trucks to be crushed into sugar, golden syrup molasses and so many things are made from sugar cane. My father decided to return to Sicily in 1925. There he met my mother, who was a very beautiful young lady. He fell in love and they were married in 1926. After us two children were born, he returned to Home Hill in Queensland in 1927 to make enough money for a better future for our family as life was becoming much more difficult in Sicily

When my father returned to Sicily in 1929, my mother wanted him to stay in Linguaglossa, but he liked Australia and wanted his young family to join him. He returned to Queensland in 1930. So Mum decided after a few years to join him, with the understanding that if she did not like the place we would return home. We sadly said goodbye to all our relatives, knowing that we may never see them again. My brother was eight, and I was ten years old. At that age, I remember that I was happy to be going to a new place to live. In April 1937, my grandpa and my uncle escorted us to board the ship *Orama* in Naples. I had mixed emotions. It was very sad to see my family's faces for the last time as we slowly set sail into the Bay of Naples towards a new life in the Southern Hemisphere. We made some friends on the voyage to Brisbane. Some were going to Home Hill and one young girl I made friends with was going to Innisfail in Queensland.

Our sea voyage was long but pleasant with plenty of activities for children. We were doing drawing, painting, and just enjoying the sunny days on the ship. One day, I got seasick and Mum had to take me to the doctor on the ship. I had to stay in bed. I was only 10 years old and wanted to play all the time; I wore out a pair of shoes because I used to go up and down the stairs on that ship so many times. That's how much we played around! I still remember those days so well. We had left Italy at the end of April, and finally arrived in Brisbane in the first week of June in 1937.

Home Hill

A friend of dad and his wife came to pick us up from the ship at Brisbane. We met the family, had lunch and dinner and stayed one night in Brisbane. The next day we were taken to the train north to our new home in far northern Queensland. The weather in Queensland was cooler in June so Mum, my brother and I wore the coats that Mum had made before we left Italy. We caught the train to Home Hill and travelled for two nights. We arrived in the early morning on 11 June 1937. I can't forget when I saw my father again. I remember that I was so excited to see my father after all that time. I didn't recognise him at all because he had left when I was very little. Dad came with his friends in a car to pick us up. It was strange for me to meet my father again. I remember that when we arrived home, my father had presents for us. For me, dad had a little black piano with little white keys and my brother got a little grey and red car to drive. The little car lasted until Giuseppe grew up, but children who came to visit ruined my little piano that I loved so much. Eventually, I learned to play a real piano.

It was good to be with my father. He had a property with a home ready for us to live. There were fruit trees, pineapples, vegetables, and fresh eggs from our fowls. Being June, the climate in northern Queensland was cooler so vegetables grew well. I was as happy as a young girl can be. Unlike my hometown in Sicily, we had no neighbours with girls my age. So I played alone making little mud cakes out of soil and toys that I got in the Christmas stocking. I remember that many times I missed the lovely ancient Sicilian town we left at the foot of Mount Etna with all our relatives and the many traditions and festivals that bonded us together.

Soon after we arrived in Home Hill, I ended in hospital many times because of mosquito bites and the harsh climate. I missed six months of school while I recuperated. But my legs were really in a bad condition from the mosquito bites. A doctor from another town came every second day to treat my wounds with olive oil, and cover them with cotton wool. I finally went back to the Sisters of Mercy Catholic School. It was only a small school because there were only 3000 people in our town, but I enjoyed my time there because they taught me how to paint and embroider which later helped my skills as a dressmaker. We had been in Australia three years and my mother talked of going back to Italy when war broke out. Italy sided with Germany against Britain and Australia.

Figure 15.2: Mariano Emmi, Home Hill, Queensland, c. 1935.

June 1940

One day in June 1940 our peace was shattered. June is the start of the cane harvest. I remember that day well. Having had an appendix operation, I was in bed recovering. Two policemen came to take my father away to a concentration camp. It was utterly devastating for all of us. Dad was not a Naturalised British Subject, so he was taken away from us to Brisbane in prison trains for transfer to the Loveday Camp in South Australia.

We didn't even know where he was taken; let alone how to get there or how to find the money to visit him.

Hidden Lives

Figure 15.3: Rosa, Maria Rosa, and Giuseppe Emmi, Home Hill, Queensland, 1940.

It was as if the heart of our family had been ripped out of our chests. We began to metaphorically bleed to death as he was torn away from the sanctuary of our family home. My mother's world was shattered into a millions pieces. She was in shock and we had no one at all to turn to. We had no relatives in Australia and could not speak the language, and other Italian families were in the same situation. Because of fear of being interned, many friends would not visit us in case they would be taken away as well. So mum got very depressed. I don't think she ever fully recovered from her shock. One of our British neighbours that had been nice to us before the war would have nothing to do with us after my father was interned. It was like a war within a war.

I was thirteen years of age and the entire burden of the family was now mine. I had to look after my younger brother and my mum, cook, go to school and help with chores. It was a huge responsibility for a young girl, but I tried my best to rise to the challenge. The tragic thing was that after my father was taken and we didn't have the cane harvested, money ran out quickly. So what were we going to do? I told mum to let us go to the local Home Hill police station to ask them for help. We told them the situation and they gave us ten shillings a week to live.

I remember the fowls that we raised. We had black and white and red Leghorns. We used to send a letter to a chicken farmer in Bundaberg saying that we wanted mixed or Leghorn chicks to raise for the table, or to produce eggs. We usually purchased two dozen (24 chicks) each time. We would send the money and the poultry breeder would send the chicks in a cardboard box via the local post office. When it was time to cook the male birds, mum made a feast even though we have very little money to buy meat. As I was the older sister, I used to give my brother most of the chook and I ate the legs. He was hungry as was growing so fast and I needed to look after my little brother.

Seeking support

In those days we had no electricity; only a kerosene lamp and a wood stove. I recall my brother Giuseppe helped me to cut the wood for the stove, but one day he cut his foot very badly with the axe. Mum fainted, so I ran down the road to get help from a nice lady who had a car. She quickly came to get my brother and took him to hospital, where he stayed for a month. It was a huge trauma for our family, as we thought my little brother was going to lose his foot or what was even worse, that he would die.

After this frightening incident, with no father to protect us, I remember going to the local priest at St Colman our local Catholic church to plead for his support, because our family was in such a critical situation. We were almost destitute and Mum could not go on any longer. Mum went to a lot of people to sign a petition to get my father released from internment. We asked the priest to sign our petition to help have my father sent home to take care of us. This priest flatly refused to support our request. Still with the pen in his hand, in a sudden burst of rage, he flung it violently across the room shouting: "I'm not going to sign that!" Mum was extremely upset and burst into tears as we left devastated and humiliated. We thought that the priest would help us because we had no relatives and no one wanted to help us, as we were Italians. The way that he treated us was our family's biggest disappointment during our darkest hour. We never returned to that church. We quietly returned home, emotionally wounded but still mentally intact and just got on with surviving. What else could we do? We later discovered that this particular priest had misbehaved badly in every town he was placed.

Life went on, even if it was like a numbing haze of frost in the wind. We were in survival mode much of the time, especially my mother, who did not seem to manage well without my father in a hostile nation with little command of the language. I must have been 14 at the time. At my school that was run by the Sisters of Mercy in Home Hill, I learnt to cut patterns and make clothes. I used my skills to work and start making money to survive without anyone's help. The nuns helped with my piano lessons, as long as I was a student in their school, but they could or would not help us with anything else. It was not like today; we were 'enemy aliens'.

Maybe because letters began to arrive from Dad who was sent to the Loveday concentration camp, Mum started to get better slowly. So we began to cultivate the land to produce enough food to keep us going. We grew beans and tied them into small bundles to sell. My little brother went to nearby homes to sell the beans for three pence a bunch. Three pence had value in those days! I remember one day when Mum sent my brother back to find the three pence that he had lost. Like many Italians whose men were taken away, my mother needed help to run the family and earn money. Without any savings, it was so hard to survive without our breadwinner.

The letter

At fourteen, I left school although I wanted so much to continue. I loved playing the piano at school but I had to stop that as well. So at home I played the mouth organ, as my love of music was great. I had to find work, so I went to the farms down the road to ask for a job. There was a farming family from Greece living nearby. I packed tomatoes and picked cotton for them. They were very nice to me and paid me well. I would give my mother the money I earned. She was very happy with any extra money, as we could survive just a little better. This helped us to get through the weeks and months, which slowly turned into years during my father's internment. We were always trying in desperation to try to get my father home. We tried writing a letter to the authorities.

In November, we wrote a letter to Mr Wake, who was the Major General of Victoria Barracks in Brisbane. I wrote it on behalf of my mum. This is what I wrote:

> Dear Sir,
>
> I wish to make application for the freedom of my husband Mr Mariano Emmi from the Internment Camp. We are very lonely since he left, as he was a good husband and a good father to his children. He is thirteen years in Home Hill and he has not been in any trouble. So I know that he is innocent and that he would not do anything to harm his country Australia.
>
> We are very badly off and now that Christmas is coming, I do not know what we will do. My daughter Rose has had an operation this year and she is not better yet. She has been in hospital for some weeks again. I write these lines in all sincerity and I should have sent them with the list of names of people who would love to see him at home with us again.
>
> Please Mr Wake, do the best for us and we shall always be grateful.
>
> Yours Sincerely
>
> Mrs M. R. Emmi,
> Box 207 Home Hill, N Qld
>
> P. S. Please answer back.

Hidden Lives

Figure 15.4: Emmi family, Home Hill, Queensland, c. 1945.
Left to right: Rosa, Giuseppe, Maria Rosa, Mariano Emmi (seated).

But we had no reply. We still had a bit to pay on the property we owned. The agent demanded his money and he wanted us to leave the place. Mum was not well and we pleaded with him. He felt sorry for us, so we stayed. People were not allowed to speak our language Italian in the street that was Home Hill 3000 people 4 hotels few shops. As I got older I started to do dressmaking with mum's help. I also did some embroidery that I learned on the machine and paper roses, paper belts and hairnets. In 1942, people wore these fancy items, as they were fashionable in those days. I offered full range of dressmaking and fine embroideries as there where no boutiques like we have today. My brother, young as he was, also found odd jobs to do to earn money.

Time ticked by slowly: 1941, 1942, 1943, 1944, and 1945. Finally, the war was over and dad was sent home from Kalgoorlie in 1945 where he was forced to work on conditional parole as a released internee. Dad said that in one job, he was sent out to put traps for foxes in the outback. One good thing that came from this job was that he brought back a fox skin and I made a fur out of it. To pass his time he used to sew raw cotton flour bags together. He made them into bed sheets and brought them home so that we could have cotton sheets on our beds even though we had no way of buying anything else for our home. At one time after his conditional release from the concentration camp, my father was working in South

Australia on the railway for the government. He said that he got no pay for his work during that time as the men paid a very high fee for tent lodgings and basic meals, so no money was given to them to send home to the family. Our family suffered enormously during the time when our father could not support us, even though he was working. So we continued to suffer in silence waiting quietly for the day of our dad's return.

Dad returns

When Dad returned home after the war had ended in 1945, we almost did not recognise him. I remember the day that dad returned home. We went to the train station in the morning with friends of mum with their car. We greeted him with so many hugs and kisses. Out tears ran freely. Then we went home to cook a good Sicilian meal, which my father had yearned to share with us for such a long time. Mum had prepared a Sicilian feast for dad's return. Mum made very delicious Polpetti di Manzo. These are big meatballs made with beef mince, grated Italian cheese, parsley, 'mollicha' (Italian bread crumbs) and eggs. The polpetti were fried in olive oil and brazed in a rich Sicilian tomato sauce. The sauce and polpetti were poured on top of the homemade Maccaroni al Ferretto. Luckily, we had brought the ferretto (metal pasta rod) from Sicily to make our own traditional pasta. Our 'Welcome Home' feast also included fried 'melegiani' (aubergines), 'Pollo al Forno' (roast chicken) from our own coop and many Italian

Figure 15.5: Rosa Emmi, wearing the dress she tailored and embroidered, Home Hill, Queensland, 1947.

delights that my father loved. It was so good to have Dad home again.

But after we had time to recover from the excitement, I noticed that Dad was not the same as he was before the war. How different he was from the strong, healthy, energetic man who was taken away from us for five years. He returned home a sick and broken, middle-aged man with bad teeth and a lot of pain all over his body. I can still see him in my mind's eye, falling off his bike after returning from work, doubling over in pain on the ground. Soon, he had to have all his teeth extracted and his stomach was constantly in lot of pain. He was treated for stomach ulcers but the doctors found a tumour was growing in his stomach. Some years later he had to be rushed with ambulance to Townsville Hospital to be operated. It was touch and go as to whether he would survive, although he slowly managed to get better. But he never returned to the health that he had before being taken to the concentration camp. Dad didn't say much about his time in the camp. My father used to talk about all the different people that he met during his time in the camp, like the Privetera, Malaponti, Rodighiero, and other families from Home Hill. He made some very good friends while he was interned. They looked after each other in that confined space for so many years because they all wanted to return alive to their families after the war. They supported each other like a family. Father did not talk about his internment except when he spoke about the good men he had met. He had experienced enough unhappiness and pain before returning home. So he wanted to forget the past to get on with raising his children and so became completely focused on a better future for us as a family.

A young man arrives

In 1946, our family moved to a rented house, having lost our property in Home Hill because we could not pay the rest of the mortgage we had been paying had before my dad was interned. Mum and I still did dressmaking and embroidery for others and were doing well. The last time we moved was to a cane farm in 1948. For the very first time we had electricity, fridge and stove that were so good to have. With the internees back to their families young girls were now young women and young boys had grown into young men. With the fathers back there were wedding proposals. Time passed. It was 1950, and, by now, I was a young woman.

One day, I drove my father to town to do shopping and when I finished I went to call my father to tell him I was ready to go home. He was talking to a young man who had been an internee in Loveday with my father. I was introduced to Giordano Rodighiero.

What can I write about Giordano? He was born in 1920, in a village high in the mountains called Costa in the Commune of Conco, Province of Vicenza in Italy. His father had arrived in Australia in the 1920s as a stonemason contracted by the government to build the foundations of the Sydney Harbour Bridge. His father and older brothers were naturalised British subjects after so many years living in Australia.

In 1937, Giordano's father arranged for him and his brother Battista to travel to Australia to join the two older brothers, before they were due to be called up for military service by Mussolini. All was going well for the Rodighiero family until 1940 when both Battista and Giordano were interned. They took them to Orange, then to the Hay and Loveday concentration camps. In the camps, he was always in the same huts with his brother Battista and other 26 men. They looked after each other all those years behind barbed wire. Although he was called Giordano at home, he became known as George in the camps because his name was too difficult for the guards to say and remember.

While Giordano was interned, he used to work in the kitchen with a team of about eight young friends. At Loveday, he was also given a job to drive a horse driven cart to bring wood or toppings, rocks and sand to military headquarters to make the road at the barracks. It was over two miles from the headquarters to the sand pit. He drove the cart without any guards overseeing the work. He did this job from 9am to 4pm daily and was paid one shilling a day to work in the camps. He was released from Loveday late in 1943 and returned to Sydney to rejoin his family.

A proposal

Giordano was Marco Rodighiero's brother. I knew Marco quite well as I used to sew dresses for his wife Maria and their children. We greeted each other. I was so taken aback by this handsome young man, that I became quite red with shyness! Giordano was tall, blond and with such blue eyes. It was love at first sight for him and for me. He was in Queensland on holiday for Christmas in 1950, visiting his brother's family in Home Hill. He lived and worked in Sydney in New South Wales with his father and another brother. I was so taken aback that I quickly asked my dad if he was ready to drive home and I went to the car floating on a cloud.

My father invited him and his brother's family for dinner. Before the dinner appointment, Giordano surprised us by coming one night with his brother. Dad and he had a lot in common to talk about being interned together. But it was clear by his looks that he had come especially to see me, so dad asked them to dinner. Giordano's two-week holiday went too quickly. Before Giordano left for Sydney, I said yes to his marriage proposal. He returned to work in Sydney and soon sent a beautiful engagement ring and a beautiful pearl necklace that I have treasured ever since. We corresponded and set the wedding date of 9th June 1951.

Preparations began. I decided to buy my wedding dress since friends said that it was bad luck to make your own wedding dress. Mum and I went to Townsville with the motor rail that left Bowen to Townsville. The town had only one big department store and Rockmans. We went to

Like a Dream So Long Ago

Figure 15.6: The Wedding of Rosa and Giordano Rodighiero, Home Hill, 1951. Left to right: John (Giovanni) Tornatori, Joe (Giuseppe) Emmi, Giuseppe Giordano (George) Rodighiero (groom), Rosa Rodighiero, nee Emmi (bride), Mary Vonnano, Anita Vecchio. Front row: Gina Rodighiero and Lina Rodighiero (flower girls).

Rockmans to buy the wedding dress. They had only two, one in satin, and one in lace. I picked the lace since it fitted me perfectly, small size. I sewed the two bridesmaids and two flower girls all close friends and the two little girls related to Giordano's brother and sister. It was a busy time. As I taught embroidery to the Ladies' Auxiliary of the Country Association, they offered to do the catering and to make the wedding cake for our wedding. Other friends including Jane Baker's daughter, made my flower arrangement, and sang at the church.

Marco, Giordano's brother, provided the calf and pig, and we provided the poultry from our own fowl yard. We hired a cook and he prepared a king's feast! We used the local bakery in those days to do the baking of the meats and sweets. A hall was hired and the local ladies provided the catering for us. There were 400 guests invited. The wedding day was a very cool sunny day for tropics of northern Queensland. Giordano arrived with his parents one week before. At night after the wedding feast, we went to Townsville to board the boat next day to Magnetic Island for two weeks honeymoon. It was a lovely time for us. We went back to Home Hill and left for Sydney a few days later on the train.

Sydney

We arrived in Sydney the next morning from Brisbane. Since arriving at Home Hill I had never been to a city except to Naples when we left Italy, when I was only ten years old. It really surprised me to see the tall buildings, the big department stores like Mark Foy's, Anthony Horden's and also trams. Sydney was a big place for me and I enjoyed shopping in 1951. Now, other stores have replaced all the big shops and department stores that we once knew. Now it is 2012, and we don't go to the city as we have big shops where we live in the suburbs. We had three sons who were all born in Crown Street in Surry Hills, Sydney. The hospital there also was closed down.

We made our home in Reversy, then we moved to Guilford, then we built a home in Horsley Park and now in our older age we have settled in Abbotsbury. Our boys, Robert, Frank and Gary were born in 1952, 1955 and 1957 and have given us grandchildren and great grandchildren. We have come a long way together as I write we are sixty-one years married. Giordano is 92 and I am 85. We spend our time at the Marconi Club where we meet old friends and play bingo. Giordano still drives the car. Our oldest friends are Nora and Johnny. I met them in 1951. My husband had gone to their wedding. Many friends have passed away, but a few of us are still meeting each other and talking about old times. Today, 1940 is like a dream ... so long ago.

– Rosa Rodighiero

Postscript: Giordano Rodighiero passed away peacefully in 2014, aged 94.

"Hey Dago!"

Memories of an Italian Childhood

I wish I could say my childhood was a happy one. There were, without a doubt, happy times, but for the most part, I feel sad when I look back at my childhood. I am 80 years of age now and my most vivid memory of growing up was during the Second World War and the turbulent years to follow. Each time my mind wanders back to those days, I cry.

Growing up in northern Queensland, as a young Australian-born Italian, my entire world disintegrated before my eyes when war was declared between Australia and Italy. Within a few years, our family's world was completely changed forever. This story begins with my father's migration to Queensland in the 1920s.

My father Antonino Cavallaro was born in 1903, in Riposto, a beautiful seaside port town in the province of Catania in Sicily. He worked as a 'carrettiere' (cart driver) in the family business. My father, his two brothers, and my grandfather all transported barrels of wine for a living. They owned five mules, which led their five carts. In Sicily at that time, it was considered a prestigious job and my father's family were relatively well off. They owned their own home as well as having a successful family business.

In 1927, he met my mother Giuseppina at church. They fell in love and got married. Like many Sicilians, he felt there was no future in Sicily and although it was a comfortable and respectable life, it lacked opportunities. He wanted a better life for the family he planned to raise and believed all the propaganda; that if one were able to migrate to the new countries and worked hard you could become very wealthy. So, he departed on the steam ship *Maria Cristina* along with many other Sicilian men, leaving their wives behind until they were settled in their homeland.

Hidden Lives

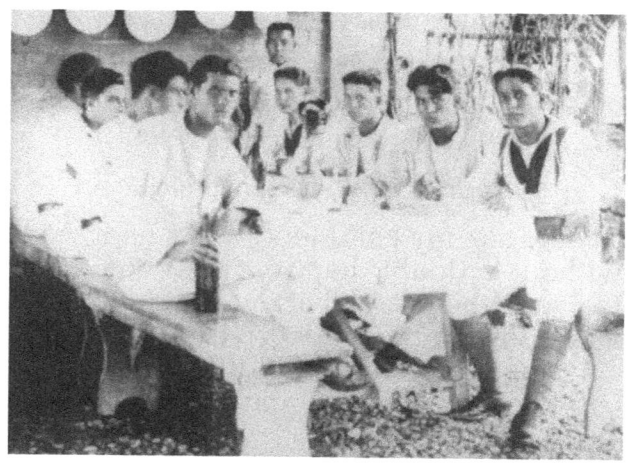

Figure 16.1: Antonino Cavallaro in Italian navy, 1920s.

Arriving in Sydney in 1928, he didn't speak a word of English, so he simply followed all the other disembarking immigrants and ended up in the cane fields of Northern Queensland. Cutting cane was hard and laborious. My father and his brother, Uncle Mick, eventually bought a farm in Midgenoo. Once they built a house on the farm, my father sent for my mother. She arrived in Midgenoo six years later, in 1934. My sister, Sarina, was born nine months to the date of my mother's arrival into Australia. I was born eighteen months later, on 1 June 1937.

Around 1939, when I was two years old, the Australian government started to get suspicious of its Italian immigrants. At that time, Italy was under the control of Benito Mussolini who was promoting Fascism to all of the Italian population. In 1940 he declared war on Britain and its allies, which included Australia. The Australian government introduced a law to send all Italian immigrants that weren't naturalised to a prison camp where they were treated as enemies of Australia. Queensland cane cutters were interned in large numbers in 1942 after Japan attacked Darwin. My father was arrested in 1942. As young as I was, at five years of age, I still recall vividly the day the police arrived at our farmhouse to intern my father. My parents were not warned of police arriving, so they were caught completely unaware.

The police pushed their way into the house and started walking up the stairs to where we all were. My mother became hysterical, yelling and screaming. She tried to push the policeman, who was at the top of the stairs, back down. However, my father went willingly; he hadn't been naturalised and, like most Italians, he didn't want any trouble. He also didn't want my mother to be arrested. Being only a child, I didn't really understand what was going on. I had never seen my mother cry so much and my sister and I felt so helpless watching our mother cry that we too started to cry uncontrollably. We had no idea where they were taking my father and whether he would return.

Figure 16.2: Giuseppina and Antonino Cavallaro, Tully, Queensland, c. 1938.

Uncle Mick never got taken away because he was naturalised, but it was impossible for him to run the farm on his own. So my mother worked on the farm every day to replace my father's labour as well as performing all the domestic duties – cooking, cleaning, washing, ironing and sewing. The tractor was taken away from our farm by the authorities to help boost the war effort. This made it even more difficult to run the farm. The tractor was never returned.

As each day passed, I saw my mother looking more exhausted and becoming so sad. A night didn't go by where I didn't hear her crying in bed. She tried her best to hide her emotions but I knew she was fretting for my father as there was no way of knowing what had happened to him and when he would be returned to his family. One day while I was playing with my next-door neighbour, Jimmy Crossan, another neighbour, Mr McBerishan, came over to talk to Mrs Crossan. He was dressed in a soldier's uniform. I overheard him say: "At least one of the dagoes next door got interned, thanks to me!" I was numb with shock.

Figure 16.3: Cavallaro family at the Tully Fair, c. 1938. Antonino holding Sam, Giuseppina holding Sarina's hand.

A few years later, when the Italian nation became neutral, the Australian government decided to release the interned Italians. After the men were released on parole in late 1943, my dad was sent to the Northern Territory with other internees to build the highway from Alice Springs to Darwin. He wanted to come home but was forced to work for the government because he was still an Italian alien. I don't remember exactly when he was released to return home. We had no knowledge of his arrival. So when we saw my father walking down the railway line walking towards our house, we all screamed with joy and ran to him. My father had aged quite considerably, he looked terribly thin, and his face was hardened. I remember wrapping my arms around his legs and he pushed me away. I was so hurt and shocked. He realised this, so he grabbed me again and tried to make up for it by giving me another cuddle, but it wasn't like the cuddles I remembered before he went away. Whenever any of us asked him questions about 'his time away', he would get angry and refuse to talk about it. I guess he didn't want to remember.

The only thing I knew about his internment was that he was taken to a prison camp for a long time, very far away from his family. I found out later that during his internment, he and the other prisoners were taken from their cells at the police station and put onto railway carriages like cattle. As they looked out through the bars, both Australian women and men alike, would swing their large cane knives around and yell out derogatory comments such as "go back to your own country, you dirty dagoes." My father was never the same after his internment: he lost the smile in his eyes. But life at home became a whole lot easier with him around. Although the war was finally over, the racism didn't seem to die down. In fact, it seemed to have become worse after the war ended.

I recall very vividly a day where racism was apparent. I was seven years old, playing with my friend, Jimmy Crossan near the railway lines where the soldiers were working on the repairs. Jimmy and I were excited to see the soldiers because in the past, the American soldiers had always chatted with us and had given us lollies. A couple of Australian soldiers were laughing and called us over. They gave Jimmy a lolly and then asked if I wanted one. I said "yes please" with my hand out, they then kicked me up the backside and one man said: "Get out of here, you dago bastard!" I ran home and cried my heart out.

A year later, at the age of eight, my mother's health started to deteriorate rapidly. I noticed, after working on the farm whilst my father was away that she had not been

Hidden Lives

Figure 16.4: Sarina and Sam Cavallaro, Tully, Queensland, 1949.

too well. She was constantly exhausted and I put it down to her doing too much whilst my father was imprisoned. Yet, she didn't get better when he returned. Although life was notably easier for her when she didn't have to perform farming duties anymore, her health seemed to be going downhill slowly each day. Some days, she would appear well and other days she would be quite ill.

At the beginning of 1947, Mum stopped having well days and seemed to be sick all the time. She was admitted to Tully Hospital with kidney problems. One morning, early in February that year, our father woke us up early to go visit our mother. We were so excited because visiting hours were only in the afternoon. When we arrived at the hospital, Mum was awake; she was very pale and she smiled weakly and looked at us one by one. She stretched out her arm and beckoned me to hold her frail hand. She squeezed my plump nine-year-old hand gently and said my name slowly three times, "Sam... Sam... Sam... " Then she passed away.

It was the saddest day of my life. Still, to this day, I don't know how she got sick. The doctors simply told us it was kidney problems. We were in shock. After my mother died, going to school became an absolute nightmare. In keeping with Sicilian tradition, my sister Sarina and I had to wear a black armband to signify that there had been a death in the family. The kids at school teased us about it and derogatory words were spat at us continually. The teachers heard and saw us getting picked on but never said anything. They didn't seem to care. I eventually told my father that I was getting picked on at school. So that Christmas, he put up a punching bag at home and gave me boxing gloves and said "Sam, you have to learn to defend yourself and fight back!"

My first fight happened soon afterwards, when I was about ten and a half years old during a lunch break at school. I was sitting by myself as usual while the other kids were playing with a tennis ball. The ball happened to land right beside me. One of the girls yelled out to me: "Hey dago boy, get the ball!" I ignored her as I always did. One of the toughest bullies in the school who was two grades higher than me yelled out: "Hey you stupid dark dago, pick up the ball!" I ignored him so he came up and pushed me off the stool. That was it for me!

I had been constantly teased but never pushed around so I got up and pushed him back. He was a lot bigger than me but I didn't care. I had so much anger and rage in me and I now knew how to throw a punch that I fought back with all my strength. The whole school crowded around to watch; even the teachers watched from the staff balcony. I wanted someone to stop the fight as I knew that I was really hurting him and it wasn't until he yelled out: "I give up!" that a teacher stopped it.

The following Christmas in 1949 was an extremely sad one for our family. Christmas of course was never the same without my mother but this particular Christmas my father became very sick. He was in constant pain with unsightly and infected boils on the back of his neck. Despite the fact that the doctors prescribed him an ointment, it didn't seem to have any noticeable effect. After Christmas, when the year 1950 began, my father lost so much weight and could no longer do any heavy work around the farm. He was perpetually tired. We didn't know what to do or where to get help for him. Dad was admitted to Tully hospital, and on 12 August 1950, he died. Sarina and I didn't really understand why he died and what made him so sick. Although I do remember that the colour had never returned to his face from the moment he returned to us from the prison camp. The day the police took our father away from us he left a healthy, strong man. He returned a very pale, frail man and was never the same again. After our mother died, Dad was all we had and I never thought for one second he would die. But we had lost Dad, too. Sarina was fourteen and a half and I was thirteen.

We were now officially orphans and I had no choice but to keep on fighting... literally.

– Sam Cavallaro

Sam's story is linked to his memoir, *Hey Dago!*, by Tina Simmons

"We were just ordinary blokes!"

Ten Italians interned in Australia during WW2

Remembrance

The first week of June 2011 marked an obscure milestone in Italian Australian diaspora history. It was seventy years after the arrival of the first contingent of Italian male civilians at Loveday Internment Camp 9 in Barmera, South Australia.[183] A group of about 900 men, collectively identified as Italian enemy alien internees, had been transferred from the Orange Staging Camp to Hay Internment Camp No. 6, in 1940, and to Loveday in 1941. The vast majority were commonplace migrants, who had been arrested as enemies of the nations because they or their parents had been born in Italy, one of the Axis nations at war with Australia as a Dominion of the British Empire.[184] A two-day event to commemorate the arrival of the first internees was prepared by a local community group. There was a bus tour of internment camp locations, an exhibition of objects from the camps, and images of the prisoners, military and medical staff. The remembrance dinner at a local hotel included a range of guests including the families of Italian and Japanese internees and descendants of the military staff.

The dinner celebrated happy memories of the Barmera community and Loveday's military staff, from a military wartime perspective. Yet, the twenty Italian internee descendants who had come from across the continent to Barmera expected a commemoration of their compatriots'

---
[183] Austral Archaeology. *Loveday Internment Camp archaeological report*, State Heritage Branch, South Australia State Heritage Branch, Adelaide, 1992
[184] Peter James Marshall. *The Cambridge illustrated history of the British Empire*, Cambridge University Press, 2001

sometimes unsympathetic, unnecessary and, for most men, a discredited indefinite incarceration without trial in Camps 9, 10 and 14 at Loveday. Clearly, there was a very stark contrast in how extra-judicial, long-term incarceration by master warrant, in prison camps were interpreted by the descendants of the captors and those of the captives. Nonetheless, a well-intentioned local historical group's festivity had revealed that more research was needed to discover how 'happy' internees were to be interned at Loveday or anywhere else. As in many other historical contexts, the event highlighted that the dominant historical narrative of internment in Australia, silenced internee experiences of personal torment that indefinite captivity at Loveday had caused thousands of Italian migrants, because they had been classified as enemies of the British Empire and its allies. Whose version of the facts about internment was the genuine? Or were they both valid? This question required further exploration, and new evidence that could corroborate the Italian internees' interpretation of how they actually experienced their wartime incarcerations.

Beginning with this backdrop, this chapter presents a fresh perspective on written and eyewitness accounts of wartime civilian internment that offer an interpretation of Italian internment in Australia from the captors' viewpoint. This discussion presents eyewitness accounts of former internees, their families, and primary documents, to illuminate the lived experiences of young Italian internees, from an Italian Australian perspective. Such an investigation requires reliable, concrete evidence.

Archives as evidence

In the earliest academic research on Italian internment in Australia published in 1980, Gianfranco Cresciani, a prominent scholar of wartime internment in Australia, argued that:

> Life in the internment camps was not physically burdensome for the internees. From the various detailed reports prepared by the International Red Cross Delegate in Australia George W. Morel, it is quite clear that the treatment of the internees by the Australian authorities was excellent ...[185]

However, this was far from the reality for most internees who were required to submit to often-harsh prisons camps conditions over many years, with some individuals confined to camps until the end of hostilities. Absent in Morel's official reports were references to mental torments, micro-aggressions, and abuses of power over the physical being of internees which remained unrecorded in military documents. It is possible that Morel was unable to speak directly with internees before writing his reports, which seem to be based on information supplied by the military. Before Dr Morel's appointment as the Official Visitor to major Australian camps, the civil courts in South Australia sent Mr K. F. Sanderson to look into internees' concerns. Sanderson's monthly reports are less than complimentary of internment conditions. In his regular reports, Sanderson noted numerous internee complaints regarding poor living conditions, rancid foodstuffs, and the harshness of military discipline imposed on civilian internees for extremely minor contraventions to prison regulations. However, the concerns raised regarding Loveday's harsh prison environment were not always well received by military authorities.[186] Similarly, Reverend Dr Martin F. Toal, the Catholic military chaplain at Loveday was met

---

[185] Gianfranco Cresciani. *Fascism, Antifascism and Italians in Australia*, (Canberra: Australian National University Press, 1980), 175; Italian edition (Roma: Bonacci Editore).

[186] National Archives of Australia, (NAA): AP613/4, 6 (Report No. 3, Official Visitor Loveday Internment Camps); NAA: AP613/4, 7 (Report No. 4 Official Visitor to Loveday); NAA: AP613/4, 8 (Complaint addressed to the Official Visitor by Internees); 255/716/58 (No. 9 Internment Camp [Loveday] - Report - Official Visitor); NAA: MP508/1, 255/716/221 (Official Visitor's Report 28th Oct. 42 Loveday).

by military authorities' resistance in respect to his role in meeting the religious needs of Catholic internees of any nationality. By early 1942, Mr Sanderson was replaced by Dr Morel, who as mentioned previously, had little or no direct access to the prisoners. During the same period, Reverend Dr Toal was forced to accept a humiliating compulsory retirement due to what the authorities called 'health issues', and was swiftly replaced by a more malleable young chaplain who complied with military rules.[187]

Such personnel changes ultimately made it possible for harsher treatment of internees to remain unrecognised, unrecorded, and unscrutinised by the two most crucial organisations that protected the wellbeing of powerless internees. Nonetheless, details of everyday life in the internment camps have been uncovered in secreted, handwritten internee diaries. These are the dairies of Mario Sardi who was imprisoned in Camp 14A,[188] and Federico Bonisoli who was detained at Liverpool, Orange, Hay Camp 6 and Loveday Camp 9.[189] Letters written in Camp 9 by Marco Panozzo[190] to his family corroborate Bonisoli's comments, while interviews with Sam Tati confirms details in the Sardi diaries.[191]

Two illustrations corroborate the suggestion that the International Red Cross reports, although seemingly written in good faith, were inaccurate. On 22 April 1942 Sardi writes in Camp 14A: 'Food today was very meagre; there is a shortage of many items.'[192] Writing in Loveday Camp 9, Bonisoli's diary on the 23 April 1942, records a previously unidentified military practice:

---

[187] NAA: MP508/1, 56/704/324 (Religious conditions at Loveday)
[188] Ilma M. O'Brien. *The Internment Diaries of Mario Sardi*, Lucerne Press, Alphington. 2013.
[189] Raffaele Lampugnani. *I diari d'internamento di Federico Bonisoli: La lingua e il "bel dire" di un fascista italo–australiano*, Arcane Editrice, Rome, 2016.
[190] Marco Panozzo. *Panozzo family - papers, 1940-1942*, Microfilm - MAV/FM4/10834, State Library of New South Wales, Sydney, 1940-42.
[191] O'Brien. *Mario Sardi*, 25.
[192] Ibid., 30.

I noticed that whenever the government controller or some other important person comes to visit us the M. C. hides the machine guns that are placed in front of the garret sentries, only to make them reappear as soon as that person has gone.[193]

Furthermore, vital information regarding internee mental and medical health was inaccessible to prisoners themselves, their families, or the official observers. Medical issues were very rarely recorded in internees' personal dossiers or other archival documents. It remains unclear where internee medical records are located or if they were destroyed after the end of hostilities.

By the time Cresciani published *The Italians* in 1985, he had modified his opinion asserting that 'Undoubtedly, internment was a trauma both for Italians who were interned and for those who were allowed to retain their freedom'.[194] Later researchers on the topic, such as Ilma M. O'Brien, Kay Saunders, Joan Beaumont, and others, corroborate Cresciani's 1985 observation, producing abundant evidence in multiple publications that show how Italians were adversely affected by internment. An even more polarising detail in an expanding debate on whether many common knowledge 'facts' about internment have been contrived into falsehoods to fit a military narrative or are true. A fact that cannot be disputed by either side of the debate is that overwhelmingly vast majority of Italian internees were later found by legally convened tribunals to be completely innocent of disloyalty to the Commonwealth. Much of the evidence against these alleged Italian Fifth Columnists was non-existent, or had been contrived. They were victims of war rather than criminals of war.[195]

---

[193] Federico Bonisoli. L'internamento in Australia e Memorie dell' internamento, unpublished manuscript, MLMSS 5288 ADD-ON 2008/Box 01, Book 1, 77, 1942, State Library New South Wales, (SLNSW) Sydney, (Translation: R. Lampugnani, 2016).
[194] Cresciani. *The Italians* (Sydney: ABC Enterprises, 1985), 80-81.
[195] Ilma M. O'Brien. The internment of Australian born and naturalized British subjects of Italian origin, in Richard Bosworth,

Yet, traditional histories on the internment of civilians in Australia during wartime remain remarkably accepting and uncritical of the large-scale arbitrary arrest of thousands of innocent migrants, to be detained indefinitely in prison camps thousands of kilometres from home. In 1940, Italian internees were far from the North African battlefields and the open oceans where Australians were fighting against the Fascists. However, from 1942 onwards, Australia was in fear of invasion not only from the Nazis in the Indian Ocean, but also by the Japanese attacking from the Pacific, the Torres Straits and on Australian shores.[196]

To investigate the lived experiences of Italians during the war, I have located eyewitness internees. Ten Italian Australian men who live in Queensland, New South Wales, Victoria, and South Australia were interviewed to explore the question of how internment was actually experienced by those who were incarcerated as Italian civilians. From 2010 to 2014, interviews were conducted with Salvatore (Sam) Tati in Mossman, Carmelo Lo Giudice, Vincenzo Fotea, Giuseppe (Joe) G., Peter Dalseno, Giuseppe Giordano (George) Rodighiero, Remo (Ray) Datodi, Leonardo (Len) De Roma, and Giuseppe, Belgio (Joe) Manca, and (Pino) Genti.[197] Still lucid in

& Romano Ugolini, *War, Internment and Mass Migration*, Gruppo Editoriale Internazionale, Rome, 1992; see Ilma M. O'Brien. "Internments in Australia during World War Two: life histories of citizenship and exclusion", in C. Elkner, I. M. O'Brien, G. Rando, & G. Cappello, *Enemy Aliens: The internment of Italian migrants in Australia during the Second World War* (Bacchus Marsh: Connor Court Publishing, 2005), 15-33; Kay Saunders, "Taken away to be shot?" The process of incarceration in Australia in World War II in *Alien Justice: wartime interment in Australia and North America*, (St. Lucia: University of Queensland Press, 2000), 152-167.

[196] Michael McKernan. *Australians at Home, World War II* (Scoresby: The Five Mile Press, 2014).

[197] Interviews were conducted from 2010 to 2014 with Salvatore Tati, Carmelo, Lo Giudice, Peter Dalseno, Vincenzo Fotea and Giuseppe Genti in Queensland, George Rodighiero and Joe G. in New South Wales, Remo Datodi in Victoria, Len De Roma and Belgio Manca in

their 90s, these men offered candid interviews on their experiences during the war. Each interviewee shared rare insights into people and events in their camps, as well as documents, ephemera, and photographs that helped to shed light their wartime stories. While some long-held secrets were revealed in very candid language, others were cloaked in metaphors and euphemisms, or nuanced in casual conversation, in gestures, or poignant silences and fleeting glances. Their wartime stories began in June 1940, with Benito Mussolini's declaration of war.[198] These testimonies commence with Salvatore Tati in northern Queensland.

Salvatore Tati

Salvatore (Sam) Tati was 94 when I interviewed him in Mossman, an hour north of Cairns in far north tropical Queensland. He was 23 years old and recently married with Mary Scarcella when he was interned in early 1942. He began the interview by explaining that his family had made financial contributions towards a charitable collection of funds by local Italians for families in Sicily, which he believed was why he had been interned. These were traumatic times for the nation at war with Italy. Italians in Australia were aware that they may be considered a risk to national security but the majority felt that the war was so far away that it would only affect their freedom of movement to the local area, whilst continuing their normal work. By late 1941, the nation was preparing for invasion by the Japanese via northern Australia and the South Pacific. British-Australians in communities with large Italian populations felt threatened, even though there was no doubt in the minds of the migrants that the nation was their new homeland.[199]

It is unknown if Sam knew the owner of a local café, Mrs Webb, as her name and the incident that allegedly

---

South Australia.
[198] https://www.youtube.com/watch?v=bYp_vN84p_U, Mussolini Declares War, accessed 20/11/2015.
[199] NAA: BP242/1, Q17157 (Tati).

Figure 17.1: Salvatore (Sam) Tati, Mossman, Queensland, c. 1939.

happened in her shop did not come up during his wartime recollections. The café owner had made a formal accusation against Vincenzo and Salvatore Tati, a few weeks after the Japanese had attacked Pearl Harbor in December 1941. Her declaration states: "On Saturday night (in) January 1942, … I heard the two men speaking Italian … and they were both laughing …"[200]. As there are no other written testimonies that refer to the woman's complaint, it cannot be proved that the incident occurred. Sam and Angelo's investigation dossiers show an absence of supporting documents that delve further into the café owner's protestation. This suggests that the brothers were not confronted with her allegation, indicating that they could respond. As a result, Mrs Webb's accusation sealed

[200] Ibid.

the young men's detention. In reality, it is likely that the Tati brothers were laughing about something personal to themselves, but this was not the issue at stake. Webb's denunciation expressed the intense vitriol and fear that British-Australians felt with young enemy alien men of military age living in their midst, whilst Australian men were actively fighting the Axis nations. By early 1942, most Italians in Queensland were perceived to be a potential Fifth Column, quietly waiting to assist the Japanese in the invasion of the continent.[201] The Webb testimony suggests that an alarmed Australian population perceived meetings between Italians and the speaking of a foreign language proof of disloyalty to the nation. At the same time as the Australians feared the Italians, the Italians feared the Australians.[202]

Mrs Webb's accusation was not an isolated case, as many archival files confirm that men and women had been reported for alleged subversion and support for the Axis alliance. Yet, not a single case of ordinary Italian migrants being spies or saboteurs proved to be true.[203] For British-Australians, the potential harmful ramifications of having Italians in their midst, while the British-Australian men were going away to fight the war was intolerable. It is possible that the previously restrained ethnic hostility against Italians in Mossman had surfaced again after the British Preference riots of the mid-1930s.[204] Given this history of ethnic animosity, it is probable that the Tati

---

[201] Antje K. Gnida. *Beastly huns, fifth columnists, and evil Nazis: Australian media portrayals of the German enemy during WW1 and WW2.* PhD thesis, (Sydney: Macquarie University, 2009).

[202] Gianfranco Cresciani. 'The Bogey of the Italian Fifth Column', in Gaetano Rando and Michael Arrighi (eds), *Italians in Australia: Historical and Social Perspectives* (Wollongong : University of Wollongong, 1993), 67–83.

[203] "Japan Claims attack on Singapore: British give ground in jungle 'North West Passage'" in *The Examiner*, Wednesday 17 December 1941, 1, accessed 13/8/2014.

[204] Lyn Henderson. "The Truth in Stereotype? Italians and Criminality in North Queensland between the Wars," *Journal of Australian Studies*, 2009, 19:45, 32-40.

men, along with thousands of other Italians, would have been interned regardless of Mrs Webb's complaint. For Sam, there were more significant events to talk about in the limited time available.[205]

Sam recollected that the vast majority of the men in Camp 14A got on well with each other and respected the mores of peaceful co-existence, no matter what their political views. He added that apart from a few fanatical Fascists and Communists, no one mentioned political issues in his circle of friends.[206] He commented on the death of Francesco Fantin with very few words: "We all needed to stick together as Italians – *restare uniti* (remain united). What happened to Fantin should *never* have happened!"[207] The only other critical incident that Sam recalled in Camp 14A was of a man named Giannotti from West Australia who one night had walked too close towards the barbed wire fence. Sam remarked:

> The guards in the tower shot at his feet with the machine gun to give him a scare and warn others not to try anything. All the internees knew that the guards would not hesitate to shoot a man dead if looked like he was trying to escape.[208]

After Giannotti's effort to challenge the limitations of security guard's tolerance, Sam recalled that no other internee neared the fence again.[209] Sam pointed out that everyone knew that it would be useless to flee to the surrounding arid country, as they would die instead of returning home to their families after the war. Sam was eventually released from internment in early 1944. He and his brother Angelo worked in hard manual jobs under strict conditions in the Civilian Alien Corps near Darwin and in Tasmania until 1946. Salvatore Tati was honoured to receive the Civilian Service Medal for his

---
[205] NAA: BP 242/1, Q17157 (Tati).
[206] Interview with Salvatore Tati, Mossman, 2011.
[207] Ibid.
[208] Ibid.
[209] NAA: MP1103/1, PWI55593 (Giannotti).

service to this nation as part of the Civilian Alien Corps during wartime.[210]

George Rodighiero

George explained how the life of an enemy alien changes once incarcerated. During the final interview with Giuseppe (George) Rodighiero, he declared with a hint of exasperation: " ... you know, (silent pause) when you are there, you've got to go along with what they do.[211] You *can't* pretend to be a *big, strong man!*"[212] His candid reflections, along with those of the other men interviewed for this project, illuminate our understanding of life in a carcerial institution during wartime. Not only did internees need to comply with military commands, but they also needed to be very mindful of the other power brokers in the camp – the camp leaders, the canteen managers, the mail distributors, the pay keepers, and the camp bullies. Life was anything but uncomplicated in all the male-only internment camps, especially as the number of inmates often exceeded 900 men in each compound.

George was 20 years old when he was arrested at his father Antonio's Sydney home in late-1940. Antonio Rodighiero had arrived from the Veneto region in the mid-1920s as a government-contracted master stonemason to work on building the Sydney Harbour Bridge (the Bridge). Notwithstanding Antonio's good standing in the Australian community, his youngest sons Battista and George were interned as enemy aliens. This was primarily because they had not been in the country long enough to become naturalised British subjects, were single and of military age. George considered, the two brothers' detention could not have been avoided because they were of military age and non-naturalised. To avoid suspicion falling on his father and oldest brother Placido, which

---

[210] https://www.pmc.gov.au/government/its-honour/civilian-service-medal, accessed 10/7/2016.

[211] George is referring to the military commanders, guards, camp leaders, and the bullies among the internees.

[212] Interview with George Rodighiero (also known as Giuseppe and Giordano), Sydney, 2012.

Figure 17.2: George Rodighiero, Sydney, New South Wales, 1940.

they feared could result in their detentions the interned brothers did not make contact with their family for the duration of their internment.[213]

Like many Italians arrested in New South Wales in 1940, the two Rodighiero brothers were incarcerated with common criminals in Long Bay Prison (Long Bay) before their relocation to internment camps. In New South Wales, Long Bay was used as a first detention centre, before detainees were transfer to the Orange Showgrounds staging camp, then to Camp 6, located in Hay by late 1940.[214]

George Rodighiero was one of the two men still living, who had been detained in both Camp 6 at Hay and Camp 9 at Loveday. During our interviews in 2012 and 2013, George sometimes found it challenging to contain his great

---
[213] Interview with George Rodighiero, Sydney, 2012.
[214] NAA: MP1103/1, PWN9107 (**Battista** Rodighiero); MP1103/1, PWN9440 (Giuseppe Rodighiero).

displeasure regarding one of the military commanders in charge of Camp 9 from 1941 to 1943. Although unnamed during the interviews, the Camp 9 Commandant was later identified as Captain Archie Dick (later Major A. Dick).[215] Although more than seven decades had passed since his internment, George's experiences in confinement still caused him considerable disquiet. His comment paints a visual picture of the camp's Commandant:

> This Captain would walk into our camp (long silence) … every time he came in he was walking in a stiff manner, with a nasty look on his face. He was with two guards – one on each side. They had rifles fixed with bayonets pointed at us men … I don't know why he acted like this! We were not **criminals!** We were just **ordinary blokes!** That's not the way to treat us![216]

George also commented on random body and hut searches that internees were regularly subjected to during their incarceration at Loveday. His voice began to calmly describe the scenario in Camp 9, but soon changed into a tone of controlled indignation:

> They were suspicious about us … (they examined) the hut - and us. This is something very, very peculiar. But, then you know, when you are there you have to go along with what they do. You can't pretend to be a *big, strong man!*[217]

His account constitutes a previously undisclosed testimony to his own and his compatriots' laboured, involuntary compliance to military control over their material possessions and themselves as disempowered hostages. There was a general view amongst internees that they were perceived as, and treated like convicted criminals in a prison rather than enemy alien civilians

---

[215] AWM: Image 030196/02, Major Archie Dick DSO, Loveday, accessed 10/10/2015.
[216] Interview with George Rodighiero, 2012.
[217] In this context, 'pretend' means 'expect'.

detained as a precautionary measure. Along with fellow internees, George endured humiliation as a war prisoner. Like many of the internees, he kept his spirits high by volunteering to work.[218] He worked in the camp kitchen where George stated that he ate better as a waiter. He also worked outside the barbed wire fence.

A photograph of George as the cart driver and two Japanese internees can be found in the Australian War Memorial. He was working, with two Japanese civilian internees from Broome, carrying wood for heating, and gravel to renew the road to the military headquarters. This image illustrates a unique moment of intercultural collaboration between European and Asian internees during wartime, particularly because the camps were organised according to racial apartheid principles, separating Asians, Indigenous, and other non-Europeans. Although an application was made for a Civilian Service Medal, George Rodighiero was not recognised for his work during his detention supporting the army's war effort.[219]

Belgio Manca

Not long after George Rodighiero was interned in Sydney in 1940, a young ship's steward named Belgio Manca was arrested in North Ryde, where he had been hiding on a farm with three other Italian men.[220] Belgio was born in Genoa of Sardinian parents, but had been raised in a Catholic orphanage after his father's unexpected death of tetanus, when Belgio was seven years old. He explained:

> I had few opportunities to be educated or to learn a trade, so I was sent to work with a mechanic when he turned 14 years old. My mother worked as a cook for a manager of the Lloyd Triestino shipping company in Genoa.

---

[218] Interviews with all internees participating in this project.
[219] AWM: Image 064827, (George) Giuseppe Giordano Rodighiero, Loveday, 1943, accessed 10/10/2015.
[220] NAA: MP1103/1, PWN9257 (Manca).

"We Were Just Ordinary Blokes!"

Figure 17.3: George Rodighiero driving a wood cart with two Japanese internees from Broome, Loveday Internment Camps, 1943. (courtesy AWM)

With his mother's help, Belgio was offered work as a cabin boy and ship's hand on a number of luxurious passenger liners including the *SS Toscano*, *SS Lombardia*, *SS Mazzini*, *SS Esquilino*, and the *SS Conte Bianco*. He recalled that on the *SS Conte Bianco*, he was the personal butler of an Indian prince. Little did he know that his final job as a ship's steward was to be on the *SS Esquilino*, on the Genoa to Sydney route. Belgio called to mind that, in early 1940, he had an altercation with a senior steward, who insisted that he make the Fascist salute. Belgio refused to do as he was told explaining: "It wasn't a military ship! It was a passenger liner. And I wasn't going to make the Fascist salute because I was a civilian! So, I jumped ship!" Fearing that the Fascists on the ship would arrest him, and that he would be in danger once he returned to Italy, Belgio deserted when the ship arrived in Sydney, hiding with an Italian family on their potato farm in North Ryde.[221]

---

[221] Interview with Belgio Manca, Adelaide, 2014.

Figure 17.4: Belgio Manca, Sydney, New South Wales, c. 1945.

Public spectacle

Belgio recounted how he and the men he was arrested with, were marched under heavily armed guard through the main street of the small townships of Orange and Hay, as they were transferred from the train to the campsites. He remembered dozens of soldiers with tanks and machine guns pointed at the internees, intensely watching them as they walked silently down the main street. Belgio stated:

> It was winter and I didn't have any warm clothes as I had walked off the ship with only the clothes on my back. It wasn't a good feeling, as we walked quietly down the street with local people watching and screaming at us![222]

This scene remained a vivid memory for the rest of Belgio's life. The parading of captured enemy as a public

[222] Ibid.

spectacle is as old as war itself. Indeed, Belgio had become an enemy of the Allies as an Italian, and an enemy of the Fascists as a dissenter and deserter. Ultimately, for Belgio Manca, humiliation, harsh prison-like treatment, and confinement were the inevitable consequences of war, no matter where he was arrested or which nation won. The three images attached to his internee dossier shows the progress from his arrest to a prisoner identified as, 'N9257'. Belgio was detained for five years in prison camps, and in 1944 was paroled to the Civilian Alien Corps, as a woodcutter for the Victorian Forestry Commission.[223]

Remo Datodi

A brief interview was conducted with Remo Datodi, whose family was interned by the British in Palestine in 1940, and deported to Australia for internment at Tatura in late 1941.[224] Remo's overwhelmingly positive commentary on his Tatura Camp 3A confirmed the dominant narrative of an enjoyable internment experience in Australian camps. However, Remo's memories of Tatura seemed to be selective, given that he was still an adolescent during his internment.[225]

Archival files disclose that conditions in Camp 3A were anything but idyllic for the majority of adults in that camp. Numerous files reveal that families constantly complained to military authorities regarding the most basic of concerns such as requests to have the unlined tin huts covered with plywood because of the extremes of temperature experienced by the children and the frail.[226]

---

[223] NAA: SP1732/1, MANCA, BELGIO.
[224] Rick Datodi. "The Internment of the Datodi Family," in *Hidden Lives*, 2017.
[225] NAA: B78, 1948/DATODI R (Datodi).
[226] NAA: MP508/1, 255/715/452; MP508/1, 255/715/396; MP508/1, 255/715/214; MP508/1, 255/715/789; MP508/1, 255/715/667; MP508/1, 255/715/596; MP508/1, 255/715/537; MP508/1, 255/726/103; MP508/1, 255/748/51 (Official Visitor's Reports, 1941-43 - No. 3 Internment Camp, Tatura).

Hidden Lives

Figure 17.5: Tatura Camp 2A, Italian and German internee group photo: (Back row left to right): Unidentified, Aldo Datodi, Henri Schubert, Remo Datodi, Martinelli. (Front row): all unidentified, 1943. (courtesy AWM)

Yet Remo, who was about 19 years old at the time, did not recall any of the troubles that were dealt with by his father and older brothers. His positive account of Tatura supports the view that the youngest adults and children in all the camps were protected from the harsh realities of internment by their parents, older siblings, relatives, paesani, and Italian leaders. In Remo's case, his father Francesco and uncle Alfredo had always taken responsibility for the family's wellbeing, and maintaining an atmosphere of relative normality within a prison camp environment. Comments made by Rick Datodi, a family member, suggest that Francesco and Alfredo consumed the family's entire life savings during their confinement at Tatura from 1940 to 1946. These funds were vital to maintain a reasonable existence with quality foodstuffs and clothing, for eleven family members including three young children.[227]

The family's emotional, social, physical, and financial protection from the harsh realities of detention allowed

[227] Interview with Rick Datodi, Melbourne, 2014.

Remo to remain a relatively untroubled youth, who regularly played sports, and pursued light-hearted romantic interests with interned teenage girls in the same camp.[228] However, this comparative calm changed by early 1942 when the affable Camp 3A Commandant, Captain Tuckerberry, was replaced with a more rigid commanding officer. According to Remo, this was because one of the girls in Camp 3 had become pregnant, resulting in the removal of all men over 18 years of age who were not interned with their wives.[229] This group of unpartnered men remained in Camp 10A at Loveday for 18 months until they were transferred to Tatura Camp 2, which was a men-only camp.

While Remo took great pleasure in sharing happy memories of his time with his family whilst they were all interned at Tatura, his voice immediately changed when asked about Camp 10 at Loveday. Remo stated, "Ask me whatever you like about Tatura, but I don't want to talk about Loveday!" After a short poignant silence he declared: "It was boring (long silence) and it was *awful*." It was evident that Remo did not want to discuss his experiences at Loveday, preferring to talk about his good memories as a carefree youth in the protection of his family at Tatura. Remo's use of the word 'awful' with emphasis, gives a clue to the active suppression of painful memories in Camp 10A.[230]

Although Remo's family had buoyed him emotionally at Tatura, this was taken away when he and his older brother Aldo were moved to Loveday. He had suddenly become a vulnerable young prisoner, who like the other inmates, was powerless to control how the Camp 10 guards treated him. Remo's very brief remark on Camp 10A clearly indicated that it was a negative experience, and that it must not be mentioned again. However, there is a written eyewitness account of events in Camp 10A in the unpublished memoirs of Vittorio Tolaini. Vittorio, a

---

[228] Ibid., 2012.
[229] Ibid., Bundoora, 2012.
[230] Interview with Remo Datodi, Bundoora, 2012.

British-Italian had been deported from Britain to Canada in mid-1940 on the *SS Arandora Star*, which was sunk by German torpedoes on 2 July that year. He survived the ship's sinking, which claimed 865 lives, including about 200 Italian male civilian internees, but was re-interned in Liverpool in the United Kingdom. Soon after, he was deported to Australia on the infamous *Dunera*, with 200 other Italian survivors of the *Arandora Star*. Tolaini offers a unique testimony that corroborates the cruel conditions experienced by the inmates of Camp 10A.[231]

> Our treatment in Camp 10 was very harsh. Bashed with the butts of rifles we were pushed into a large hall and forced to strip naked. ... Some of us were coerced to submit to an extremely degrading investigation. ... It was a terrible experience. ...[232]

Vittorio was not the only internee to put negative experiences in Australian internment camps in writing. A detailed and graphic account of body searches is found in Peter Dalseno's memoir describes a similar incidence as a Queensland internee in Camp 14D:

> Many were completely naked and paraded before officers – presumably medical doctors and orderlies. ... Fingers furrowed through the hair, ears were probed, then an instruction to bend over so that his anus was exposed and examined for articles that might have been inserted for concealment.[233]

Although Dalseno's unambiguous depiction may seem confronting, his articulation of detainee experiences at Loveday corroborates other testimonies. Added to these

---

[231] http://www.bluestarline.org/arandora.html; and http://www.bbc.com/news/10409026; accessed 10/12/2015.

[232] Vittorio Tolaini. 'Voyage of an alien', unpublished, Monash University, Rare Books Collection, 1989.

[233] Peter Dalseno. *Sugar, Tears and Eyeties* (Brisbane: Boolarong, 1994), 224-226.

three eyewitness accounts is Joe G.'s comments regarding to his own experiences of body searches.

Joe's experience

Joe G. arrived in Queensland in 1933 from Catania in Sicily. He had just turned 18 years old when he was interned in Innisfail in mid-1942.[234] His father had already been interned early in 1942 and sent to Loveday in what David Faber calls the great internment dragnet, and Ilma M. O'Brien labels the great Queensland round up.[235] I refer to this phenomenon as the third surge of Italian internment that followed the initial mass internments of 1940, and the second wave in late 1941. A few months later, Joe was arrested and was eventually transferred to Loveday Camp 14A to join his father. Joe recalled the extreme terror he felt during his time in custody, beginning with his arrest in northern Queensland.[236]

> One day, ... mum was in town to visit the doctor. After working in the fields, I came into the farmhouse for lunch and lay down to relax. ... I looked up and saw the local policeman. I was terrified. I'll never forget it, as long as I live [237]

After his arrest, he was transferred to Gaythorne in Brisbane before being sent to the Cowra Internment Camp in northern New South Wales. Joe explained that when he arrived at the prison and saw the rows of barbed wire fences:

> Oh!!! I didn't want to go in! But they pushed me in! As we went inside the gates, there were tents with doctors inside waiting for us. We were in this tent and the doctor said we had to strip to examine us all over. All over, all over! (long pause,

---

[234] NAA: MP1103/2, Q74__ (expunged for privacy)
[235] O'Brien. *Sardi Diaries*, 6.
[236] NAA: MP1103/1, Q74__.
[237] Interview with G. (Joe) Giuseppe, New South Wales, 2012.

> looking into the distance with sad eyes) … *You've got **no** idea*!! … They treated us *really badly, very rough*. I wanted to run away, but I couldn't.[238]

After this initial shock, Joe connected with a few young friends, who had also been interned without their fathers. Joe and the other boys were eventually reunited with their fathers who were detained in Camp 14A at Loveday. Nonetheless, even after joining his father, Joe remembered that he regularly woke up in terror late at night. Although he finally had the emotional protection and support of his father, his terrifying experiences at Cowra still took some time to resolve in the young boy's mind. Joe vividly describes his first few months at Loveday: "I was in a *bad* way. … The first few months, dad walked around the camp with me late at night. … I was crying and I was still scared."[239] This remark suggests that imprisonment at Cowra was terrifying for young men detained without their fathers.

In the confused detention conditions at Cowra as described by Joe G. and Carmelo Lo Giudice, the youngest internees without the protection of fathers, older brothers or relatives, were especially vulnerable to physical and mental maltreatment. While a few reported cases of abuse are not representative of all young internees' experiences, Joe's comments suggest a prevalence of similar maltreatment of internees in more than one camp. The loss of liberty contributes to the potential for abuse by authorities that may choose to employ harsh and demeaning procedures on vulnerable detainees. These accounts enhance our understanding of military practices used in a number of Australian internment camps during wartime.

Carmelo Lo Giudice

Carmelo's wartime narrative began with his sea voyage from Calatabiano in Sicily to Mourilyan in Northern

---

[238] Ibid.
[239] Interview with Joe G, NSW, 2012.

"We Were Just Ordinary Blokes!"

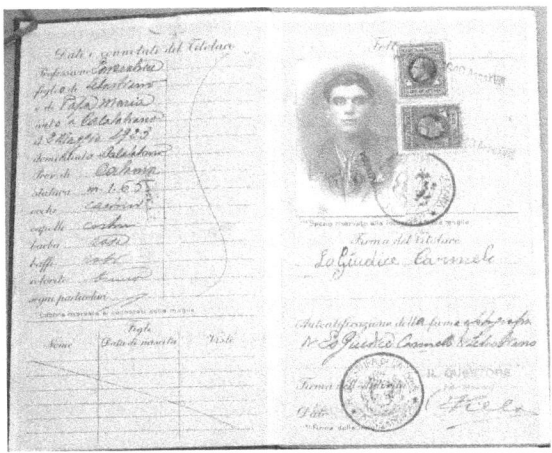

Figure 17.6: Carmelo Lo Giudice's passport 1940. (courtesy NAA)

Queensland on the *SS Romolo* in May 1940. Carmelo had joined the family of Caterina Donzuso, acting as chaperones since as a 16-year old minor he was not permitted by Italian authorities to travel alone.[240]

He recalled the enormous trauma when his father Sebastiano and uncle Giuseppe were arrested in early 1942. He was alone for the first time in his life in a foreign nation where he was an 18-year-old enemy alien. Carmelo reflected: "I got drunk for the first time when they took my father away!" He explained that he was in shock and felt very scared without his father and uncle to protect him, especially with his mother still in Italy. Carmelo had no one to turn to for safety. On the morning of 25th March 1942 the police came to arrest Carmelo.[241] Carmelo recalls the day the police took him into custody: "It was war! (long pause) You don't know what can happen in a war ... you just never know if you will ever see your family again!"[242] After some days in the Gaythorne Prison, Carmelo was transferred to Cowra.

---

[240] NAA: BP242/1, Q24750 (Lo Giudice).
[241] NAA: A435, 1947/4/1177 (Lo Giudice).
[242] Interview with Carmelo Lo Giudice, Innisfail, 2011.

The Cowra camp was an unsettling location for Carmelo who felt vulnerable without his father's support. When he arrived, it had no huts. "We were hundreds of men sleeping outside on the ground for a few nights. ... Then they brought tents and we put them up quickly."[243] Carmelo dreaded being away from his father, so he made an application to be transferred to be with his father and uncle who were at Loveday Internment Camp 14A. He recalled: "I could still picture the massive rolls of barbed wire that surrounded the camp." From this account, it is clear that Cowra was a prison camp that was still under construction and was unable to cope with the large numbers of new internees once the mass internments in Queensland had begun. When questioned about the guards at Cowra, Carmelo burst into laughter. Even though he had been constantly anxious about his imprisonment, he was alert enough to notice one characteristic of the soldiers who guarded the Cowra Internment Camp in early 1942.

> Oh! The army guards at Cowra! Ha! Those soldiers got drunk every night! They didn't worry about the internees! They were always *drunk as skunks* - every night! We could hear them from our camp! ... (they were) screaming and fighting with each other ... every night! ... ![244]

In Carmelo's judgment, he felt that the guards at Cowra were dangerous because no one could predict what they would do. He remarked: "Maybe they could shoot without thinking!" This view is supported by archival documents that indicate military concerns regarding some of the guards at Cowra.[245] This concern hastened Carmelo's application for an urgent transfer to be reunited

[243] Ibid.
[244] Interview with Carmelo Lo Giudice, Innisfail, 2011.
[245] NAA: MP742/1, 115/1/148 (Internment Camp Cowra – Transfers); (Official Visitors' Report, Cowra, May 1942); SP1714/1, N45633 Part 1, Cowra Internment Camp (intelligence file, box 42).

with his father and uncle at the Loveday Camp in South Australia. He also mentioned the fear that overcame him and five other boys being entrained to Loveday. Three armed guards, including a sergeant, accompanied them. Carmelo stated that the sergeant tried many times to touch him and the other boys in inappropriate ways. The boys resisted these advances, being careful not to anger the guards so that they would avoid being shot.

After a two-day train trip from Cowra in northern New South Wales, Carmelo arrived at Loveday Camp 14A. He clearly recalled the image of his father who was waiting for him at the gate. Carmelo uttered, with tears in his eyes: "We hugged each other tightly and both burst out crying because we were finally together. We both said: "If we have to die, at least we'll die together!"[246] Such was their relief in being reunited that this memory triggered an emotional response in Carmelo during the interview.

Although most other interviewees did not mention that they felt that their lives were in peril, this father and son couple were acutely aware of the personal risks during wartime detention. From this point onwards, Carmelo's internment story turns to sports and time spent with the other young internees from Queensland. Now that his father and uncle were protecting him, his safety concerns were no longer uppermost in his mind.

Vincenzo Fotea

On the day that he was interned, Vincenzo Fotea was working in his family's bakery in Mourilyan, near Innisfail Queensland. Vincenzo had arrived from Melicucca` in Calabria in 1937 to join his father who had arrived in the mid-1920s.[247] Speaking about what the youngest boys in the camps did in their spare time, Vincenzo reflected:

---

[246] Interview with Carmelo Lo Giudice, Innisfail, 2011.
[247] NAA: BP25/1, Italian Fotea V (Fotea); J1736, FOTEA, V (... Civil Constructional Corps CQ116028).

> The youngest boys had nothing to do. So we had fun flipping off the older men's hats as a joke. It wasn't serious stuff! We were just having fun. I liked boxing. Being one of the youngest, I wanted to prove myself as the best boxer in the camp. The Fascists dared me to go to Fantin's hut and to challenge him to a boxing match outside. I went in, and asked him to come outside to where some of the other boys were waiting to see us fight. He told me to go away. So I did! I didn't want to harm him. I just wanted to be popular in front of the boys. I didn't know that he would die the next day! I feel very sad about what happened that day.[248]

Finally, Vincenzo had made peace with the past. The young man's actions, on the day before Francesco Fantin was killed by a group of fanatical fascists, were not based on an informed appreciation of the consequences of challenging him to a boxing match in a camp where more than a few Fascists were bulling the antifascists. There are reasons why such a gentle young boy became unwittingly embroiled in an attempt to intimidate Fantin. As one of the few Calabrians in Camp 14A, every provincial group in the camp would have considered Vincenzo an ethnic outsider. So, Vincenzo needed to show the Camp Leader, Dr Piscitelli, that he was one of the team. As one of the youngest adolescents, Vincenzo was susceptible to being led into actions that supported the political agendas of the most powerful leaders in Camp 14A. Yet, Vincenzo's innate affability surfaced when he walked away from Fantin after he dared him to come outside to fight.

The evidence presented during our interviews suggests that Vincenzo and his young friends were unaware of the serious political ramifications that their boys' games would lead to. Vincenzo was released from Camp 14A just as the Italian government had signed the Armistice in September 1943, after Mussolini had been removed

---
[248] Interview with Vincenzo Fotea, Brisbane, 2012

from power. After two years of hard manual labour in the Civilian Alien Corps (CAC), he was released to return home in 1945.[249]

Giuseppe Genti

Giuseppe (Pino) Genti was an internee barber in Camp 14A. During two interviews conducted in 2013 and 2014, Giuseppe requested notes be taken rather than a video recording.[250] Pino spoke about the attack on Francesco Fantin, which he witnessed from his hut less than 20 meters away. He described the afternoon of the attack on Fantin in detail.

> It was a hot day. I lived in the hut next to the one Fantin lived in. That afternoon, I was sitting outside the hut and had just finished playing cards with my friends. I can remember that it was after lunch in the late afternoon. We were talking in the shade of our hut and didn't take any notice of what was happening at the water tap nearby until we heard men arguing. I turned around and saw a group of older men, including Paternoster, arguing very loudly with another man. I later came to know that it was Francesco Fantin. The men arguing with him were from similar background. ... A new hut was being built next to Fantin's hut and there were some wooden stumps lying around on the ground near the new construction. Suddenly a man from the group picked up a piece of stump about a meter long and about 6 inches by 6 inches thick. As he was swearing at Fantin, he threw it like a javelin at his head. The wood hit him at the back of the head and Fantin fell to the ground. Paternoster was violent against him too. He finished him ....[251]

---

[249] NAA: BP25/1, Italian Fotea V (Fotea).
[250] Initial interview with Giuseppe Genti, Stanthorpe, 2013.
[251] Interview with Giuseppe (Pino) Genti, Stanthorpe, 2014.

This noteworthy eyewitness account of a man who was sitting outside a hut close enough to have a good view of the altercation, offers another perspective on a critical incident that changed the history of Italian internment in Australia. Other assumed eyewitness accounts recorded in a dossier on Fantin's death corroborate the use of a piece of wood to strike down Fantin.[252] The Fantin dossier notes that he may have been kicked in the stomach or torso. David Faber explains that no mention is made in the autopsy report of damage to soft tissue on the torso.

However, Pino insisted that Giuseppe Paternoster had struck the victim after he received a blow to the head and that he killed him. Carmelo Lo Giudice offered another comment on the incident. He was on the soccer field where he was playing with other young internees. He noticed a brawl between a few internees from the corner of his eye, but was too involved with the game and too far away to see any details. Joe G. who was playing with Carmelo, stated that he was focused on winning the soccer match, and was disinterested in a fight between older men somewhere else.[253] The same can be said of Mario Sardi's interest in the incident. He does not even mention the striking of Fantin or his death in his diary. Given the eyewitness accounts by Pino Genti, Vincenzo Fotea, Carmelo Lo Giudice, Joe G., and the earlier mention by Sam Tati, there is still more to unearth about this needless death in custody.[254] Archival documents suggest that Paternoster's anger was easily triggered by the anti-fascists, resulting in belligerent behaviour.[255] Nonetheless, the facts from all perspectives need to be examined further including Paternoster's intentions and role in this tragic

---

[252] NAA: A373, 10913 (Death of Francesco Fantin - Segregation of Fascists and anti-Fascists in internment camps).
[253] Interviews with Carmelo Lo Giudice and Joe G, Innisfail and NSW, 2014.
[254] David Faber, (forthcoming). *An Anarchist Life: FG Fantin 1901-42*, Adelaide.
[255] NAA: MP1103/1, PWN9419 (Paternoster).

event.²⁵⁶ Although Camp 14A was troubled by political problems with a strong Fascist leadership, but a largely apolitical Queensland inmate population, Camp 14D was somewhat unresponsive to the call for political unity. In 14A were Jewish Italians, disaffected former Fascists, those who had always been apolitical, and a range of nationalities.

Len De Roma

One of the youngest men in Camp 14D was Leonardo De Roma who was interned with Alfio De Roma his father and older brother Antonio. Before being arrested, they worked as contract cane cutters near Fishery Falls in the Cairns area in far northern Queensland. In the evenings, the three De Roma men played in a band at the local Fishery Falls Hotel to earn a few extra shillings.²⁵⁷ Similar to most of the other Queensland Italians, they were detained soon after the Japanese attack on Darwin in January 1942. They were transferred to the Gaythorne Prison before being sent to Loveday Camp 14D. Like other adolescents who had been interned with relatives, Len's father and brother Antonio protected him as much as possible from the harsh prison camp conditions. Alfio and his two sons were the camp's favoured musicians. According to Len, they experienced few challenging situations whilst interned. The De Roma trio was focused on producing a monthly musical event throughout their incarceration from March 1942 to November 1943 when they were transferred to the Civilian Alien Corps.²⁵⁸ Len

---

²⁵⁶ NAA: A367, C18000/174 (Paternoster).
²⁵⁷ NAA: BP242/1, Q14635 (De Roma, Leonardo [or Deroma]); BP242/1, Q27526 (De Roma, Alfio - Queensland investigation case file); BP242/1, Q23021 (De Roma, Antonio - Queensland investigation case file); J1732, DE ROMA L (De Roma, Leonardo - born 1924 - Civil Constructional Corps CQ117042).
²⁵⁸ NAA: BP242/1, Q14635 (De Roma, Leonardo [or Deroma]); BP242/1, Q27526 (De Roma, Alfio - Queensland investigation case file); BP242/1, Q23021 (De Roma, Antonio - Queensland investigation case file); J1732, DE ROMA L (De Roma, Leonardo -

Figure 17.7: Len (Leonardo) and Tony (Antonio) De Roma, doing hard labour in Civilian Alien Corps work gang, c. 1944.

described his daily routine as one of practicing the music for next month's concert, playing soccer, and doing a number of sports with other young internees. Leonardo explained:

> ... to clear our heads from worries, our group of friends, the ones in our soccer team, would sometimes go out with a few guards who were our age outside the camp for a walk. ... Look, the blokes were our age and we used to have fun, as a group ... they (the young guards) were just like us ...[259]

These recollections evoke images of a war that was as distant as it could be from the daily experiences of both the young Australian military guards and the Italian adolescent internees under their charge. Fraternisation between captors and captive was strictly forbidden,

---

born 1924 - Civil Constructional Corps CQ117042).
[259] Interview with Leonardo De Roma, Adelaide, 2012.

but the Camp 14D guards and the internees eventually became friends regardless of the situation.

However, the De Roma men with other members of the camp 14D band, were able to create an extraordinary atmosphere that took their listeners to another space in time and a level of altered consciousness if only for the moment that they were playing Italian and local tunes. On concert nights, the desert night air was filled with musical joy created by Len's saxophone, Alfio's guitar, and Antonio's piano accordion. The De Roma trio was as well respected behind barbed wire as they had been in the community at home. The power of their music became their strongest tool in negotiating good conditions for themselves within the camp. Their music was better than a tonic, because it kept emotions buoyant and light-hearted for both inmates and guards. Len recalled that when internees were transferred to another camp because they were classified as pro-Fascist, they would play *Giovinezza*, a Fascist song, as the men were marched out of the gates. Len and Antonio were released to the Civilian Alien Corps in 1943, returning home in 1945. They were later awarded the Civilian Service Medal after two years of hard manual work for the nation's war effort.[260]

Peter Dalseno

I have had many discussions with Peter and Gladys Dalseno about their wartime experiences.[261] Peter generously offered many valuable clarifications about his internment.[262] As an educated man, Peter has been able to document his family's story their experiences of wartime internment experience in his published novel-memoir.[263] Although Peter insists that he has written all he needs to

---

[260] https://www.youtube.com/watch?v=PtS1G0F7wT4, accessed 18//1/2016 (*Giovinezza*).
[261] Peter Dalseno was a bookkeeper and baker before internment. He graduated as an accountant in the 1960s.
[262] NAA: MP1103/1, Q8228 (Dalseno).
[263] Dalseno. *Sugar, Tears and Eyeties*, passim.

say in his book, he still has one unanswered question to ask the Australian government.²⁶⁴ Peter remarked:

> If the Yanks could compensate Japanese internees in spite of the atrocities committed by their nationals in the sphere of war, then it would be reasonable to expect some consideration for the work performed by the Italians on Australian soil and for the paucity of belligerency by the Italians on the battlefield.²⁶⁵

Discussions concerning the many types of losses incurred by Italians, solely due to their status as enemy aliens, have remained a moot point since the war's end. Peter Dalseno's unanswered question is evidence of the importance this issue still holds for those who were affected, after more than seven decades. Recent political acknowledgements of 'regret' were recorded in both the South Australian and Western Australian State Parliaments.²⁶⁶ According to Peter, and others interviewed for this project, these political commentaries are of little consequence because they were not followed with affirmative action to remedy injustices that resulted from internment. A number of other interviewees had hesitantly mentioned their desire for reasonable compensation for the actual financial losses incurred by those who were found to be innocent of disloyalty, as was done for the Japanese families affected by internment in the United States of America.²⁶⁷ Whilst it is now accepted that a wrong had been visited on interned Italians, political silence has persisted on this controversy.

---

²⁶⁴ Details in Dalseno's book referring to Camp 14D are corroborated in interviews with Leonardo De Roma.
²⁶⁵ Peter Dalseno, email received Thursday, 17 July 2014.
²⁶⁶ http://www.academia.edu/5546156/Il_Globo_-_newspaper_article_30_Nov_2011 (*Il Globo*); Also: W.A. Hansard: 20 June 2012, p4100a-4117a.
²⁶⁷ Interviews with Sam Tati, Carmelo Lo Giudice, Vincenzo Fotea, Leonardo De Roma, George Rodighiero, Belgio Manca, various dates at locations, 2012-2014.

Barbed wire memories

Both unpleasant and happier memories of life behind barbed wire were discussed in each of the interviews and conversations. Life was not always bad in the prison camps, but it was not good either. It was a mental torment to be incarcerated indefinitely for committing no crime other than being Italian. While all ten men interviewed were thankful not to have been fighting in a war, they believed that they could have been more gainfully employed in society, rather than being imprisoned. Each said that they could have been given non-military work to support the nation instead of being watched over by almost 1,500 guards who could have been employed in more productive wartime activities.

This belief was evident in a letter written by Salvatore Tati in camp 14A in 1943. Sam wrote to the Attorney General: "Sir, … As I am all but a weakling, since then (my detention) I could have given a huge amount of work to the country …"[268]

Salvatore's letter gives an insight into the opinions of many internees during the seemingly endless days, weeks, months, and years of their indefinite detentions. We do not know if his letter was delivered to the Attorney General, but no reply was lodged in his case file. Other Italians did not receive replies from letters sent to the Attorney General's office, which suggests that he did not answer internee correspondence as a matter of practice.[269] Sam's sentiments resonate in a letter written by my grandfather Antonino (Antonio) Spizzica, from Camp 9 at Loveday, to his wife Maria Angela, who remained in Italy with their teenage son Domenico. He remarks:

> … they (Australian government) have not realised the mistake that they have made by confining all us workers who would do more good than bad

---

[268] NAA: BP242/1, Q17157 (Tati).
[269] Andrew Campbell. "Dr HV Evatt-Part One: A Question of Sanity." 2007, *National Observer* 73: 25.

to this nation. They have found a way of costing themselves many thousands of pounds Sterling, each day to the Australian government by even interning those that were born here so that they don't even know if they are doing the right thing or not. ...[270]

This letter written in December 1941, by a self-educated shopkeeper, was remarkably accurate on the subject of the financial and social costs of internment to the nation. It is probable that the men in Camp 9 had often discussed their views on what they perceived as the irrational incarceration of able-bodied men who had no intention of waging war against their new homeland. This point was made throughout Federico Bonisoli's diaries. It was clear to every internee that they could have been more gainfully employed in non-military civilian works instead of languishing in a prison camp constantly guarded by 1,500 military personnel. Furthermore, Lt. Col. Dean's confirmation of the Loveday camps' economic success with a profit of over £59,000 after all costs were deducted from 1941 to 1946 illustrates that the military authorities had no sense of the practicality of incarcerating enemy aliens who were low, if any, risk, to the nation's military security.[271] Examples of how low risk Italians were to national security abound throughout each state with thousands of men detained, without being imprisoned, by Manpower, the Civil Construction Corps, and the Civilian Alien Corps. While conditions were harsh, these men were able to move beyond the Bush Camps for short periods to attend religious services or go to the local hotel for a drink once a fortnight.[272] Furthermore, thousands of Italians farmers were allowed to stay home in relative freedom to produce food all over the nation with no incidence of trouble reported anywhere on the continent during the war.[273]

---

[270] My translation from the original letter.
[271] Austral Archaeology. *Loveday Internment Camp archaeological report*, 1992.
[272] Interviews with Giuseppe Tesoriero, Melbourne, 2015.
[273] Interview with Grazia Zappia, Melbourne, 2014; Interview

Figure 17.9: Antonino Spizzica, Sydney, New South Wales, c. 1945.

Conclusion

The ten men interviewed for this study were fortunate because they had youth, strength of body, mind, and character. Commonly, fathers and older brothers ensured that the youngest men were protected from the mental ravages of 'barbed wire disease' while confined in the prison camps.[274] Another common thread in their stories was the dichotomy between the ways in which senior military officers and the ordinary guards treated the internees. The consensus in most interviews was that the regular guards treated the men reasonably well in Camps 9, 14A, 14D at Loveday and Camp 3A Tatura, although this was not true of Camp 10A. In contrast, some senior officers were reported in the Bonisoli diaries, (corroborated

---

with Agata Previtera, Sydney, 2014; Interview with Roy Cardillo, Charters Towers, 2016, See Francesca Musicò-Rullo's chapter in this book.

[274] John Yarnall. *Barbed wire disease: British and German prisoners of war, 1914-19*. History Press, Stroud, 2011; Barbed wire disease is a psychiatric condition resulting in depression and mental illness in incarcerated populations.

Hidden Lives

by George Rodighiero and Belgio Manca) to be harsh and sometimes unnecessarily cruel in their attitude and behaviour towards detainees.[275] The eyewitness testimonies of the men in this chapter illustrate that deep reserves of resilience, mental and physical health, and the on-going support of others are vital elements in overcoming wartime internment. Nonetheless, their endurance against a backdrop of arbitrary imprisonment based solely on ethnicity underscores the futility of war and its adverse consequences on migrants, later found to be innocent of disloyalty to this nation.

– Mia Spizzica (peer reviewed)

---

[275] Interviews with Belgio Manca and George Rodighiero regarding Camp 9, Adelaide and Sydney, 2013, 2014.

Tears and Sadness

A Story of Family Resilience

To Australia

Salvatore Previtera's only brother, Alfio, had already departed for Australia in 1929 at the tender age of seventeen. During the intervening years, news from Australia heralded great work opportunities and the chance to work hard and become economically successful. Salvatore continued with his labouring job of fruit picking in Sicily, and served in the Italian Army in the Italo-Abyssinian War in 1935. In a conversation with his son Mario many years later, Salvatore said that during his deployment in this war he saw many tears and sad faces among the subjugated people of Abyssinia, now named Ethiopia. Their human suffering would haunt him for some time to come.

Figure 18.1: Salvatore Previtera in Italian military uniform, Italy, 1920s.

Salvatore was born in Mascali in Sicily in 1913 to parents Filippo and Maria but not much is known of his early life. In 1937, he married Orazia Crimi in Fiume Freddo. Soon they welcomed their baby son, Filippo with much joy and excitement in the household. After the First World War, times were economically depressed in Sicily. Work opportunities were very limited and hunger often reared its ugly head. With this in mind, Salvatore finally made the decision to create a better life for his new family and leaving them in his parents care, he departed for Australia to join his brother Alfio. He had sponsored Salvatore's trip through a migration sponsorship plan, known in Italian as the "l'atto di richiamo". This meant that the person who was sponsoring needed to supply accommodation and paid work for at least two years.

Salvatore, then aged 25, travelled on the ship *SS Romolo*, arriving in Sydney on 31 March 1938. During the period following his arrival from Sicily, Salvatore worked on a cane farm in half shares with another Italian named Domenico Pozza. Long, hard, manual labour cutting cane and working on the land in a relentless hot, tropical climate was the norm for cane cutters. Life was hard but good. Cousins were soon sponsored to come out to Australia and there was many a joyous reunion with news from Sicily warmly welcomed with each new arrival. Marriages and christenings of the new generation followed and times were happy.

The family reunites

By 1939, Salvatore had saved enough money to bring Orazia and Filippo out to Australia. Orazia's happiness at finally being able to join her husband was overshadowed by Nonna Maria and Nonno Filippo's sadness at their grandson Filippo's departure. Little did they know that this would be the only grandchild Nonna Maria would ever meet, and that fate would once again step in and she would wave him off for the last time. Orazia had packed all her belongings into two Oregon pine trunks, which are still in the family's possession today. The voyage on the *SS Remo* was long and arduous, eventually arriving in Brisbane on 29 September 1939. The North Queensland landscape and tropical climate were astonishing, as it was so different from their Mediterranean homeland. The new language was a major hurdle and they pined for family left behind in Sicily, most of whom they would never see again. Arriving in Ayr, much happiness flowed, Salvatore, Orazia and Filippo reunited and Alfio and his wife Nellie (Sebastiana) and their infant daughter Maria (Mary), also welcoming them.

Figure 18.2: Orazia and Salvatore Previtera holding Filippo (centre) with other Italian cane cutter families at their home in Chippendale Street, Ayr, Queensland, 1939.

The photograph of the three families in the foreground and workers on the verandah was taken in 1939, just after Orazia and Filippo had arrived in Australia. It was taken at Alfio and Sebastiana's house on their farm at the end of Chippendale Street, Ayr, in northern Queensland. The two people in the back left of the photo are unknown. Next to the two men are Orazio Finocchiaro, (Sebastiana's father) and Alfio Romeo, who were both interned during the Second World War. Left to Right in the front of the photo is Alfio Previtera, holding daughter Maria (Mary) and wife Sebastiana. In the centre of the photo, are Orazia and Salvatore Previtera with infant Filippo in Salvatore's arms. The family to the right are unknown. As the photo shows, family life at Ayr was happy in 1939.

Aliens

Both the work and settling into a new country were hard, but the family was together again and their dreams for a better future were being realised. Finally, life had some normality, but this peaceful existence was soon to be shattered. Fascist Italy declared war on Britain in June 1940. In the midst of this international chaos, Salvatore and Orazia created more joy in their family with the birth of Leonardo on 26 September in 1940. WWII was now raging, but the cane cutters were still left free under 'alien' control conditions to cut sugar cane as it was an essential service for the nation. However, things would soon change. Italians and other immigrants who had not been naturalised and had links to the country of their birth, at war with Australia, were seen as a security threat. Japan attacked Pearl Harbor in December 1941 and Darwin in January 1942. Word got around that Italian men were to be rounded up and interned without warning. Suddenly, the men of Ayr and surrounding district were taken to Stuart Creek Prison in Townsville to be processed. Salvatore was captured on 11 March 1942, along with most of his friends and cousins.

The families left behind were distraught. News that the men would travel south by train resulted in the families of the prisoners waiting at the Ayr Railway Station to catch a glimpse of the men and wave goodbye as they passed. An elderly family friend, who as a child went to the Ayr Railway Station to wave her father Alfio Pappalardo goodbye, told us that the carriages were boarded up. But the families still managed to throw food and clothing parcels on board to show their loved ones that they were thinking of them. It was heart wrenching with wives and children extremely distraught as their men were confined like criminals in a prison-train. Why were their husbands, fathers, brothers, relatives, and friends being taken away? These men had been leading a peaceful existence and were all employed, hard-working men. Thus, it came to pass that Salvatore would finally arrive at Loveday Internment Camp located at Barmera in South Australia. His internment period spanned from 11 March 1942 to 29 November 1943. While interned, the men planted vegetables, played sport, learned to speak and write English, and participated in many other activities that the prisoners organised. This was to keep them busy and sane.

A rusty nail

In the meantime, Orazia lived a lonely life by herself with Filippo and Leonardo in a small tin shack with a dirt floor, which was commonplace in this era. Life was extremely harsh working in the fields, cane cutting and doing other heavy manual work. Without Orazia's own physical strength and the support of her brother-in-law and sister-in-law Alfio and Sebastiana, the stress may have become impossible to bear. This became evident when in September 1942, Orazia was working in the paddock when Filippo, now a four-year old, wandered off to pick wild passionfruit. He stood on a rusty nail. While the injury did not draw blood and nothing was thought of the incident at the time, it soon developed into a tetanus infection.

When it was obvious Filippo was ill and required medical intervention, Orazia and Sebastiana walked several miles carrying the sick child to the doctor. People were extremely poor in this era and walking was the main mode of transport. Leaving the child in the doctor's care, they later went back in Alfio's truck possibly with the expectation of bringing Filippo home. The doctor, upon handing a wrapped Filippo to Orazia, said "I can't

Hidden Lives

Figure 18.3: (left to right) Filippo Previtera with his infant brother Leonardo and cousin Maria (Mary) Previtera, Ayr, Queensland, 1940.

do anything more for this child." Upon feeling her son's forehead, Orazia realised that her son was dead. He died on 22 September 1942, aged 4 years and 2 months. The doctor showed absolutely no compassion for a woman who had just lost a child. With Filippo's death, her world imploded. Her husband was confined thousands of miles away in an internment camp and she did not have enough command of the English language to make the necessary burial arrangements.

Orazia was inconsolable, and she was on her own with two-year old Leonardo to care for. The Sicilian community was in shock, as Filippo's illness and death were incomprehensible to anyone. How could an injury while playing happily lead to such tragedy? A cloud of sadness descended upon the town. Filippo was buried in the Ayr Cemetery. Still a baby, Leonardo could not comprehend what had happened to his big brother and the grief of the people around him. It was hard for Orazia to visit the cemetery because of distance and no transport, but she gratefully accepted offers when people could take her there. News of his son's death was sent to Salvatore but he was not allowed to return home from Loveday to attend the funeral or comfort his wife. Given the distance and many days that it would take to return home, it was impossible for him to attend the funeral. How isolated he must have felt, so far from home, grief-stricken for his son and not able to console his wife.

Grief

Salvatore was finally home, but he was a very different man after the war. His anguish manifested itself into anger when he learnt how the doctor who attended to Filippo had treated Orazia. After his release from internment, Salvatore alighted from the train in Ayr, and wanting to go straight to the doctor and have it out with him. Relatives and friends rallied around to console Salvatore and help him move forward in his life. They tried to reason with him that tetanus had no inoculation and was very hard to treat. By the time that his mother was aware that something was wrong with her little boy and medical help was sought it would have been too late.

He was bitter about being interned, being separated from his family and the loss of Filippo. If he had been home, would this tragedy have happened? He never spoke of his time in the internment camp and the only memory we have of this time in his life is a ship in a bottle, which was made while he was interned. Inside the bottle is a ship docked off the coast of Sicily with houses along the coastline and Mount Etna in the background and the detail is meticulous. Salvatore named the ship the 'Leonardo P' and on the neck of the bottle wrote, 'Greetings from Papa'. More than seventy years later, the bottle remains with the family in perfect condition. Salvatore's anger towards the doctor's treatment of his wife never left him, but slowly he and Orazia picked up the pieces and had two more children, Joseph and Mario.

Hidden Lives

Figure 18.4: Salvatore (Sam) Previtera harvesting sugar cane, Ayr, Queensland, 1939.

After the war

After being released from the Internment Camp, Salvatore first worked for his brother Alfio and later as a farm labourer for Herbert Grey of Ayr. When Salvatore applied to be naturalised as a British subject, Grey, who was a well-known farmer in the district, spoke very well of Salvatore. The relentless hard work paid off and in 1946 Salvatore and Orazia purchased five acres of land that they cleared in their spare time. Later, they grew vegetables on this land, again in their non-existent spare time, later building their first home. Salvatore bought a truck to haul sugar cane. Leonardo, Joseph, and Mario were growing up and helped their parents with the vegetables. Salvatore's father migrated and lived with his sons, after the death of his wife in 1950. As time went on, life slowly resumed its usual family and farming cycles.

In 1960, Salvatore and Orazia sold their land in Ayr and a sugar cane farm was leased for seven years on Colevale Road, Brandon. Leonardo became a diesel mechanic, Joseph worked on the farm, and Mario was at high school. Family life was busy but happy. On the morning of 19 December 1964 the family awoke to another normal busy day. That afternoon, after returning from a funeral, Salvatore and Orazia were changing out of their attire when news was sent to the house of another family tragedy. Joseph, who was 19 years old, had just been electrocuted and Leonardo had been badly burnt trying to save him. The old nightmare had re-surfaced again. Salvatore's memory of the tears and sad faces in Abyssinia had once again shattered the family's peace.

Joseph had been working on the family farm when the Toft-Loader, which was mounted on a truck, made contact with overhead power lines resulting in the vehicle becoming a live electrical conductor. He had descended from the truck and as he made contact with the ground he was electrocuted. Leonardo had been hospitalised and made a full recovery but the tragic event would haunt the family and many others forever. Relatives and friends visited the family often to help in the healing process. Flowers were lovingly taken to Filippo's and Joseph's graves at the cemetery every Sunday. Perhaps for the sake of her two remaining children, Orazia slowly picked up the pieces and looked forward to happier days. Salvatore, however, was a broken spirit and true happiness eluded him for the rest of his days. Orazia passed away in March 1987 and Salvatore grieving for the loss of his wife, passed away in July four months later.

Salvatore and Orazia came to Australia in search of a better life, little did they know how hard it would be to attain and the many hurdles they would have to overcome. Starting with Salvatore's internment, their lives became a struggle to overcome many things out of their control. They left behind an immense legacy of hard work and strong family values and are fondly remembered. Leonardo and Mario, although branching out with their own families, still work on the family farms with their children. Every year we all remember the anniversaries of Joseph and Filippo's deaths and know that Salvatore and Orazia are looking down on us all.

– Susan & Mario Previtera

Hidden Lives

Figure 19.1: (left to right) Carmelo (John) Elpi Fortuna holding her infant son Concetto (Con), and Mafalda, interned at the Bethlehem convent, Palestine, 1940.

Childhood Recollections of Tatura Camp 3A

It was on 10 June 1940 when my life was to change irrevocably. I, Mafalda Fortuna, born on 14 October 1936, am endeavouring, with the help of my brothers, to relate our recollections from the period mentioned above until the end of the Second World War.

My father, Domenico Fortuna and my mother, Elpi Lambros with my two brothers, Carmelo (John) born 30 April 1938 and Concetto (Con) born 1 February 1940 and I were living in Jaffa, Palestine. Dad was leasing a small garage where he worked as a motor mechanic. Palestine was then under British Mandate and as we were Italian Citizens we were regarded as aliens.

On the abovementioned fateful day, my father was captured and interned in a camp in Acre, Palestine. On 10 July 1940, my mother, brothers, and I were also captured and interned in an old convent named 'Casanova' in Bethlehem. We remained separated for over 12 months, so we enjoyed and treasured visits to my father's camp on a monthly basis.

On 23 August 1941, we boarded a ship named the *Queen Elizabeth* and amidst bewilderment as to our destination, we arrived in Sydney, Australia. Subsequently we were transported by train, to Tatura in Victoria, arriving on 25 August 1941. Camp 3 was to be our new home until the War ended in 1945. I have to admit that for us children, the duration was a happy peace-filled existence. We were with both of our parents revelling in the security of being a family again.

On many occasions my father recounted that on arrival we were allocated rooms in the barracks according to the size of each family. These were sparsely furnished, cold and draughty. Each woman and child was issued with a kapok mattress, while the men were given straw-filled mattresses. The vast majority who made up the camp

Figure 19.2: (left to right) Elpi Fortuna far left, with Mafalda, Concetto and Carmelo Fortuna, interned in Tatura Camp 3A, Tatura, Victoria, c. 1942.

were of German background, while the Italians numbered approximately one hundred.

The men were assigned a variety of jobs on a roster system including wood chopping, general cleaning, maintenance, cooking and cleaning duties in the kitchen, shoe repairs and carpentry. The initial task undertaken was the construction of latrines. For their labour, they received fifteen shillings a fortnight, with any materials required supplied through the canteen. Con called to mind seeing all the men assembled in the morning before being dismissed to carry out their particular task.

Many of them were very resourceful, and an exhibition was held to display the various handiworks. Having done some shoe repairing, it was here that Dad's expertise in making girls' and women's sandals was discovered. As a result, orders poured in and Dad would request leather soles, a variety of coloured uppers and wooden heels through the canteen to ensure that he could satisfy the demand. My mother and I were the very proud owners of some attractive sandals. There existed a shortage of rubber at the time and hot water bottles were in demand because of the cold winters. As the need for them to be replaced arose, Dad suggested they keep the screw tops and he ingeniously made the hot water bottles from flattened corrugated iron.

We were permitted to go for walks at set intervals accompanied by two military personnel. On one of these occasions we saw a baby rabbit scuttle into a burrow. Dad succeeded in catching it and intended to take it back with us to keep as a pet but to our disappointment, this was disallowed. It was also during one of our walks that John remembers seeing a dead horse lying in the bottom of a gully. Being at an impressionable age the image touched him deeply and remains with him. It was believed that the horse had stumbled and fallen.

John recollects seeing men riding motorcycles across the other side of the barbed wire fence, of course not realising that they were Japanese Internees in the next compound. Con also had a vivid memory of seeing a plane flying very low with obvious engine trouble. We found out later that it had crashed close by. He also remembers being touched by the friendliness of one of the soldiers on guard who evidently loved children and who they nicknamed 'Margherita'. Being young and full of mischief he recollects with glee that when the bread was being delivered, he and John would hitch a ride on the van to the perimeter of the camp.

A drama group was formed, with annual performances in the community room adjacent to the kitchen. This rather large area, warmed in the winter by a square black wood-burning stove with a flue, served as a dining room, recreation room, as well as a school and church. It was here that two clergy celebrated Mass on Sundays and Holy Days and nurtured us spiritually. A memorable experience was Bruno D'Elia and I made our First Holy Communion. I felt very special, dressed in a beautiful but simple white frock and veil made by Mum.

We would enjoy Easter, Christmas, and New Year celebrations here with an abundance of good food. The

Figure 19.3: (left to right) Elpi Fortuna with children Mafalda, Carmelo, Concetto with their father Domenico Fortuna, Tatura.

merriment continued with dancing to lively music provided by Mr. Dellafiore and his button accordion.

Christmas was a very special occasion when toys made lovingly by all the fathers during the year were distributed to us children. My favourite toy, one particular Christmas, was a deep blue tea set comprising of cups, saucers, a coffee pot and tray to match. I delighted in serving cordial to my family and friends. John and Con experienced similar pride and joy when each received a rifle magnificently carved by Dad and admired by all. Looking very realistic, they were painstakingly finished in French polish. On 6 January, the Feast of the Epiphany, the '*Befana*', an old Italian folklore character, similar to Santa, visited the children in our camp. An internee dressed in black with a pointed hat just like a wizard delivered small gifts to all the children.

We attended school for a few hours from Monday to Friday and I completed Grade 3 in the camp. I learnt to read and write in Italian, Arithmetic and a little History and Geography. I can remember reciting poetry at one of our end of year concerts.

There were a variety of sources of entertainment including a Puppet Theatre, which enthralled us children, as well as film nights held in the adjacent camp. Movies with Deanna Durbin and Shirley Temple, as well as a film about the story of Pinocchio were shown. John and Con remember movies with Tom Mix and Charlie Chaplin. Fairs were held annually in the same compound and it was here on one occasion that I proudly won some sweets by turning a small wheel in a racehorse competition.

Girls tended to be included in the boy's games as they were outnumbered. It wasn't unusual to see us all as a gang brandishing hand-made wooden swords led by an older boy named Peppino Centonse. We all looked up to him and responded to his leadership. We played endlessly with marbles and kite flying was a popular pastime. We were always eager to help Dad make the kites with any paper available, in various shapes and all with long tails. Only occasionally did we girls play with dolls.

My youngest brother, Mario was born on 16 July 1943 at the Waranga Hospital. I desperately wanted and prayed for a little sister and although disappointed, I welcomed and loved Mario immensely. It's ironic that Mario died on 23 October 1984 and is buried in Rushworth Cemetery, not far from where he was born.

My mother was always there for us, providing all the loving tender care for our wellbeing. She didn't appear to have much free time, constantly occupied with washing, ironing, mending, knitting and sewing. She was always eager to help anybody when the need arose and was admired and respected by all.

My mother was born in Jaffa, Palestine of Greek parents. She spoke Greek, French, Arabic, and English fluently. After completing school, she was employed as a telephonist until I was born. At first, when interned in Bethlehem, the Italians scorned her. In Tatura, scorn turned to admiration and respect. Sadly, Mum left her parents and siblings in Jaffa never to see them ever again.

Figure 19.4: (left to right) Domenico Fortuna, with his children, Mario, Carmelo, Concetto and Mafalda at the Tatura Internment Camp 3A, Tatura, Victoria, c. 1944.

My brothers and I were susceptible to tonsillitis with severe coughs. In September 1944, the three of us were admitted to 28 Camp Hospital for Tonsillectomies. The chloroform mask used as an inhaling anaesthetic was a terrible experience.

We certainly did not lack any food. Initially, the internees were provided with mutton for their meals. The Italians were unhappy and protested and requested flour to enable them to make their own pasta. We had an ample supply of dairy products, including milk, butter, and cheese. Eggs were plentiful but as there was a limited supply of vegetables, families were encouraged to grow their own. To the envy of all, Dad proved to have a green thumb. He grew the biggest and most luscious strawberries, sweet succulent tomatoes, silver beet, sweet corn, capsicums, zucchinis, cucumbers, and watermelons.

The kitchen was available each afternoon for a certain time for anyone who wished to use it. To our delight and after a few disastrous attempts, Dad succeeded in baking the most deliciously moist rock cakes. He would also indulge us with slices of bread topped with thick slices of cheese, which he would pop in the hot oven until it was toasted and all the cheese melted. We all devoured this.

Alcohol was not permitted in the camp but there was an exception to the rule and at Christmas, Dad recounted that each adult male received a pint of beer.

I wish to acknowledge the Italian Families and

Childhood Recollections of Tatura Camp 3A

Figure 19.5: Interned Fortuna and Sabatini families: (back left to right): Elpi Fortuna, Domenico Fortuna, Liliana Sabatini, Enrico Sabatini. (front left to right): Mario Fortuna (youngest child), Concetto Fortuna, Carmelo Fortuna, Mafalda Fortuna, creator: R. L. Stewart (courtesy AWM).

individuals that were interned with us. Some of these families include: Casati, Calandra, Centonse, Grilli, Dibella, Dellafiore, Riboni, Longodorni, Datodi, Paoletti, Delia, Andrea and Giuseppe Librio and Mr. Sabatini.

At the end of the War, we were released on 3 August 1945. Dad decided to come to Melbourne to find work and accommodation. On 25 September 1945, we left the camp and joined Dad in Melbourne to recommence our life of freedom. The Australian government offered to return us to Palestine, but Mum and Dad chose to remain and make a new life here in Australia, primarily for our welfare. Both our parents are no longer with us, Mum died on 13 July 1980, aged 67 years and Dad on 8 February 1993, aged 82 years.

May this be a tribute to them and all the Italians who were interned in Camp 3, Tatura, in Victoria during the Second World War.

– Mafalda Fortuna

Figure 20.1: Francesco Belligoi (with dog), and Italian Australian cane cutter families, Ingham, Queensland, 1930s.

Shattered Dreams

From Friuli Land of Emigration to Australia Land of Promise

I am Marino Belligoi and I was born in Italy in Canebola a small mountain town in the area of Faedis, Udine in the Region of Friuli Venezia Giulia in Northern Italy. I am the grandson of Francesco Belligoi who was born on 30 October 1893. This is his Australian story.

Friuli Venezia Giulia is a small region of Italy situated in the north east of the country bordering Austria, Slovenia, and the Adriatic Sea. During its history it has endured poverty and invasion by Barbarian populations from Northern Europe. It was from this land that Francesco left at 31 years of age in 1924 from the Italian port of Genova aboard the steamship *Caprera*. Its destination was the far away and mysterious 'promised land': Australia.

Francesco had completed his military service during World War One, serving in the 'Great War' of 1915 that involved two opposing factions: Germany, the Austro-Hungarian and Ottoman Empires, and Bulgaria against the Allied Forces of Great Britain, France, Imperial Russia, Serbia, Italy and the United States. This worldwide conflict took the lives of nine million soldiers and seven million civilians through combat, hardship, and sickness. Having survived this dark period, which ended on 11 November 1918, my grandfather returned to his home at the age of 25.

On 21 March 1920, he married Maria Cont and they had three children, two girls, and a boy, who was my father, Marcello. The Great Depression of the 1920s was affecting everyone. Supporting a family in such a time of crises and economic difficulty was so great a challenge that on advice of unknown people, Francesco came to the equally difficult decision to migrate to Australia. Together with a friend named Luigi Topatigh, both determined and confident of having made the right decision for their future and that of their families, with the hope that one day they would be reunited with their loved ones in Australia. As Christmas approached on 20 December 1924, boarding the ship *Caprera*, with suitcases full of little more than hopes and dreams, they departed the port of Genova to traverse seas and oceans, bound for Australia. What feelings and emotions must have touched the heart of Francesco having to leave behind his wife Maria, who was 28 years old, daughters Amorina who was three years old, Maggiorina, aged two years and my father Marcello, who was nine months old.

Finally, after 45 days, the long voyage ended when the ship docked in the port of Sydney, Australia on 6 February 1925, having called into the ports of Colombo, Fremantle, and Melbourne. The two friends, Francesco and Luigi, then travelled on to Brisbane and from there, they took the train to North Queensland to the small town of Tully, a sugar-cane growing farmland where Francesco found work as a cane cutter.

In this area, not too distant from Cairns, my grandfather worked for about 17 years, adapting to the new reality and the incredible world that was completely strange and diverse from his previous life. In Tully he mixed with other immigrants, Australians, and Indigenous People, in a land of tropical climate, inhabited by incredible fauna, kangaroos, koala, crocodiles, dingoes, spiders, sharks and the inevitable rats and mice attracted by the sugar cane. This land was also home to snakes among the world's biggest and most poisonous. Francesco soon came to feel a part of this country of the great tropical forests, oceans and deserts.

His hard work on the sugar cane farms allowed Francesco to send money home to his family in Italy, thereby permitting his children to have a more comfortable life, notwithstanding the physical absence of their father. The money sent home also allowed his wife Maria to purchase land on the plains surrounding Canebola, which she rented out to local farmers thereby supplementing the family income. This part of the story was easy for our family to understand. But, my grandfather's story of his life in Australia was a mystery to all of us back in Italy. When he died on 14 February 1963, I was only 12 years of age and I don't remember that he ever spoke of his experiences. I could never have imagined the details of his story until by pure chance I came across a document stating what had really happened to him and to thousands of Italians who had migrated to Australia for work to support their families here and those left behind in Italy.

In December in 2008 during a short holiday in Cairns, Far North Queensland, my partner Pina suggested we enter the Cairns Public Library and try to find information on Francesco Belligoi. After only minutes of searching the National Archives of Australia website the librarian found and printed out a document relating to my grandfather that was dated 9 March 1942. The document was issued by Australian Military Forces and was titled: 'Report on Prisoner of War'. Surprised and fascinated by our discovery of this first document, my curiosity spurred me on to commence further research and as a consequence brought to light other documents relating to my grandfather's life in Australia. A particularly important discovery was the story of Italian civilians interned in Australia as 'enemy aliens' on the outbreak of WWII at the declaration of war against the British Commonwealth by Mussolini in 1940.

Civilian Italians in Australia numbering almost 5000 out of a population of about 33 000 were interned as enemy aliens from 1940 to 1946. These stories of unjust suffering, all but ignored by the history books, were lost to subsequent generations as many of the internees have chosen to forget, convincing themselves that they were at the very least, fortunate to have survived. My research led me to understand that my grandfather and thousands of Italians were interned in what were in effect concentration camps overseen by the Australian military. The largest

Hidden Lives

camp was named 'Loveday' in a remote and desolate area near the Murray River in South Australia. This group of camps also held German and Japanese civilian prisoners.

Among the many official documents to be found online at National Archives of Australia website regarding Francesco Belligoi was one document that in particular made an impression on me. Reading it, I imagined my grandfather's shocked reaction at that moment in his living quarters in Tully when he was arrested as an 'Enemy Alien'. The following is a copy of this report:

> Cairns District, Tully Police Station-2nd March 1942
> Sir
>
> I have to report in connection with the above referred to matter, that a 9.30am on 28/2/42 in company with Constable Kimlin, I proceeded in my private motor car to a hut occupied by Francesco Belligoi, an alien of Italian nationality, at Lower Tully, via Tully. Upon arrival there I saw Francesco Belligoi who was arrested by me by virtue of a warrant issued under the National Security (Aliens Control) Regulations, for his internment.
>
> After making a careful search of the hut occupied by Belligoi, I then and there took possession of the property mentioned hereunder, and which was handed to Constable Purcell, of Cairns, who was returning off escort from Townsville, and who was instructed to convey same to Cairns and to be handed in by him to your office on his arrival there.
>
> Hereunder is a list of the articles seized by me:-
> 20 envelopes containing 20 letters
> 16 sheets of writing paper, with foreign writing
> 8 certificates in foreign writing
> 1 book written in foreign language
> 1 small two cell electric torch
>
> No 'Order to enter and Search' was received by

me in connection with this internment.

Sergeant1/C 2140

COMMISSIONER:

Forwarded:

This Italian alien, Francesco Belligoi, was arrested for internment and left under escort from Tully on 2/3/42. The property mentioned as having been seized has been handed over to an Officer from the Local Intelligence Office and his receipt filed in this Office. No expenses were incurred.

Signed
Inspector

Signed
Chief Inspector

After his arrest, Francesco Belligoi was taken to the Gaythorne prison on the outskirts of Brisbane and then transferred to an internment camp at Loveday, in South Australia. He arrived in Barmera near Loveday on 16 March 1942 where he remained until 1943. His internee number was: Q136699. The military confiscated all money from internees, so they had no control over their own money and were not allowed to communicate freely with their families for

Figure 20.2: Francesco Belligoi, 'mug shot' on internment form, Queensland, 1942. (courtesy NAA)

six years. The few letters that got through to their families were via the Vatican or the Red Cross and were heavily censored by the military. We do not know what his life was like during his internment as few written documents have been located. After Mussolini was removed from power in June 1943 and the Italian Armistice in September 1943, Italians were no longer enemy aliens. They were considered no longer a military threat and so became aliens on parole.

Following orders issued by the Deputy Director of Security on 7 September 1943, Francesco was conscripted into the Civilian Aliens Corps as part of his conditional release from the internment camp. One document states that Francesco worked with the Commonwealth Railways at Port Augusta in South Australia. He worked as a labourer on the construction of the great railway that traverses from Adelaide to the centre of Australia to join Darwin in the Northern Territory. Francesco during this time lived in Marree, a small town in the arid desert district of the South Australian outback, about 700 kilometres from Adelaide and bordering Lake Eyre National Park. Here he was probably paid just enough for his food and for the tent he slept in.

As documented in the National Archives of Australia, on 12 September 1945 at the end of WWII, the Government of the Commonwealth of Australia ordered the release and return of the objects confiscated from Francesco in Tully on 28 February 1942. By the same token, my grandfather returned to being an immigrant and free man in Australia and continued to work in the outback of South Australia employed as a labourer by the Commonwealth Railways until 1950. After 25 long years residing and working in Australia, Francesco felt the nostalgia for Italy and his family. His pay had not been enough to enable him to save for the funds to go home. A ship's ticket to Italy would have cost at least a year's wages, which would take about five years to save. Having been rendered destitute by his wartime experience, he worked hard to be able to earn the £25 for his return voyage to Italy.

Passenger ships were put into service to return the 18 000 prisoners of war back to Vietnam, Indonesia and all of South East Asia. There were no passenger ships available until about 1950, as many were fitted out as hospital ships to bring back soldiers and produce. On 11 May 1950, Francesco departed the port of Adelaide for his long awaited journey back to his beloved family and Friuli. His return was a great joy but also a huge shock to his family and friends. He was seen as an immigrant who had not made his fortune in Australia. The passing of 25 years found his wife was now 54 years old; his children were adults and had all married. Amorina was 29, Maggiorina was 28, and my father Marcello was 26 years old. He also found the grave consequences of war that had brought the Italian people to their knees with destruction, poverty, insecurity, many thousands of lives lost and many more injured in body and spirit.

According to the memories of my relatives still alive, my grandfather at the age of 57 was greatly aged and worn out from many years of hard physical labour. His work as a cane cutter was tough on the body as was the forced physical labour after his release, as he was already a middle-aged man. The work in the South Australian and Northern Territory Outback was tough indeed. He stood with difficulty and walked with the aid of a walking stick. He remained introverted and closed within himself. His rapport with his newly reconnected wife and children was distant and cold. His 25 years away in Australia remained a complete mystery of which he spoke to no one, keeping his story to himself. For many years during the Second World War, his family and friends not having received any direct communications had thought him lost or worse killed. Consequently, for a long time his family endured the absence of his financial support, causing them much hardship and suffering. Despite the misery imposed on all

Hidden Lives

Figure 20.3: Belligoi family: (top) Francesco and Maria Belligoi, (bottom left to right): Amorina, Marcello and Maggiorina Belligoi, Udine, Friuli Venezia Giulia, 1950s.

concerned and the difficulty Francesco had re-established the relationship with his family. I feel that he was at peace having returned to his home to live the last years of his life in the place of his birth close to his dear ones until 14 February 1963 when he departed this life at the age of 70 years.

Fifty years have now passed since the death of my grandfather. After having researched and reconstructed some of his life in Australia, I now understand how this man, with courage and determination, managed to overcome incredible adversities, being forced to accept imprisonment because of his origin, notwithstanding all his hard work and the good intentions he had invested in Australia.

On 23 March 2011, because of these noble motives, I am proud to have at last obtained in the name of my grandfather, Francesco Belligoi, an honour bestowed posthumously on him - the 'Civilian Service Medal – 1939–1945'. This award is granted by the Australian

Government Department of the Prime Minister and Cabinet of Canberra, for Civilian Service during the war. It is recognition of his contribution and that of many others like him made to Australia during WWII.

As if in a movie, after having received the honour on behalf of my grandfather, the Barmera Branch of the National Trust of South Australia invited Italian internee descendants to attend a commemorative ceremony from 11-12 June 2011, entitled 'Loveday Internment Camps – 70th Anniversary.' This ceremony commemorated the arrival of the first internees at Loveday Camps on 11 June 1941, from the military's perspective. I attended the ceremony with great pride and deep emotions as an Italian internee descendant with Pina and families who shared this wartime history. We also visited the sites of the various internment camps in memory and tribute to our loved ones. I was however disappointed to discover that the commemoration in fact only honoured the soldiers with little or no tribute to the suffering of the internees. The moments I passed in these remote places of Australia imagining the presence of my grandfather in that land 70 years before were filled with emotion and touched my heart profoundly.

In concluding this incredible story of Francesco Belligoi, I have come to the understanding that, in the end, he didn't achieve his dreams of a new life with his family in Australia, but he fought with all his strength to survive and to reunite with them in Italy after 25 long years. I am honoured and happy to have had a grandfather like Francesco Belligoi, a simple migrant but a great man with great ideals and dreams and I hope with his spirit to realize here in Australia the dreams that he was not able to realize. At this point of the story of my grandfather, I wish to add some details of my own story. From Italy, at the age of 21, my destiny brought me to Australia in 1972, then in 2008 and finally in 2010. From this date I have lived in Australia on the Gold Coast, Queensland.

– Marino Belligoi

Italian internees, Loveday Internment Camp, 1943.
(courtesy AWM)

Selected Further Readings

Alafaci, M. *Savage Cows and Cabbage Leaves: An Italian Life*. Melbourne: Hale & Ironmonger, 1999.

Alcorso, C. *The Wind You Say*, Melbourne: Angus and Robertson, 1993.

Andreoni, H. "Le italiane nelle campagne d'Australia: un cuore e una capanna." *Studi Emigrazione*, vol. 31, no. 114, 251-268, 1994.

Andrighetti, J. *Italians in New South Wales: a guide to the archives in the Mitchell Library*, Sydney: State Library of New South Wales, 1995.

Baldassar, Loretta. *Visits home: Migration experiences between Italy and Australia*. Melbourne: Melbourne University, 2001.

Baldoli, C. *Exporting Fascism: Italian Fascists and Britain's Italians in the 1930s*. Oxford: Berg, 2003.

Beaumont, J., I. M. O'Brien, and M. Trinca, eds. *Under Suspicion: Citizenship and Internment in Australia during the Second World War*, Canberra: National Museum of Australia, 2008.

Bevege, M. *Behind Barbed Wire Internment in Australia during World War II*. St. Lucia: University of Queensland Press, 1993.

Blagg, Janet, ed. *The Child is Wise: Stories of Childhood*. Fremantle: Fremantle Arts Centre Press, 2005.

Bonutto, O. *A migrant's story. The struggle and success of an Italian-Australian, 1920s-1960s*. St Lucia: University of Queensland Press, 1994.

Borgia-Griguol, C. *To Set the Record Straight: The Story of Francesco Borgia: Pioneer Pasta Maker in South Australia*. West Lakes, S. A.: Seaview Press, 2008.

—. "War, Totalitarianism and 'Deep Belief'." *European History Quarterly* 34, no. 4, pp. 475-505, 2004.

—. "'Per necessita' famigliare: Hypocrisy and Corruption in Fascist Italy." *European History Quarterly* 30, no. 3, 357-387, 2000.

Bosworth, R., & Ugolini, R., eds. *War, Internment and Mass Migration: The Italo-Australian Experience 1940-1990*. Rome: Gruppo Editoriale Internazionale. 1992.

Bosworth, R. *The Italian Dictatorship: Problems and perspectives in the interpretation of Mussolini and Fascism*. London: Arnold, 1998.

Brinson, C. "A Woman's Place...? German-speaking Women in Exile in Britain, 1933–1945." *German Life and Letters*, vol. 51, issue 2, pp. 204–224, April 1998.

Bunbury, B. *Rabbits & spaghetti: captives and comrades, Australians, Italians and the war, 1939-1945*, Fremantle: Fremantle Arts Centre Press, 1995.

Cannistraro, P. V., and G Rosoli. "Fascist Emigration Policy in the 1920s: An Interpretive Framework", in *International Migration Review*, vol. 13, no. 4, Winter, 1979.

Castles, S., C. Alcorso, G. Rando, and E. Vasta, eds. *Australia's Italians: Culture and Community in a Changing Society*, Sydney: Allen and Unwin, 1992.

Castles S., and M. Miller. *The Age of Migration: International Population Movements in the Modern World*. New York: Palgrave MacMillan, 2003.

Cappello, A. 'Rome or Ireland? The Religious Control of the Italian Community.' *Journal of the Australian Catholic Historical Society* 23: pp. 58-73, 2002.

Cavallaro, F. "Italians in Australia: Migration and Profile." *Altritalie*, no. 26, pp. 65-87, 2003.

Cecilia, T. *We Didn't Arrive Yesterday*. Victoria: Sunnyland Press, p. 257, 1987.

Cigler, M., and N. Randazzo. *The Italians in Australia*. Blackburn: Stanley Thornes and Hulton, 1987.

Cooper, R. P. "Italian Women and Mass Migration." *War, Internment and Mass Migration: The Italo-Australian Experience 1940-1990*, edited by R. Bosworth and R. Ugolini. Rome: Gruppo Editoriale Internazionale, 1992.

Cosmini-Rose, D. "Italians in the Civil Alien Corps in South Australia: the 'forgotten' enemy aliens." *Journal of the Historical Society of South Australia* 42, pp. 43-52, 2014.

Cresciani, G. "Refractory Migrants. Fascist Surveillance on Italians in Australia."*Altreitalie*, gennaio-giugno, 2004.

—. *The Italians in Australia*. Cambridge: Cambridge University Press, 2003.

—. "The Bogey of the Italian Fifth Column: Internment and the Making of Italo-Australia." *War, Internment and Mass Migration: The Italo-Australian Experience 1940-1990*, edited by R. Bosworth and R. Ugolini. Rome: Gruppo Editoriale Internazionale, 1992.

—. "Italian Fascism in Australia 1922-45." *The Attractions of Fascism: Social Psychology and Aesthetics of the 'Triumph of the Right'*, edited by J. Milful. New York, Berg, 1990.

—. *The Italians*. Sydney: ABC Enterprises, 1985.

—. *Fascism, Anti-Fascism and Italians in Australia*. 1922-1945. Canberra: Australian National University Press, 1980.

—. "The Internment of Italians in New South Wales." G. Cresciani (ed.), *Australia, The Australians and the Italian Migration*, Quaderni di Affari Sociali Internazionale, Milan: Franco Angeli Editore, 1983.

Cooper, R. P. "An Australian in Mussolini's Italy: Herbert Michael Moran." *Overland*, no. 115: pp. 44-53, 1989.

Dalseno, P. *Sugar, Tears and Eyeties*, Brisbane: Boolarong Publishing, 1994.

Darian-Smith, K. *On the Home Front: Melbourne in Wartime: 1939 - 1945*. Melbourne: Melbourne University Press. 2009.

Dewhirst, Catherine. "The 'Southern Question' in Australia: The 1925 Royal Commission's Racialisation of Southern Italians." *Queensland History Journal* 22, no. 4, 316-332, 2014.

Dewhirst, C., C. Kennedy, and F. Ricatti. "150 years of Italians in Queensland: an introduction". *Spunti e Ricerche*, 24 (1). 8-21, 2011.

Dewhirst, C. "Italians in north Queensland." *Queensland Historical Atlas*, 2010.

—. "A sense of being Italian: the value of family history." *Ozhistorybytes* 12, 2009.

—. "Collaborating on whiteness: representing Italians in early White Australia." *Journal of Australian Studies* 32, no. 1, 33-49, 2008.

—. "Inventing Italians: Experiences and Responses in Australia's Colonial and Federation Societies." Paper presented at the conference of Social Change in the 21st Century, Brisbane: Queensland University of Technology, November 2002.

Dignan, D. "The Internment of Italians in Queensland." In *War, Internment and Mass Migration: The Italo-Australian Experience 1940-1990*, edited by R. Bosworth and R. Ugolini. Rome: Gruppo Editoriale Internazionale, 1992.

—. "Italians: Historical Perspectives." In *Multicultural Queensland 2001: 100 Years, 100 Communities: A Century of Contributions*, edited by M. Brundle. Brisbane: GOPRINT, 2004.

Di Stasi, L. *Una Storia Segreta: The Secret History of Italian American Evacuation and Internment during World War II*, Berkeley: Heyday, 2001.

Douglass, W. A. *From Italy to Ingham: Italians in North Queensland.* St Lucia: University of Queensland Press, 1995.

Elkner C., I. M. O'Brien, G Rando, and A. Cappello, eds. *Enemy Aliens: The Internment of Italian Migrants in Australia during the Second World War,* Bacchus Marsh: Connor Court, 2005.

Everett, S. *Not welcome: a Dunera boy's escape from Nazi oppression to eventual freedom in Australia.* Melbourne: Hybrid Publishers, 2010.

Faber, D. "F G Fantin: A historical legacy retrieved." *Journal of the Historical Society of South Australia* 44, 77-88, 2016.

—. "The Italian anarchist press in Australia between the wars". In *Italian Historical Society Journal*. 17 (2009), 5-11, 2009.

Fitzpatrick, G. "Inky Stephensen's internment experience in Australia: Letters to his wife, 1942-45." *ERAS* 9 November 2007.

Gabaccia, D. R. *Italy's Many Diasporas*. London: University Collage London Press, 2000.

Gatt-Rutter, J. "You're on the list!" Writing the Australian Italian experience of wartime internment." *Flinders University Languages Group Online Review [FULGOR]* vol. 3, issue 3, 1-11, 2008.

Genovesi, P., W. Musolino, I. M. O'Brien, M. Pallotta-Chiarolli, and M. Genovesi. *In Search of the Italian Australian into the New Millenium: Conference Proceedings*, Victoria: Grow Set Pty Ltd, 2000.

Gentile, E. "Fascism as Political Religion." *Journal of Contemporary History* 25, no. 2/3: 229-251, 1990.

Glenk, H., H. Blaich, and M. Haering, eds. *From Desert Sands to Golden Oranges: The History of the German Templer Settlement of Sarona in Palestine 1871-1947*, Victoria, B.C.: Trafford Publishing, 2005.

Gorecki,V. M. "Black Italians in the Sugar Fields of North Queensland: A Reflection on Labour Inclusion and Cultural Exclusion in Tropical Australia." *Australian Journal of Anthropology* 5, no. 3: 306-319, 1994.

Hasluck, P. M. with Australian War Memorial. "Appendix 4, The Wartime Treatment of Aliens." *Australia in the War of 1939-194, Series 4 – Civil – Volume 1, The Government and the People, 1939-1941,* Canberra: Commonwealth of Australia. 1965.

Henderson, D. *Nazis in our midst: German-Australians, internment and the Second World War.* North Melbourne, Victoria: Australian Scholarly Publishing Ltd, 2006.

Henderson, L. "Italians in the Hinchinbrook Shire, 1921-1939: Motives for Migration." *Lectures on North Queensland History.* vol. 3. Townsville: James Cook University, 1979.

Iacovetta, F., R. P. and A. P. *Enemies Within: Italians and Other Internees in Canada and Abroad.* Toronto: University of Toronto Press, 2000.

Jupp, J. *From White Australia to Woomera: The Story of Australian Immigration.* Cambridge: Cambridge University Press, 2002.

—. "Immigration and National Identity: Multiculturalism." *The Politics of Identity in Australia.* Cambridge: Cambridge University Press, 1997.

Kahan-Guidi, A. M. and Weiss, E., eds. *Give me strength. Italian Australian women speak.* Forza e coraggio, Sydney: Women's Redress Press, 1989.

King, S. and O'Connor, D. J. "Building blocks of settlement: Italians in the Riverland, South Australia" *Italian Historical Society Journal,* vol. 11, no. 2, July-December, 24-29. 2003.

Koehne, S. P. "You have to be pleasing and co-operative: Australia's vision splendid for post-world war II migrants", *Traffic: A vision splendid,* no. 5, 27-45, 2004.

Kweit, K. "'Be patient and reasonable!' The internment of German-Jewish refugees in Australia." *Australian Journal of Politics and History,* vol. 31, issue 1, 61-77, 1985.

Lampugnani. R. *I diari d'internamento di Federico Bonisoli: La lingua e il "bel dire" di un fascista italo–australiano,* Rome: Arcane Editrice, 2016.

Larsen, S. U. (ed). *Fascism Outside Europe: The European Impulse against Domestic Conditions in the Diffusion of Global Fascism.* New York: Columbia University Press, 2001.

Latham, J. G. Foreword to The *Peopling of Australia,* edited by P. D. Phillips and G. L. Woods. Melbourne: Macmillan, 1928.

Loh, M., (ed). *With Courage in their Cases: The Experiences of Thirty-Five Italian Immigrant Workers and their Families in Australia.* Melbourne: Italian Federation of Emigrant Workers and their Families, 1980.

Menghetti, D. "Italians in North Queensland." *The Australian People: An Encyclopedia of the Nation, Its People and their Origins*, edited by J. Jupp. Sydney: Angus and Robertson, 1988.

McKernan, M. *This War Never Ends: the Pain of Separation and Return*. St Lucia: University of Queensland Press, 2001.

—. *Australians at Home: World War II*. Scoresby: Five Mile Press, 2015.

Mees, B., & S. P. Koehne, & Australasian Association of European Historians. *Terror, war, tradition : studies in European history*. Unley, S.A.: Australian Humanities Press, 2007.

Menghetti, D. "Their Country not mine." In *Lectures on North Queensland History*. vol. 3. Townsville: James Cook University, 1984.

Moore, A., & J. Perkins. "Fascism in Interwar Australia." *Fascism Outside Europe: The European Impulse against Domestic Conditions in the Diffusion of Global Fascism*, edited by S. U. Larsen. New York: Columbia University Press, 2001.

Morrissey, M. "Italian Migration to Australia and Argentina." *Australia's Italians: Culture and Community in a Changing Society*, edited by S. Castles, C. Alcorso, G. Rando and E. Vasta. Sydney: Allen and Unwin, 1992.

Murphy, B. *The Other Australia: Experiences of Migration*. Cambridge: Cambridge University Press, 1993.

Musicò, F. "The Contribution of the History of Italian Settlement in Australia to the Formation of an Italo-Australian Identity." *In Search of the Italian Australian into the New Millenium: Conference Proceedings*, edited by P. Genovesi, W. Musolino, I. M. O'Brien, M. Pallotta-Chiarolli and M. Genovesi. Victoria: Grow Set Pty Ltd, 2000.

Myers, A., and Moshenska, G., (eds). *Archaeologies of Internment*, New York: Springer, 2011.

Nagata, Y. *Unwanted Aliens: Japanese Internment in Australia*, St Lucia: University of Queensland Press, 1996

Nelli, A. "Tristine Clubs in Melbourne." *The Passeggiata of Exile: The Italian Story in Australia*, edited by R. Pascoe & J. Ronayne. Melbourne: Victoria University of Technology, 1998.

Neumann, K., and G. Tavan. *Does History Matter? Making and debating citizenship, immigration and refugee policy in Australia and New Zealand*. Canberra: ANU Press, 2013.

Selected Further Readings

Neumann, K., "Jan Lingard, Refugees and Rebels: Indonesian Exiles in Wartime Australia." In *Labour History: A Journal of Labour and Social History* 96: pp. 251-254, 2009.

—. *In the interest of national security: civilian internment in Australia during World War II*. Canberra: National Archives of Australia, 2006.

O'Brien, I. M. (ed.), *The internment diaries of Mario Sardi*. Alphington, Victoria: Lucerne Press, 2013.

O'Brien, I. M., "Italians in Ingham and Innisfail in World War II: Selective and not Mass Internment?" *Spunti e Ricerche, 150 years of Italians in Queensland*, vol. 24, 2009.

—. "Citizenship, Rights and Emergency Powers in Second World War Australia." *Australian Journal of Politics and History* 53(2): 207-222, 2007.

—. "The Enemy Within: Wartime Internment of Enemy Aliens," Crotty & Roberts *The Great Mistakes of Australian History*. Sydney: UNSWP Sydney, 140-41, 2006.

—. "Internments in Australia During World War II: Life Histories of Citizenship and Exclusion." C. Elkner (et al.), *Enemy Aliens – The Internment of Italian Migrants in Australia during the Second World War*. Bacchus Marsh: Connor Court, 2005.

—. "The Internment of Australian Born and Naturalised British Subjects of Italian Origin." *War, Internment and Mass Migration: The Italo-Australian Experience 1940-1990*, edited by R. Bosworth & R. Ugolini. Rome: Gruppo Editoriale Internazionale, 1992.

—. *Australia's Italians*. Carlton: The Italian Historical Society, 1988.

O'Connor, D. "Outsiders no more: the establishment of the Italian community in Port Pirie, South Australia." *Scandinavian and European Migration to Australia and New Zealand: Conference Proceedings*, edited by O. Koivukangas & C. Westin. Turku: Institute of Migration, 1998.

O'Connor, D. J. "Viva il Duce: The Influence of Fascism on Italians in South Australia in the 1920s and 1930s." *Journal of the Historical Society of South Australia*, vol. 21, 5-24, 1993.

—. *No Need to be Afraid: Italian Settlers in South Australia between 1839 and the Second World War*. Kent Town, Wakefield Press, 1996.

Paganoni, A. *The pastoral care of Italians in Australia : memory and prophecy*. Ballan: Connor Court, 2007.

Palombo, L. "Mutations of the Australian camp." *Continuum: Journal of Media & Cultural Studies,* vol. 23, issue 5, 613–627, 2009.

—. "The Fasci Femminili in Australia: Re-Imagining the Past Creating the Future." *In Search of the Italian Australian into the New Millenium: Conference Proceedings,* edited by P. Genovesi, et al. Victoria: Grow Set Pty Ltd, 2000.

Pascoe, R. *Buongiorno Australia: Our Italian Heritage.* Victoria: Greenhouse Publications, 1987.

—. "Place and Community: the Construction of an Italo-Australian Space." *Australia's Italians: Culture and Community in a Changing Society,* edited by S. Castles, et al. Sydney: Allen and Unwin, 1992.

Pesman, R. "Italian Studies in Australia: Past, Present and Future." *In Search of the Italian Australian into the New Millenium: Conference Proceedings,* edited by P. Genovesi, et al. Victoria: Grow Set Pty Ltd, 2000.

Pretelli, M. "La risposta del fascismo agli stereotipi degli italiani all'estero." *Altreitalie 23,* gennaio-giugno, 2004.

Papalia, G. "Imaginary Colonies: Fascist Views of Australia in Italian Diplomatic Correspondence 1922-1940." *Eras Internet Journal 6,* November 2004.

—, *Peasant Rebels in the Canefields: Italian migrant involvement in the 1934 and 1935 Weil's Disease cane cutters strikes in Queensland.* Melbourne: Catholic Intercultural Resource Centre, 1985.

Pieris, A. "Australian architectures of internment." *Architecture Australia,* vol. 104, no. 4: 64, pp. 67-68, Jul-Aug, 2015.

Phillips, D. "The Effect of immigration on the family: The case of Italians in rural Australia." *The British Journal of Sociology* 26, 218-226, 1975.

Phillips, T. L. "Symbolic Boundaries and National Identity in Australia." *British Journal of Sociology,* 47, no. 1, March 1996, 113-134.

Pollard, J. F. The *Vatican and Italian Fascism 1929-32: A Study in Conflict.* Cambridge: Cambridge University Press, 1985.

Price, C. *Southern Europeans in Australia.* Melbourne: Oxford University Press, 1963.

Rando, G. "Italo-Australians during the Second World War: Some perceptions of internment." http://ro.uow.edu.au/artspapers/120, 2005.

—. "Tales of Internment: The Story of Andrea La Macchia." Elkner, C, O'Brien, IM, Rando, G and Cappello, A (eds.), *Enemy Aliens. The Internment of Italian Migrants in Australia during the Second World War*, Connor Court Publishing, 35-54, 2005.

Rando G., and M. Arrighi (eds), *Italians in Australia – Historical and Social Perspectives*, University of Wollongong, Wollongong, 1993.

Rando, G. "Narrating the Migration Experience." *Australia's Italians: Culture and Community in a Changing Society*, edited by S. Castles, C. Alcorso, G. Rando and E. Vasta. Sydney: Allen and Unwin, 1992.

Ricatti, F. "Elodia and Franca: Oral histories of migration and hope." History Australia 7(2), 33.1-33.23, 2010.

Saunders, K., & Daniels, R (eds.). *Alien Justice: Wartime Internment in Australia and North America*. St Lucia: University of Queensland Press, 2000.

Saunders, K. "The Dark Shadow of White Australia: Racial Anxieties in Australia in World War II." *Ethnic and Racial Studies* 17, no. 2, pp. 325-341, 1994.

Simmons, T. *Sam Cavallaro Hey Dago!!! The untold story*, Tina Simmons, 2010.

Spizzica, M. "Italian Civilian Internment in South Australia Revisited." *Journal of the Historical Society of South Australia*, (41), pp. 65-79, 2013.

—. "On the Wrong Side of the Law (War): Italian Civilian Internment in Australia during World War Two." *International Journal of the Humanities*, vol. 9 (11), 121-134.

Sponza, L. "The Internment of Italians in Great Britain." In Franca Iacovetta, Roberto Perin, & Angelo Principe (eds.), *Enemies within: Italian and other internees in Canada and abroad*. Toronto: University of Toronto Press, 2000.

Thompson, S. L. *Australia Through Italian Eyes: A Study of Settlers Returning From Australia to Italy*. Melbourne: Oxford University Press, 1980.

Twomey, C. "'In the Front Line?' Internment and Citizenship Entitlements in the Second World War." *Australian Journal of Politics and History*, vol. 53. issue 2, 194-206, June 2007.

—. *Australia's Forgotten Prisoners : Civilians Interned by the Japanese in World War Two*. Cambridge, Cambridge University Press, 2007.

Ugolini, R. "From POW to Emigrant: The Post-War Migrant Experience." *War, Internment and Mass Migration: The Italo-Australian Experience 1940-1990*, edited by R. Bosworth & R. Ugolini. Rome: Gruppo Editoriale Internazionale, 1992.

Valli, R. S. "The Myth of Squadrismo in the Fascist Regime." *Journal of Contemporary History* 35, no. 2, 131-150, 2000.

Vasta, E. "Multiculturalism and Ethnic Identity: The Relationship between Racism and Resistance." *The Australian and New Zealand Journal of Sociology* 29, no. 2, August 1993.

Vellar, I. *Adventures in Two Worlds: My battles with the D word.* Melbourne: Ivo Vellar, 2008.

Ventresca, R. A. "Mussolini's Ghost: Italy's Duce in History and Memory." *History and Memory* 18, 86-119, 2006.

Ward, R. "The Internment and Repatriation of the Japanese-French Nationals Resident in New Caledonia, 1941–1946." *PORTAL Journal of Multidisciplinary International Studies* 14, no. 2, 2017.

Yarnall. J. *Barbed wire disease: British and German prisoners of war, 1914-19.* Stroud: History Press, 2011.

Selected websites

http://www.naa.gov.au/collection/snapshots/internment-camps/index.aspx; see Wartime Internment Camps in Australia

https://www.awm.gov.au/research/guide/pow-civilian; see civilian internment in Australia

http://www.abc.net.au/news/2011-11-18/push-for-loveday-internment-camp-museum/3680542

http://www.ww2places.qld.gov.au/homefront/internment/#aboriginal_internment; see Aboriginal internment

http://ergo.slv.vic.gov.au/explore-history/australia-wwii/home-wii/refugee-internment; see Refugee internment

http://www.theaustralian.com.au/arts/review/world-war-ii-internment-camps-became-home-to-germanaustralians/news-story/35f8207dfaaede1e1add2fb233d591ad, see: German internment in Australia

http://www.migrationheritage.nsw.gov.au/exhibition/objectsthroughtime/dunera/index.html; see internment history https://www.slideshare.net/ecagd/tony-pccolo-loveday-internment-motion-published-format-3-august-2011, accessed 19 December 2012.

http://www.parliament.wa.gov.au/Hansard%5Chansard.nsf/0/26975d3c173ad0ee48257a46002d164d/$FILE/A38%20S1%2020120620%20p4100a-4117a.pdf

http://theconversation.com/when-ethnicity-counts-civilian-internment-in-australia-during-ww2-3273

Appendix 1: Australia Location Maps

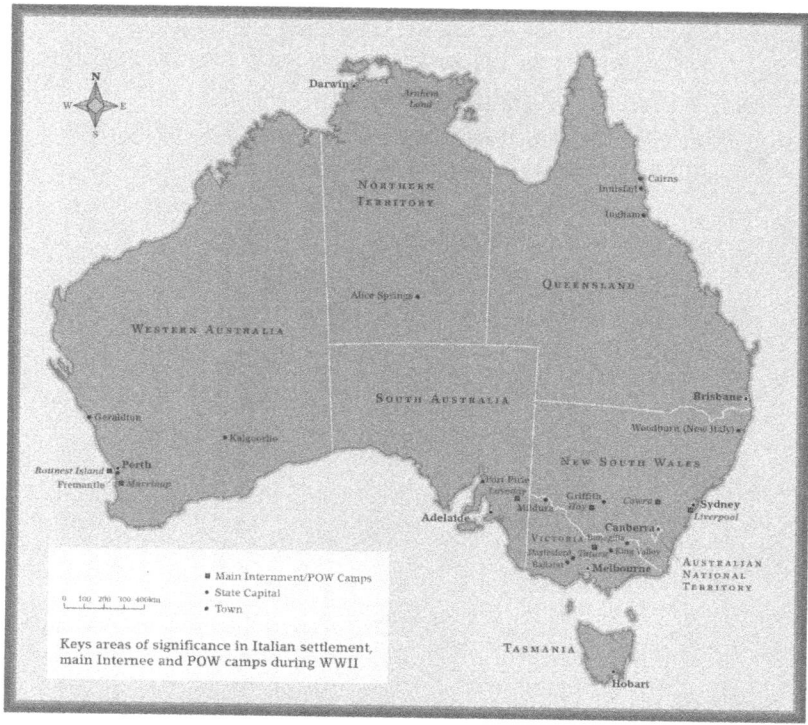

Figure A1.1: Major Internment Camps and Key Australian Cities (courtesy Italian Historical Society).

Appendices

Figure A1.2: Major Internment Camp locations relative to where the authors of narratives in *Hidden Lives* live. (artwork courtesy I. Lam)

Appendix 2: Map of Italy

Figure A2: Map of Italy Showing Regions and Capital Cities
(courtesy Italian Historical Society)

Appendix 3: Loveday Camp

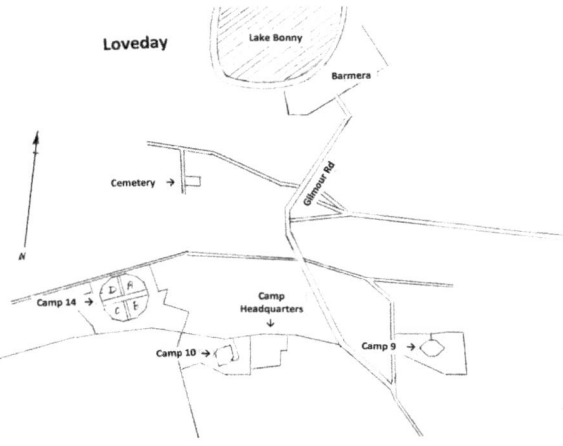

Figure A3.1: Loveday Camps 9, 10, 14 A, B, C, D and Military Headquarters. (courtesy R. Datodi, based on National Archives map)

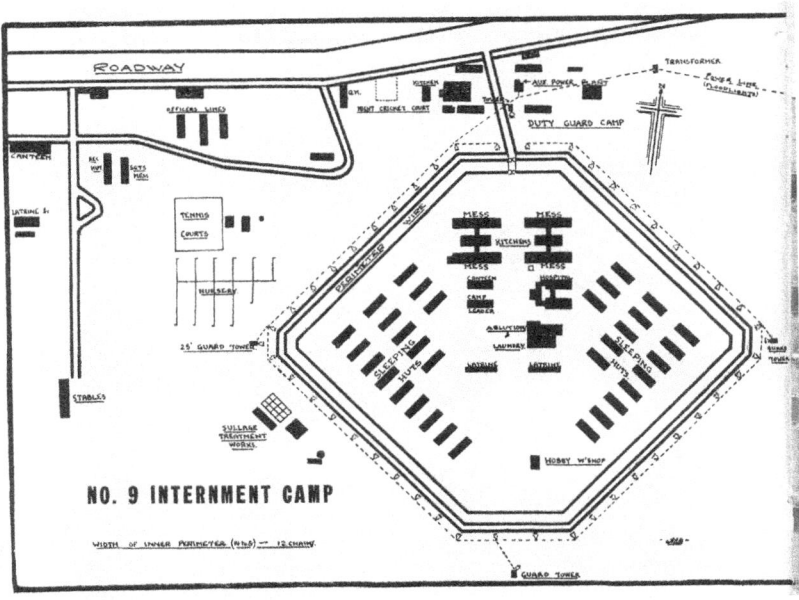

Figure A3.2: Loveday Camp 9
(courtesy State Library of South Australia)

Hidden Lives

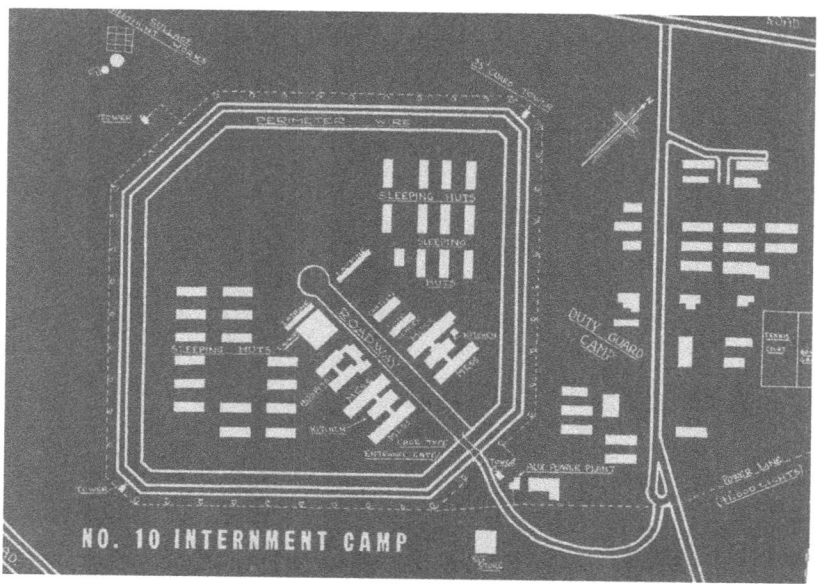

Figure A3.3: Loveday Camp 10.
(courtesy State Library of South Australia)

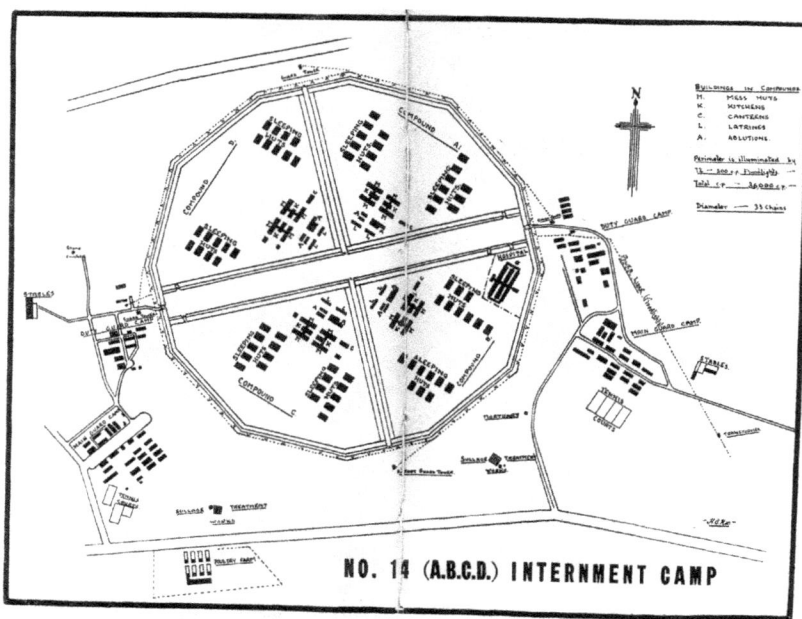

Figure A3.4: Loveday Camp 14 A, B, C, D. (courtesy SLSA)

Appendices

Appendix 4: Cowra Camp

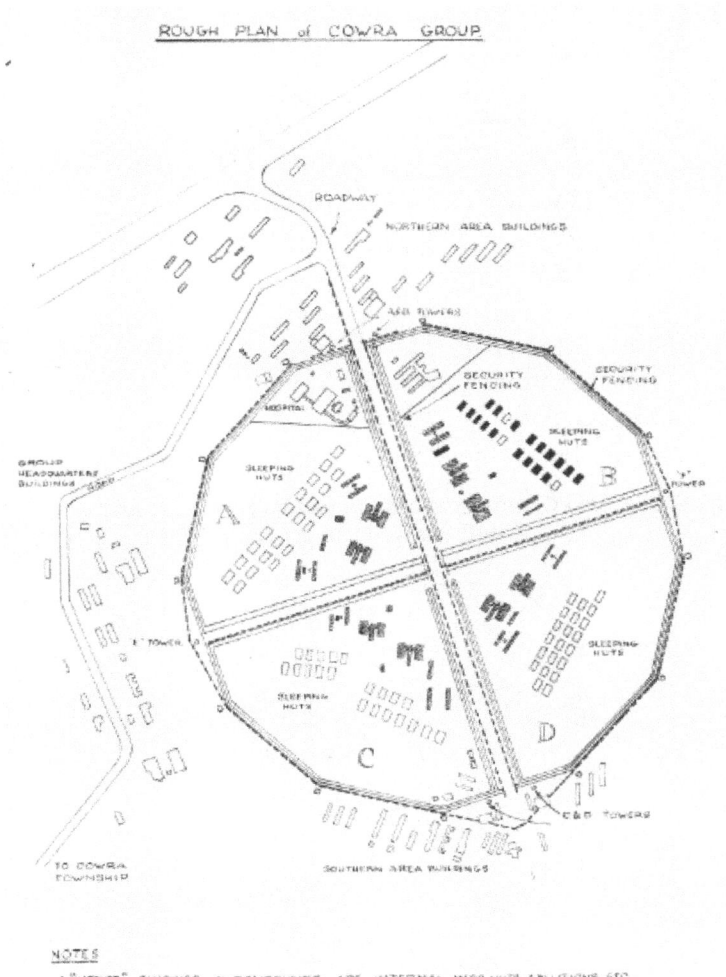

Figure A4: Cowra Interment Camp 12 A, B, C & D.
(courtesy National Archives Australia)

Hidden Lives

Appendix 5: Hay Camp

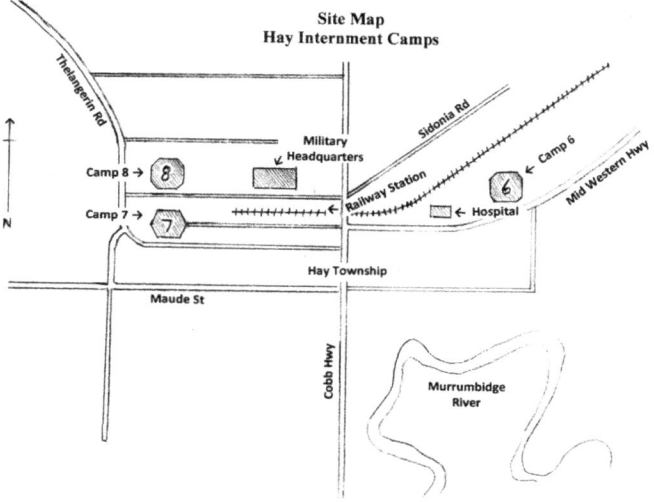

Figure A5.1: Hay Camp Locations. (based on Hay Museum map, courtesy R. Datodi)

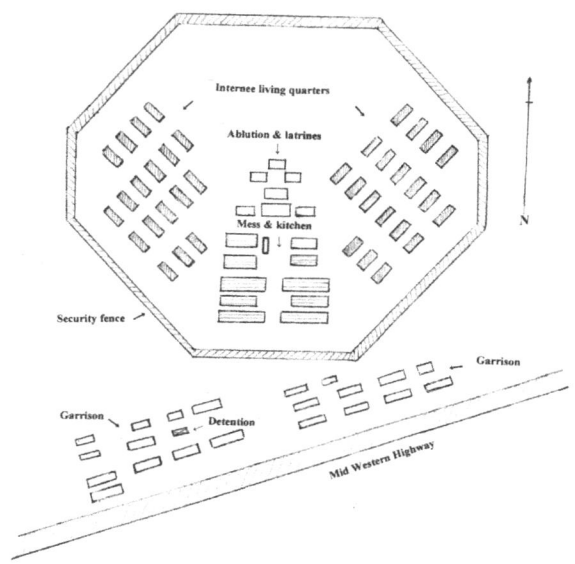

Figure A5.2: Hay Camp 6. (based on Hay Museum map, courtesy R. Datodi)

Appendices

Appendix 6: Tatura Camp

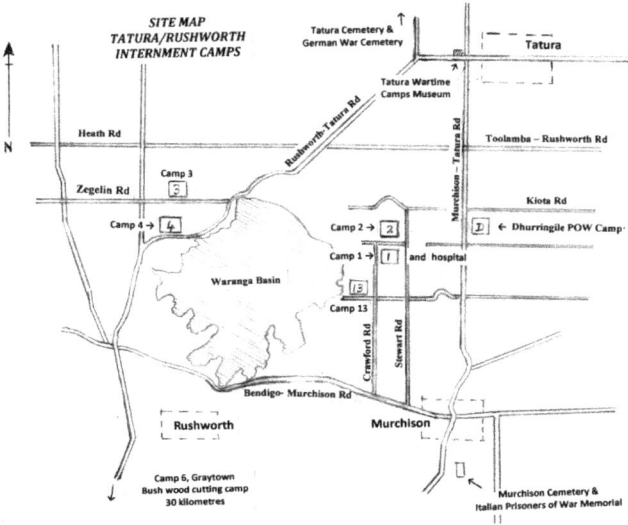

Figure A6.1: Tatura Camps 1, 2, 3, 4 and other camp locations. (based on Tatura Museum map, courtesy R. Datodi)

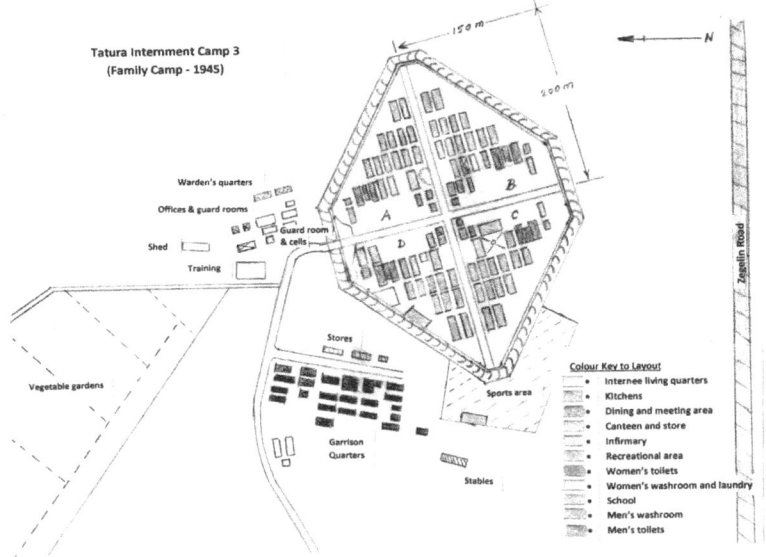

Figure A6.2: Tatura Camp 3 A, B, C, D. (based on Tatura Museum map, courtesy R. Datodi)

About the Contributors

Simone Alcorso was born in Tasmania and now lives in Canberra. She has worked as a lecturer, researcher, policy analyst, writer, and editor. She has researched her family's history both in Australia and Italy.

Claudia Barker (nee Marsella) and husband Ken live at their Caldermeade farm where they run Bazadaise Angus-cross cattle and grow Shiraz grapes for their winery. Claudia has taught at Kooweerup Secondary College since 1965. caldermeade@gmail.com

Marino Belligoi was born in Faedis in Friuli, in Northern Italy. After working 35 years in the Health Care Department in Udine, he moved to Australia in 2010. He became a citizen in 2015, and is happily living on the Gold Coast in Queensland.

Ross Calì was born in Innisfail and is the eldest son of Giuseppe & Anna Calì. He and wife Mary live in Innisfail and have two adult children. Ross is interested in raising awareness of the unfair internment of Italian civilians during WW2.

Roy Cardillo was born in Ingham, Queensland. After leaving school in at 15 years of age with dyslexia in Grade 5 primary, he worked as a corn farmer, stockman, drover, and in his own business as a windmill mechanic until 1985. After his retirement, he travelled the country for 15 years.

Sam Cavallaro was born in Tully, North Queensland and moved to Sydney in 1952 to follow his boxing career. He changed his career for love and a family life with wife Margaret. They have 3 children and 8 grandchildren. They celebrate 60 happy years of marriage in 2018. tinashouseofbeauty@bigpond.com

Rick Datodi was born in Tatura Internment Camp 3, and now lives in Melbourne with his wife Deirdre. After establishing a successful import business, Rick is now retired and is researching his family's genealogy.

Dr David Faber is an Adjunct Senior Lecturer at Flinders University. He won the 2016 Wakefield Essay Prize for a paper on Francesco Fantin, the anarchist anti-fascist activist assassinated at Loveday Internment Camp 14A in 1942. He is working on a critical biography of Fantin.

Mafalda Fortuna was born in Palestine and now lives in Melbourne. She has been happily married to Italo Malavisi for 60 years. They have 5 children, 18 grandchildren, and 3 great grandchildren.

Nora Lo Giudice (nee Carbone) is 90 years old. She left school at 14 years of age. She married Carmelo Lo Giudice in 1947. They have 3 children, 6 grandchildren, 4 great-grandchildren. The family lived happily in Innisfail.

Francesca Musicò Rullo has taught History at the University of Sydney, Macquarie University, and Western Sydney University. She has published widely on Italian migration and teaches History at St. Patrick's College in Campbelltown, NSW.

Nicole Musitano lives in Brunswick in Western Australia. She enjoys researching family history and has relished discovering information on her Nonno's life.

Mario and *Susan Previtera* have successfully run a sugar cane farm near Brandon in North Queensland for more than 46 years. Mario is passionate about his farm, and Susan enjoys genealogy, reading and gardening. They have 3 children and 3 grandchildren.

Francesca Puccini (nee Salvemini) was born in Port Pirie, South Australia. Francesca and her family moved to Adelaide in 1960, when she was 20 years old. Happily married to Frank Puccini, they have 2 children and 5 grandchildren.

Associate Professor Gaetano Rando is Honorary Senior Fellow, Wollongong University and has published extensively on Italian Australian studies. His latest book is *Filicudi facts fiction and fantasy: Pen Portraits of a Magic Italian Island* (2015).

Rosa Rodighiero (nee Emmi) migrated with her family from Sicily to Queensland. She and George (Giordano) Rodighiero have been happily married for 65 years in Sydney. They have 3 sons, 3 grandchildren, and 3 great grandchildren.

Rina Scagliotti (nee Tibaldi) was the youngest of Rico and Maria Tibaldi three children and the only one of their three children to be born in Australia (Ingham). Rina and Sid Scagliotti were happily married for 56 years.

Mia Spizzica has taught at the University of Siena in Italy, the University of Melbourne, and RMIT University in the Humanities and Social Sciences. She is a Melbourne Museum Research Associate. Her PhD at Monash University has focused on the internment of Italians in Australia. See: http://monash.academia.edu/MSpizzica;

Josie Verbis was born at Stawell in Victoria at the end of the war. Her family farmed in Shepparton for 7 years, moved to Melbourne for 11 years, and finally settled in Adelaide in 1964. Josie and husband Ennio have 2 daughters and 6 grandchildren.

www.ingramcontent.com/pod-product-compliance
Lightning Source LLC
Chambersburg PA
CBHW051036160426
43193CB00010B/959